DOG
SMART

Also by Jennifer S. Holland

Unlikely Friendships

47 Remarkable Stories From the Animal Kingdom

Unlikely Loves

43 Heartwarming True Stories From the Animal Kingdom

Unlikely Heroes

37 Inspiring Stories of Courage and Heart From the Animal Kingdom

Unlikely Friendships: Dogs

37 Stories of Canine Compassion and Courage

DOG SMART

Life-Changing Lessons in Canine Intelligence

JENNIFER S. HOLLAND

NATIONAL GEOGRAPHIC

Washington, D.C.

Published by National Geographic Partners, LLC
1145 17th Street NW Washington, DC 20036

Library of Congress Cataloging-in-Publication Data
Names: Holland, Jennifer S., author.
Title: Dog smart : life-changing lessons in canine intelligence / Jennifer S. Holland.
Description: Washington D.C. : National Geographic, [2024] | Includes
    bibliographical references and index. | Summary: "This investigative narrative
    explores the latest research on dog intelligence"-- Provided by publisher.
Identifiers: LCCN 2023038552 (print) | LCCN 2023038553 (ebook) | ISBN
    9781426222719 (hardcover) | ISBN 9781426224256 (ebook)
Subjects: LCSH: Dogs--Behavior. | Animal intelligence. | Dogs--Psychology.
Classification: LCC SF433 .H644 2024 (print) | LCC SF433 (ebook) | DDC
    636.7/083--dc23/eng/20240105
LC record available at https://lccn.loc.gov/2023038552
LC ebook record available at https://lccn.loc.gov/2023038553

Since 1888, the National Geographic Society has funded more than 14,000 research, conservation, education, and storytelling projects around the world. National Geographic Partners distributes a portion of the funds it receives from your purchase to National Geographic Society to support programs including the conservation of animals and their habitats.

Get closer to National Geographic Explorers and photographers, and connect with our global community. Join us today at nationalgeographic.org/joinus

For rights or permissions inquiries, please contact National Geographic Books Subsidiary Rights: bookrights@natgeo.com

Interior design: Sanàa Akkach/Anne LeongSon

ISBN: 978-1-4262-2271-9

Printed in the United States of America
24/MP-PCML/1

For JB,
for both my dads,
and for Mom, always

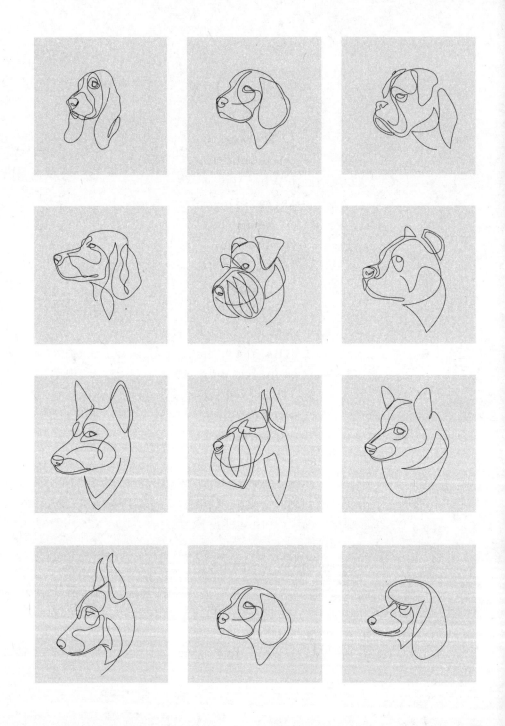

CONTENTS

AN EYE-OPENER

"Loosen your hold," Oscar Pelaez, the dog trainer for The Seeing Eye, says. I ease my death grip on the harness handle. "There you go. Now, say 'Forward' and stay close to her side. Let her work."

And then we're flying along the Manhattan sidewalk—me in the slip-stream of a petite, shiny-coated black Lab named Jesse, feeling her every move through the stiff harness. My legs seem out of my control, scrabbling to keep up. I have a strong urge to stop short or let go, and an even stronger impulse to open my eyes.

I fight both urges and keep trotting with my eyes squeezed shut, letting the dog decide our path. It's disconcerting to move like this—I can't tell how straight our trajectory is, how fast we're going, what we're passing—but apparently, we zoom by light poles and sidestep hydrants, thread through a knot of other pedestrians, dodge uneven sidewalk. I'm relieved when Jesse finally stops at an intersection. I know we're there by the downward slope toward the street and the safety bumps under my feet. (And, OK, fine—I peeked.)

Oscar has kept up on my other side, and per his direction, I tap my foot and tell Jesse she's a goooood girl and scratch behind one floppy ear to reward her for stopping at the crosswalk. I get the *thwack-thwack* of a tail wag against my leg in reply. Then we wait together. I listen. When I hear traffic to my right cough to life, I gesture ahead with my hand and say "Forward" once more, as Oscar has instructed. The little dog cheerfully complies and guides me across West 45th Street and up 9th Avenue without incident.

The adventure lasts just two blocks, but when I open my eyes and look back, I can't believe I'm still upright. Even with the gift of sight, I could easily have tripped or run into something or someone on that crowded stretch of New York City concrete at that speed. "Wow," I say. And because it's the only suitable word I can think of at the moment, I say it again. "Wow."

Oscar smiles. "It's intense, isn't it? You have to put your faith in the dog, your life in her paws. That's when you really see, and feel, what she can do."

I look at the pup standing proud in her harness, ignoring the platoons of people jostling us on either side. She's a pretty little thing, barely to my knee, her muzzle longer than square (Lab snouts can go either way), her head supersmooth.

Jesse! She's a dog anyone would be lucky to have tucked next to them on the sofa, a dog who could easily learn all sorts of tricks. But Jesse is destined to use her brain for something more. If she makes the cut, as I suspect she will, she will give her all, ear nuzzles and tail wags included, to a person with a visual impairment who needs her. Combining what she's learned with what she's always known, and putting it all to work, she'll make that someone's life better, safer, more filled with freedom—and love.

What a very smart girl.

DOG SMART

*S*it, *Geddy, sit. Good boy.* Ah, dogs. Sometimes they do all we ask. Even when they choose not to, they often know *how* to do as we ask. They know our names for things, where we hide their snacks, that they're not allowed on the couch, and how to convince us they should be. Especially in their dealings with us, dogs are such intelligent creatures. Aren't they?

Certainly, their abilities to learn from us and remember, to receive instructions, understand them, and carry them out, are signs of smarts. Relating to humans is a signature part of a dog's natural repertoire and one aspect of their cognitive ability that we truly value. But is performing for us, no matter how impressive the trick, really the hallmark of intelligence in a dog?

In asking this question, it helps to consider our point of view. After all, we're in the habit of assessing intelligence through a human lens, in which cognitive abilities—based on types of problem-solving and achievements that are meaningful to us—by default make sense for our species. This isn't surprising—we are humans, after all, for better or worse—and our perspective is a perfectly valid one. Unless you're another species entirely, dismissed as "just a dumb dog" when you display your smarts in a way that doesn't match our vision.

"We are obsessed with pinnacles," says Emory University primatologist and animal behavior expert Frans de Waal. "We are obsessed by things *we* are good at, *our* specialties. And then we judge other animals based on whether they can do those things." In other words, though we may be cousins to monkeys and descendants of shrews, we like to suppose that we've climbed a very tall tree from which to enjoy the grand view—and to proclaim ourselves unique, superior, and (definitely) smarter than all that we survey.

Even as many nonhuman species prove able to make tools, solve math problems, and communicate specific details about a lurking predator, *Homo sapiens* continue to claim that top branch, unwilling to scoot over and make room for beings with other sorts of smarts. Which is a failing on our part, de Waal says. "Really, intelligence is bushier than that, with all kinds of cognitive and sensory components that may have nothing to do with what we *usually* think of as intelligence," he explains.

Cognitive ethologist Marc Bekoff, who has studied a broad spectrum of behavior in dogs for decades, likewise sees value in broadening our perspective on animal capacities. "Intelligence can be viewed as an evolutionary adaptation whose expression differs for each species," he writes in *Canine Confidential,* pointing out that dogs exhibit multiple intelligences depending on context. He describes them as having "active minds, senses of humor, and significant smarts." Continually thwarting attempts to define them as nothing more than stimulus-response machines, dogs routinely prove themselves to be thinking, feeling beings "who assess different situations and experience a wide range of emotions similar to our own," he observes. Their minds are rich, and their hearts are deep.

Inspired and informed by scientists like de Waal and Bekoff; by dozens of researchers, trainers, breeders, handlers; by many other humans who devote much of their lives to their four-pawed pals; and by an array of the good boys and girls themselves, my quest in writing this book has been to discover what it means to be "dog smart." By this, I mean smart in the world of the dog—both among us and separate from us—using the perceptual and physical tools that make up the cognitive and behavioral repertoire of the dog.

My own two dogs are, of course, part of this story. And by that dog smart measure, one of them is a friggin' genius. Let me explain.

Most mornings, my sweet pup Monk, a fluffy black Japanese Kai Ken, likes being up on the bed with me, a warm lump against my side. Somewhat less sweet Geddy, a toast-colored Korean Jindo, also likes that spot. And he's not big on sharing. In fact, the canine power balance being what it is at our house, Geddy's growl dictates whether Monk is allowed in the bedroom at all. If Geddy is feeling generous and permits Monk entrance, the latter comes in looking meek, his feathery tail dipped low. He stays against the wall, eyes averted, and slinks around to the far side of the bed to lie on the hard floor.

But don't feel sorry for Monk. He knows exactly what he's doing. All he needs is for Geddy to be lured away, and he's poised to grab the coveted seat. So, one day Monk got creative. Banished from the bedroom by a Geddy growl, he began doing excited circles at the bottom of the stairs, yipping as if someone were at the door. (Nobody was.) When Geddy jumped down to investigate, Monk zoomed right past him and leaped into his place.

If Geddy could have given Monk the finger on returning from his fruitless venture, he would have. But now he accepted Monk's presence: Some kind of canine-fairness doctrine seems to rule that, even if ill gotten, order onto the bed matters. The pair remained there together, back-to-back, for the rest of the morning.

But would Monk's wily ruse, if that's truly what it was, work another time? Well, yeah. It has, in fact. Because Geddy just isn't as smart as Monk. As my husband puts it, "Geddy plays checkers. Monk plays chess." Geddy is all about the now; Monk plays the long game.

Watching this scenario unfold made me reflect on our typical definition of intelligence, and how *we* might adapt *our* thinking when examining another species. What if we consider a different standard for intelligence that is wholly relevant to dogs to help us better explore the myriad ways they are extraordinary, both within and outside of the human context? Educational psychologist Howard Gardner long ago proposed that humans can have multiple kinds of intelligence, many of which standard IQ testing ignores. Why not apply that same kind of inclusive approach to our pups and learn to appreciate their social and olfactory intelligence as much as we do their ability to respond to our commands? Or, more generally, to respect their *adaptive intelligence,* which has allowed them to thrive so beautifully in such diverse contexts: by our sides, on the streets, and across the planet?

Though it's understandable that we zoom in on dogs learning *our words* as a primary marker of canine intelligence, acting on command is just one small part of the *Dog Smart* story. In fact, sometimes being smart is *not* doing what you're told. As I learned while spending time with Seeing Eye dogs and their trainers, dogs may know more than the people they're with, and sometimes their most intelligent move is to trust that knowledge and respond accordingly, regardless of the insistence of their human companion. The idea of "intelligent disobedience" was, for me, one surprise among many about what dog smart really means.

Many dogs were interviewed, in the most doggish way possible, for this book. Outside of those within arm's reach, how did I choose my subjects?

Early in my investigation into canine cognition, Cat Warren, whose fascinating book *What the Dog Knows* details her work with cadaver-sniffing dogs, advised me, "If you want to learn about dog intelligence, you've got to start with intelligent dogs." I took that excellent logic, leashed it, and ran with it by seeking out the country's most capable and adaptable dogs: those who have had opportunities to take their natural aptitudes to the highest possible levels.

That took me into the wide and wonderful world of working dogs, where I was able to meet and marvel at individuals representing a host of talents: the seeing eyes, the bomb sniffers, the sheepherders, the duck hunters, the child protectors, the scat trackers, the cadaver finders, the disease detectors, the trick doers, the mood readers, and the pain easers, among others. I was astounded not only by these dogs' ability to go beyond what they're trained to do, but also by their cross-species social intelligence and the bond that grows out of it—a relationship renowned dog training expert Patricia McConnell says, "seems miraculous."

That social connection with dogs has given us entry into a world of extreme possibility. And when Julianne Ubigau of the Seattle-based Conservation Canines told me that chasing obscure scents with her detection dog was like "having access to a superpower," the word "superpower" struck me as exactly right. I began to think of many dog cognitive abilities—especially ones like olfaction that surpass ours by leaps and bounds—as *canine superpowers*. And as you'll see, many of the pups in these pages have proved themselves worthy of a superhero's cape.

But even those of us who appreciate dogs' superskills, who love dogs profoundly, can forget that these animals inhabit an entire universe of their own. Each day they are plunged into sights, sounds, smells, urges, needs, and experiences that overlap with ours but are also very different. The biologist Jakob von Uexküll used the term *umwelt* in 1909 to describe other animals' unique perceptual experiences of the world, reminding us that nature has bestowed on humans just a fraction of what's sensorially possible. The rest belongs to others. The dog's umwelt, like that of any other animal, will always remain at least partly beyond our ken. Still, it pays to step inside a dog's world as far as we can and have a look (and a sniff) around.

I've attempted to do just that with the dogs I've met these last few years, trying to discern—and illuminate—their inner dogness. And in these pages, I've written my best understanding of what it must be like to straddle the species line so deftly. Does any other animal do it so well?

To borrow McConnell's term, I find it miraculous how members of *Canis familiaris* apply their many kinds of intelligence as they toggle between being dogs and being *our* dogs.

To document this story, I visited farms, hunting grounds, military bases, and centuries-old cemeteries where dogs were working. I let one dog be my eyes, another sniff me out in a crowd, and another peg me as a "bad guy" and nearly take me to the ground. I *oohed* and *ahhhed* over dogs who dance, dogs who "talk," and dogs who fly. I joined training sessions and workshops and expert presentations on everything from dogs' evolutionary journey to how a chip in our phones, modeled after a dog's nose, will someday assess our health. I *booped* the *snoots* of dogs with the olfactory intelligence to unearth an endangered salamander or an environmental toxin, or who know diabetes, COVID-19, or cancer when they smell it. I gazed into the eyes of pups whose emotional intelligence lets them be an anchor to people unmoored by tragedy.

I also traced the paths that scientists have taken to learn more about these animals' capabilities, which led me to realize this: We have to tweak our thinking if we are to become smart enough ourselves to understand what it's like to be a dog. Chew on that!

And we're getting there. As perspectives have changed on cognition and sentience in nonhuman animals—and as new, noninvasive technologies have become more accessible in the last few decades (think doggy fMRI)—researchers are asking more sophisticated questions about dogs' thoughts, feelings, needs, and preferences. And the answers are letting us add color and texture to the portrait of our best friends.

Once we accept the fact that dogs are very smart indeed—both within and outside our usual definitions—we'd be wise to open our minds. Not only to such practical applications as how to build better detection technologies (which we've learned by way of dogs' noses), but also how to use our own senses and brains in a smarter way, for a richer experience of life's broad and glorious variety.

I've certainly learned a lot along the way. By delving into myriad forms of dog intelligence, I've discerned how to examine my own perceptions and navigate my own day-to-day experiences a little differently. The super-dog interactions have inspired me to notice what dogs notice, to try reading them as they do one another and us, and to become more mindful of my own physical space, movement, and sensory responses. How refreshing it is to look to canines as role models for an intelligent existence—even to consider how we measure up against them rather than the other way around.

Finally, the more I learned about dogs' remarkable adaptive intelligence, the more I wondered if we could be more intelligent in how we approach our roles as their owners, trainers, partners, and friends. Can we become more dog smart ourselves—by learning their language instead of only teaching them ours, and by appreciating them not just for their ability (and readiness!) to do as we command, but also for their ability to adapt and thrive as dogs, in whatever context they find themselves? Our failure to comprehend why they do what they do doesn't mean a behavior isn't smart. Assuming there's no good reason to lick the carpet or roll in squirrel bones may be a misstep on our part. Shame on us for not trusting their process!

This work has made it clear to me that in shaping dogs to be our companions, we have tamped down some of the doggiest aspects of their intelligence. Put another way, dogs have given up key parts of their *dogness* to fit snugly in our niche. I wonder: Is it possible to give them back some of those pieces? In the final chapter of this book—intended to be gently inspiring rather than finger-waggingly prescriptive—I'll suggest ways we can let our dogs' natural intelligences sparkle by giving them opportunities to be the nose-forward, curious, tireless, sometimes smelly, muddy-pawed creatures they prefer to be when humans loosen the leash just a little.

In the end, it's not an exaggeration to say that what I've learned about dogs through this work has changed both my life—my thinking, my actions—and, where we overlap, theirs. I would love for you to have a similarly meaningful experience. I promise it's not a chore—it's a surprising and joyful journey into the world of a friend like no other. So, please, with a hand on your furry companion, open your mind (and nose and heart) to a dog smart approach to intelligence.

Sit. Stay. Read.

CHAPTER ONE

WHAT MAKES A DOG A DOG?

On a tropical beach some years ago, I met what may be the doggiest dog of all my canine acquaintances. My husband, John, and I got married at an ecolodge in Costa Rica, and after the little ceremony, our hosts arranged a special excursion for us—a boat trip to a private beach with a picnic lunch and a return trip at dusk.

But we weren't quite alone. Three dogs showed up soon after we arrived and hung around nearby. They were scruffy and skinny, gritty with dirt and sand. They spent the day nosing around in some trash up the beach and wrestling with one another and lying in the sun biting at their various itches. I thought they'd all beg from us, but two of them kept their distance. The third dog was friendlier than the others. Pretty quickly he was taking baby carrots from my hand, and shortly after that he allowed us to pet him. By day's end, he'd had a relatively full lunch, a cup of fresh water, and some good back scratches. He trotted off and checked in with his pals now and then but soon returned to the hands that were feeding him. Smart pup! We named him for his very unneutered status: Mr. Ball Dangles (apologies).

Two things struck both John and me about this experience. First, it seemed likely that Mr. Ball Dangles's behavior was mirroring that of his ancestors as they crept toward domestication thousands of years ago, which was a fascinating thing to consider. Second, it was interesting just to watch the dogs *exist,* as comfortable doing their thing "in the wild" as any pet dog would be lolling on the couch. Eating trash may seem a rather unfortunate way to make a living, but the animals had nothing to compare it to and appeared unfazed by their lot. The trio mostly got along: Brief spats were resolved without bloodshed through the masterful modes of communication that dogs share. Really, why be surprised by the beach dogs' comfort in their own skin? Animals exist in all sorts of conditions we might find unpleasant. And of the estimated one billion dogs on the planet, some 85 percent are free roamers.

I'll repeat that, because in my little Western dog-on-my-pillow bubble, both of those figures shocked me (and maybe they do you, too). By many estimates, there are a billion dogs on Earth, and they occupy every continent except Antarctica (and pups have visited even there). The vast majority of the world's dogs—as many as 850 million of them—live on their own, unleashed, uncollared, unspayed, unneutered, untrained, and without benefit of kibble deliveries or routine veterinary care. Free roamers are also known as street dogs and village dogs, and by evolutionary standards, they're doing just fine. Better than fine. In fact, the number of free-roaming *Canis familiaris* across the globe is many times that of all the other members of their genus combined—including wolves, coyotes, jackals, and dingoes. They are clearly doing something right. Something smart.

Smart about us

When I ask cognitive ethologist Marc Bekoff what he thinks is at the heart of intelligence in animals, he doesn't hesitate. "Adaptability," he says. "Those animals that adapt, win." Winning for any living thing means getting along in its niche; that skill requires creativity, problem-solving abilities, and the flexibility to navigate day-to-day complexities. It means being able to learn, remember, and adjust as needed. It means being capable of choosing and then making smart choices based on context— knowing when to hold back and when to go full force. Adaptability is the piece at the very center of the survival puzzle for nonhuman animals. Being flexible is smart because being flexible means making it through.

Especially for animals living among us or even at the edges of environments shaped and dominated by humans, survival requires a big dose of cognitive curiosity and behavioral plasticity. We see it in wildlife adapted to urban and suburban living all the time. Raccoons challenged to breach tight-fitting trash can lids or squirrels raiding "squirrel-proof" bird feeders must use their smarts to win a meal—and the harder we try to outwit them, the more innovative they become. Dogs, like other animals that have learned how to benefit from our presence, live particularly creative, thoughtful, and flexible lives. Intelligent lives.

But for dogs, intelligence also means taking full advantage of an inter-species relationship that gives them a leg up in the struggle for survival. Do dogs learn and adapt *better* than others? Not necessarily. But they do it differently, because of what they are and how they came to be, and much of what they think and do is shaped by this extraordinary history— by their willingness to associate more closely with humans than do any of their kin.

Consider the gaze. What is it about a dog's eyes that makes them seem to say so much? Partly it's about muscle movement: Dogs have the musculature to raise their inner eyebrows and create that puppy dog face. You know the one: It makes you forget you were about to yell at your dog for grabbing the whole roast chicken off the counter. It makes you want to scoop him up and cuddle him and rub his chicken-filled belly (poor baby is so full!). That's no accident. Pups with the tiny mobile muscles that power the "adore me" face likely flourished better than their less expressive kin, because humans with lots of resources to share responded to That Look. (Let's call it intelligent anatomy!) We selected for that face by loving it so much. Wolves can't produce it. *Canis familiaris* is the master of it. And though scientists once dismissed dogs' facial expressions as mere "involuntary displays," more open-minded researchers are now finding evidence for intent—and intelligence—behind those signals.

When a dog and a human gaze into each other's eyes, both experience a bump in endorphins, dopamine, and prolactin—all feel-good brain chemicals—along with oxytocin, the so-called "love hormone," according to influential research out of Japan. Scientists call this phenomenon a "gaze-mediated hormonal feedback loop"—the very same one that operates between human mothers and their infants. Duke University canine cognition researchers write that over the course of their evolutionary journey and ours, dogs appear to have "hijacked the human bonding pathway," adopting behaviors like that puppy dog gaze that trigger our nurturing instincts. And because we are looking back at them, the effect is mutual, and mutually reinforcing. Dog feels good. Human feels good. Give a dog extra oxytocin to sniff, and she'll gaze at you all the more.

This trick didn't work on wolves tested in captivity (they rarely make eye contact with their human handlers anyway). A study published in the journal *Science* found that when human mothers looked at photos of their children and photos of their dogs, the same brain areas related to emotion, affiliation, and reward were activated. "Aspects of our biology appear to be tuned into dogs and children in remarkably similar ways," the study authors write.

We know that dogs know when we're paying attention to them and when we're not. Research has shown that a dog told to leave food alone will snatch it more readily when the tester has her eyes closed or her back turned, or when she's distracted. Dogs also know the scents of human emotional states. A study of golden retrievers and Labradors tested how armpit-sweat odors generated by happy or fearful male strangers affected the animals' interactions with those men and with their owners. Pups exposed to fear smells showed more signs of stress and had higher heart rates than those who sniffed happy or neutral smells. The fear sniffers were less interested in novelty, less confident, and needier, seeking more contact with their owners. They were less apt to socialize with the strangers than were the happy-sweat sniffers.

Moreover, our emotions are specifically represented in dogs' brains: Functional MRI studies show that viewing a "happy" human face sets off distinctive brain activity in our pups, mainly in the temporal cortex, where complex visual information is processed. Stroking your dog can lower stress hormones like cortisol and insulin, and even slow your heart rate and lower your blood pressure. It's another manifestation of the mutual love fest between us and our very good boys and girls. How incredible is that? Over generations of coevolutionary selection both inadvertent and purposeful, we have forged a bond with dogs so powerful that *our mutual feelings alter our physiologies.*

So it seems that dogs have evolved to know us inside and out. And the urge to befriend us starts remarkably early. In what must have been the most fun and chaotic dog study ever, Evan MacLean and Emily Bray and their colleagues at the Arizona Canine Cognition Center borrowed 375 golden retriever puppies from Canine Companions, a nonprofit that breeds dogs to assist people with physical disabilities and post-traumatic stress disorder (PTSD), to try to tease out whether there is a genetic basis for the dog-human bond. MacLean later told *Science:* "Working with puppies is a lot like having young kids. It's a balance between extraordinarily cute and rewarding moments, and frustration that leaves you at the brink of insanity. There is nothing that will not be chewed or peed on, including all of your research equipment, your clothes, and your body." The team's goal? To determine whether *Canis familiaris* comes with "interspecies social intelligence" encoded in its DNA, or if domestic dogs are born blank slates. They considered whether the puppies, barely eight weeks old and having had limited human interaction, would look at human faces, follow human gestures, and approach people for help and attention. The animals did all these things. They understood human-initiated social signals without having prior experience "reading" people, suggesting dog pups are biologically primed to socialize with us.

And wherever they live, dogs learn who their friends are. Pups who belong to no one in particular are simply part of the fabric of the community in much of the world; adaptive intelligence is clearly their superpower. Some adopt a person or family and become a sort of at-a-distance pet, getting fed regularly as a result of their social savvy. In *What Is a Dog?* longtime canine researchers Raymond and Lorna Coppinger write that the village dog is "a natural species ... with a self-tailored lifestyle that suits it just about perfectly." It is not a "stray"—it has its own identity. That independent identity didn't stop John and me from fantasizing about scooping up Mr. Ball Dangles from that Costa Rican beach and whisking him home with us to give him a new life. But some ethologists would take issue with such good intentions, arguing that village dogs are not lost souls needing to be "rescued." Trying to shoehorn them into restricted lives with owners and leashes and fenced-in yards often backfires when the dogs don't take to the life that *we* think is best for them.

People often argue over whether to rid the streets of these wandering pups or leave them be. I'm very sensitive to the fact that free-roaming dogs may bite and spread diseases—rabies being the most devastating— and may harass livestock and threaten native species. It would be naive to suggest that the impacts of unhomed dogs are entirely benign, especially where they are present in large numbers. Ask experts like conservation biologist Abi Vanak whether these roaming pups are a concern, and he'll describe them as an invasive species across India—pointing to their role as predators, competitors, aggressors, and pathogen reservoirs among wildlife—and stress their very real threat to people.

Also, let's be real: Life isn't always a walk in the dog park for these animals. Friends of mine, Pia Sethi and Nadir Khan, who live in Gurgaon, near Delhi, India, have spent more than two decades catching street dogs to provide needed care, to vaccinate them against rabies, and to neuter or spay them. They've witnessed high mortality rates among the dogs they call "Indies," whose lives are cut short by accidents, diseases, parasite infestations, exposure, and starvation. It sure puts a darker spin on the romantic idea of the animals' "freedom." No matter how intelligent the dogs are at navigating the streets—and they are very intelligent at it—in Sethi and Khan's experience, "they are rarely thriving." The average life span of free roamers, if you include puppies, is only around three years. (Adults do a bit better.) That's typical for small- to midsize carnivores in the wild, but it's a much shorter life than most well-homed pet dogs enjoy.

Still, street dogs are *dogs,* uninterrupted. Instead of learning human vocabulary or how to shake a person's hand, they put their intelligence and creativity toward what's relevant to *them:* day-to-day survival. "Street dogs know the lay of the land and map the availability of food," Sethi says. "They know the spots where people throw food and garbage, and they know the houses where people might feed them scraps." One especially intelligent Indie named Pipli, she says, heads out every night and comes back with a bunch of flatbreads, knowing exactly the time and place to collect her meal. Remarkably, she shares her spoils with an unrelated paralyzed dog, another Indie, even regurgitating food for him. Though the village- and city-born dogs are skittish and slow to trust, Sethi isn't surprised that their tendency toward humans is in their DNA. "Even the wariest are human commensals in urban areas," she says. Dogs living in a pack will quickly shift their alliances to a person if it benefits them. She notes that during Diwali, the festival of lights, when firecrackers light up the city, "we are often tracked down by our Indies who spend the night in the safety of our home. The next morning, they are back on the streets." Adaptable and open to an interspecies relationship that has proven to be beneficial to them, contemporary street dogs offer us a glimpse of their ancestors' smarts as well.

Studies of these street dogs have suggested key aspects of the domestication story that led to the remarkable human-canine relationship. In *What Is a Dog?* the Coppingers pulled together research done by various groups over the years on populations of free-roaming dogs in Mexico, Italy, and elsewhere around the world. Those study subjects were mostly scavengers on human refuse heaps. The researchers noticed that dump-diving dog populations included many chubby puppies and a solid cohort of adults, but very few juvenile dogs. Most of the weaned pups simply didn't make it on their own; they weren't mature enough at two to three months old, when their mothers stopped providing care, to compete successfully for food, water, and shade. And yet some individuals were clearly surviving to adulthood, because adult dogs were plentiful.

"How does the pup make the transition from a fat neonate to a repro-ductive adult?" the researchers wondered. What they found seems to offer a key insight into the process of domestication: As soon as the mothers stopped feeding their puppies, the youngsters' best shot at surviving was to solicit care from some receptive person, they explained, adding that it helped if the human thought the pup was cute. It follows that establishing a friendly relationship with the people who were already generating food resources may well have been critical for juveniles among the earliest dogs, too. That would mean that the social intelligence to understand the behavior of members of another species—and ultimately the ability to trust and elicit help from that species—was foundational to the evolution of domestic dogs, as it remains essential to the survival of their mod-ern descendants.

Not that dogs are unique in exploiting anthropogenic opportunities. As early humans altered all corners of Earth we occupy, we inadvertently created new niches that begged to be filled. And other animals happily obliged: Everything from cats to rats to houseflies to pigeons to bedbugs adapted to fill the new spaces—not because humans consciously decided they should, but because evolution made it so. That is, natural selection acted on natural variation, and the creatures that adapted best to human-dominated environments settled in for the long haul. That it's such a well-worn evolutionary path supports the idea that dogs took a similar one. (Evolution is efficient that way.)

Deliberate human activity has certainly modified *Canis familiaris* into hundreds of breeds displaying an extraordinary range of sizes, styles, and behavioral tendencies. But my sense is the earliest dog was not so much a wolf turned woof by human direction as it was a product of the natural order of things, at least at first. And some of the group's earliest members almost certainly took the first and biggest steps toward domestication themselves. As Kathryn Lord, an evolutionary biologist at the University of Massachusetts at Amherst, puts it, "Dogs did not predate us, but we didn't need to have any direct control or contact with them for them to evolve."

Either way, I have a new respect for how dogs have molded themselves to fit into the niches available to them all over the world. Isn't that how nature defines the best and the brightest—the ones who demonstrate the capacity to "make it work"? Nicely done, really.

The family tree of friendship

Thinking about the beginnings of dog-human relationships got me wondering: Who exactly are these beasts sprawled on my couch and begging at my table? Where did their kind come from? And does their ancestry have anything to do with their intelligence?

The current "official" taxonomy of mammals, now nearly 20 years old, classifies dogs as a subspecies of the modern gray wolf, *Canis lupus,* and it's certainly popular to talk about our pets as "tame wolves." The vision of a bold Stone Age person choosing a youngster from a wild wolf litter and raising it to guard the cave and help hunt mastodons still exerts an almost mythic hold over the minds of some authors. It's a great story, acknowledges professor of psychology Clive Wynne, founder of the Canine Science Collaboratory at Arizona State University, but he says it falls apart completely if you've ever gotten anywhere near a real, live wolf. The only way a human could survive an attempt to seize custody of a wild wolf pup from its mother, he writes in *Dog Is Love,* is if the mother wolf were dead (and maybe several other pack members, too). That's not to say it *never* happened; maybe it did. (People today still take young animals from the wild as pets, after all.)

But is it an efficient way to found a species?

Meanwhile, modern dogs and gray wolves are kin, sure, in much the same way that modern humans, bonobos, and chimpanzees are kin. We share the overwhelming majority of our DNA with our closest great-ape relatives. But that doesn't mean humans are a subspecies of chimps; it means we share a common ancestor. Most of the scientists I talked with believe, based on the most current genetic analyses, that this is the case with *Canis familiaris* and *Canis lupus:* The two share a relative, now extinct, from which the two lineages split off somewhere between 40,000 and 27,000 years ago. Dogs have been their own kind of animal for a very long time.

Regardless of ancestry, we can all agree they didn't leap as fully formed friends into the lives of prehistoric peoples. How the relationship developed is surely complex, and there's no consensus on the narrative. Is it the man-tames-wolf scenario? More than a decade ago, Mark Derr wrote in *How the Dog Became the Dog* that "the dog is inherent in the wolf"; in other words, the ancestral wolf contained the dog's nature from the get-go, and people took those wolves in and found the friendliness waiting within. Or were dogs on their way to dogginess genetically, as some more recent studies propose, before humans glommed on to and further shaped them? A sort of chicken-egg mystery? Perhaps.

Exactly how the "proto-dog" stairstepped from community edges to couches will likely remain a subject of energetic debate among experts, from archaeologists to zoologists, for many more years. Still, scientists have learned about physiological and behavioral differences between dogs and their wild cousins that can help us understand how they came to cross the species divide, and later offered their impressive range of cognitive gifts to help humans. That's of course my interest here, because partnering with humans is an intelligent move (one could even call it "dog smart"!). So let's consider it—that willingness to simply be near us.

Driving south from Atlanta, Georgia, on a reporting trip for this book, I spotted a lone pup running along an empty stretch of highway. She was white with random black splotches and a compact, blocky build that suggested a pit bull mix. Dirty, wearing a tattered collar but no tags, she had "that look about her"—a certain something my mother always saw in the eyes of lost animals she knew needed her help. Mom taught me to see it, too.

I turned the car around and parked so that she was heading toward me. I had some kibble in the back of my rental car (long story) and I scattered a bit, hoping the smell might convince her of my good intentions. As she got closer, I called to her in a happy voice and made kissy and clucking noises. I clapped. I threw more food. She was about 50 feet from me when she stopped. She stood stiffly, watching me slap my thighs and listening to my high-pitched calls. She sniffed the air. I moved toward her a little. She backed up. I squatted and called more softly, putting all the love I could in my voice. She took a few steps forward. We eyed each other. I was confident that, shortly, she would be eating out of my hand.

I was wrong. As I stood, she abruptly dove into a stretch of tall grass lining a ravine and was gone. Anyone who has tried and failed to catch an unfamiliar dog has experienced what animal behaviorists call "flight distance." The term refers to how close an animal will let any novel stimulus get to them before they flee. In this situation, I was the new thing, and the black-and-white dog's flight distance was about 47 feet. That's roughly the length of a Greyhound bus, and though it might seem an unfriendly distance, it's unusually close for strangers from two different mammal species to get voluntarily (at least when neither one means to eat the other).

As a group, dogs have an even closer flight distance than my highway pup: In a study of street dogs in Ethiopia, researchers reported an average of 16 feet. If one trait paved the way for domestication, this tolerance of humans must be it. It may be the smartest of dogs' many smart choices: a primary driver of their immense success across the globe.

Had she been a wolf, I'd probably never even have seen the wandering animal, much less gotten close enough to decide if she was too dirty to put into the rental car (not that dirt would have stopped me). Wolves' flight distance is vastly greater than dogs': One Swedish researcher reported them fleeing with 650 feet between them and a human. And my friend Dan Cox, a wildlife photographer who over many years has amassed a portfolio of gorgeous images of wild wolves, never saw a single wolf when he was growing up in Minnesota, despite his home state having the largest concentration of the animals in the lower 48.

As an outdoorsy kid living on a small farm that backed up to wolf habitat, Cox heard howls at night now and then. But going out to look for wolves, he told me, was like chasing ghosts. They remained mostly outside of the human domain, and those that did come close were often persecuted by farmers who believed the predators posed a threat to their livestock. Distance suited the wolves, and having wolves remain far away suited the landowners. Cox only spotted his first wild *Canis lupus* years later, in a surprise encounter while he was tracking and photographing black bears. "There it was, getting ready to cross the road," he recalls. "Thinking back, it seems incredible I'd never seen one before. But that's how wolves are."

How did *Canis* become *familiaris*?

"No matter how intensely you socialize a wolf," says Kathryn Lord, "you don't get a dog." Flight distance is just one of the many traits that separate the two. All members of the genus *Canis,* including not just wolves and dogs but also jackals, dingoes, and coyotes, can breed and produce fertile offspring, given the opportunity and a shortage of more familiar prospective mates. But behaviorally, wolves and dogs are worlds apart. "People tend to glorify wolfiness," Lord says, "but dogs are evolutionarily ridiculously successful in comparison to wolves. They certainly aren't *less than* wolves. They are just different."

How different? Lord knows. For 19 years, she raised captive-bred wolf pups at various zoos and educational facilities for her research, and can attest to the unique challenges of trying to socialize them to humans. It's not that it can't be done, she says. In her own 2010 dissertation on the subject, she notes that it's doable, "but wolves require more intense exposure to reach a less intense attachment." And a recent study by Swedish researchers concurred, showing that with extreme socialization, wolves are capable of human-directed attachment.

But with wolves, Lord says, it has to start *extremely* early and be a full-on commitment. That includes always smelling like yourself—skipping showers and deodorant—when they're pups, as wolves don't respond well if they no longer recognize someone's scent. To get wolves to apply their social intelligence to people, "you have to be with them 24/7 for the first four to six weeks, and then all waking hours until 16 weeks, and then daily contact for the rest of their lives," Lord says. "And what you get isn't a dog, but a canid with its hunting instincts intact. You shouldn't even enter a wolf enclosure if you have an injury or a cold." Even if you raised them and they know you well, she says, "your altered movement could trigger their predatory behaviors. They may not realize they know you until you're on the ground."

The two canids are also unalike cognitively. "Dogs and wolves have very different kinds of intelligence," Lord says. "A wolf completely understands cause and effect, and will watch a situation and figure out what's going on." He'll also persist in trying to solve a problem independently no matter how impossible it may be. A dog? "He cheats," Lord says. If the two were taking a test, the wolf would work its tail off "while the dog would be glancing around the room asking, 'Psssst, what did you get for number nine?' And he'd cheat off the smartest kid in class! Which is a totally successful strategy but uses a completely different kind of brainpower."

Lord is referring in part to research in which wolves proved tenacious in trying to solve problems on their own while dogs "gave up" and looked to human observers for help. A 2019 study by animal behaviorist Friederike Range at the Wolf Science Center in Vienna, Austria, suggested that human-socialized wolves are just as *capable* as dogs of cooperating with people on tasks—specifically, coordinating their actions with a human partner in a food-getting trial. But Range's study wolves were less than half as likely as dogs to look to people for guidance and would move on to a new task solo, whereas the dogs let a person make the first move. As Lord noted, independence doesn't necessarily mean superior intelligence—just a different kind. Indeed, one might argue the reverse is true: Especially if efficiency matters, the smart move is to ask for help if a source of help is nearby. It's the canid version of stopping for directions. *Wolf: It's around here somewhere, dang it! Dog: Pull into that gas station and ask. Wolf: I've lived here all my life; I can find it. Dog: You're being ridiculous. We're going to be late. Wolf: Shhhh! Let me concentrate! Dog: Eye roll.* And so on.

Having learned firsthand just how difficult it is to get wolf pups comfortable with people, Lord went in search of the underpinnings of *Canis familiaris*'s friendliness. In doing so, she connected some very important dots that help to explain the interspecies social intelligence of dogs.

Like many mammals, both wolves and dogs are born blind and deaf: It takes weeks for all their senses to come fully online. But little wolves, whose legs gain strength early and quickly, enter roaming mode sooner—at just two weeks old—when their eyes and ears are still sealed shut. Dog pups aren't strong enough to begin actively investigating their surroundings until they're about four weeks old.

That timing matters because it means that when the two animals go through a stint of rapid brain development and fearless exploration called the primary critical period of socialization, they experience it very differently. As with roaming, for wolves it begins at about two weeks, when only their noses are gathering information; when the primary socialization window closes about four weeks later, they're only just beginning to see and hear. That means much new sensory information arrives during the subsequent "fear period," making wolves wary of novelty for the rest of their lives. Dogs enter their critical period two weeks later, with all their senses in working order. So, puppies amass a lot of detail about their world when they're still filing pretty much everything in the "Ain't life grand?" folder.

Wariness—useful for self-preservation in the face of the unknown—naturally replaces this all-out curiosity after about six weeks in wolves and about eight weeks in dogs. By then, the latter are well-versed in all sorts of odors, sounds, and sights. Compared with young wolves, dogs are more comfortable with novelty and less fearful—including of people. In fact, during the critical period it takes well under two hours of exposure to a reasonably pleasant person *on a single occasion* for a pup to decide that humans in general are just fine.

So, the timing of the critical period supports dogs' interspecies social intelligence. And so do their genes. The whole dog genome was first sequenced in 2005, and since then scientists have been poking around in it, trying to better understand which genes do what jobs. Rarely is there a simple relationship of cause and effect between one or a handful of genes and a particular behavior—genetics and behavior are both complex, and many genes are typically involved.

But Princeton evolutionary biologist Bridgett vonHoldt and colleagues, including Arizona State's Clive Wynne, found a rare exception to that rule, which they reported in 2017: The team linked a trio of genes to dogs' "exaggerated interest" in humans, and at least one of those genes changed significantly during the long process of domestication. The same genes in humans are involved in something called Williams-Beuren syndrome (WBS)—a condition that results in, among other things, hypersociability.

"This finding suggests that there are commonalities in the genetic architecture of WBS and canine tameness," the authors write in their *Science* paper, adding that "selection may have targeted a unique set of linked behavioral genes of large phenotypic effect, allowing for rapid behavioral divergence of dogs and wolves, facilitating coexistence with humans." Translation? Part of that social intelligence that lets dogs connect peaceably with other species, including us, very likely comes from this tiny section of the genome.

The researchers also found that structural variants in these genes are probably responsible for different *levels* of sociability in different dog breeds in ways that fit nicely with our typical descriptions of breeds' tendencies toward friendliness or aloofness. So, your golden retriever's *Gtf2i* and *Gtf2ird1* genes—on chromosome 6, for those who were wondering—aren't quite the same as those in your neighbor's chow chow or in my Jindo, Geddy. The gene variations in these latter breeds are at least partly responsible for their relative reserve in interspecies relationships. Maybe this explains Geddy's refusal to meet my loving gaze as many other dogs will do. When he responds to my emotional overtures by coolly turning his head away, I can give those variants on chromosome 6 some serious side-eye.

Scavenger, hunter, partner

With the genetic architecture to support sociability in place, "step one to becoming a dog is adapting to the anthropogenic niche, living off our garbage," Kathryn Lord tells me. "And then step two, once you're a dog, is to take advantage of those niches closer to humans," giving someone puppy dog eyes and "possibly getting a little favoritism."

Especially considering how today's street dogs make their living, it's sensible that many experts have replaced the idea of the wolf-whispering caveman with a story of smart ancestral dogs making use of nutrient-rich refuse generated by human settlements. You can imagine how the *naturally* more human-tolerant dogs would get the freshest scraps and, perhaps, special tidbits from early dog lovers. Better nourished, those dogs would be more reproductively successful, with natural selection helping to weed out the misanthropes cowering at the far edges of the dumps.

It's not terribly romantic, but trash most likely brought humans and dogs together first, those experts say. "It makes sense to any of us with a dog and a kitchen trash can," Wynne says. "Scavenging is very, very salient in dogs' repertoire." Scavenging our trash ultimately changed dogs on the inside too: With the rise and spread of agriculture, and particularly the cultivation of grains, dogs evolved the capacity to digest our starchy leftovers—something meat-dependent wolves can't do—through tweaks in key carbohydrate-processing genes.

And somewhere along the way, *Homo sapiens* and *Canis familiaris* would have begun locking eyes in a way that just doesn't happen with most wild animals unless there's aggression behind the stare. Early dogs' willingness to match our gaze with friendly intent would have been significant in the domestication process, nurturing a sense of connection that has led to partnerships across a staggering range of undertakings—from protecting us to helping us relocate to securing the foods we share. Some experts speculate that prehistoric dump dogs would have barked or growled at the approach of unfamiliar animals or people—helpfully, if unintentionally, warning their neighborhood humans of the potentially dangerous intrusion. And in 2017, researchers in Arctic Siberia found evidence that humans were using husky-like dogs to pull sleds as long as 9,000 years ago.

But Wynne believes that the beginning of cooperative hunting marks the moment "when the connection between human and dog really kicked up a notch into the strong emotional bond we are accustomed to today." He suggests that dogs and humans pursuing prey together likely started out accidentally, with some early village canines trailing a group of humans as they set out on a hunt. "But I'm sure it quickly grew into a powerful relationship," he writes in *Dog Is Love*. While scavenging provided human-tolerant animals with an evolutionary niche, "hunting would have given these proto-dogs a chance to prove their worth to people."

Curious to get a sense of how such primordial partnerships might have worked, I turn to hunting dogs, which are abundant in my part of the country. On a cold, blustery day in late spring, I slog up a muddy farm drive in Remington, Virginia, to Shady Grove Kennels, where dozens of pups are slated to be tested on retrieving, a key hunting skill. The vast majority are Labradors, including all three sanctioned breed colors and a curly-coated or two. Two judges sit bundled up under a small tent at the edge of a field, clipboards in their laps for scoring, hot coffees and a bag of brownies propped between them.

Each dog's field trial also relies on a set of distinctive tools: a duck whistle, a shotgun, a mechanical slingshot, and three dead mallards. The dogs are tested on their ability to wait at the line while three birds are "shot," then to retrieve them one by one, following their handler's instructions. Platforms out in the field each hold a mechanical duck slinger (something like a tennis ball launcher angled toward the sky) and a guy with a duck whistle and a 20-gauge shotgun.

"Number 17 to the line," yells a judge, and a woman steps up with a slim black Lab quivering against her left leg. The dog sits at her "heel" command—used to mean "hold position" in the working dog world—and the judge raises a paddle to signal "ready" to the people staffing the field platforms. The trial begins.

Platform one comes to life—think Angry Birds with a morbid twist. The duck whistle quacks, which gets the dog's attention; then *thunk,* the first deceased mallard is launched over the field. As it "flies," *pop-pop,* the shooter knocks it out of the sky. From platform two, then, the same series—*quack* (dog looks), *thunk* goes the duck-apult, *pop-pop* goes the shotgun, bird falls. Last, from platform three: *quack, thunk, pop-pop,* duck down. With three birds now somewhere in the grass, far from one another, the dog's job is to quickly retrieve them on command. By now, I've completely lost track of ducks one and two. Even duck three, if I'm honest. But Dog 17 hasn't lost track. He knows exactly where they were.

An aside: I'm not anti-hunting, but I'll admit I am relieved that the birds were already dead before their "flight." Even watching the dead birds launched like cannonballs is distressing. They spin beak over tail on the rise and, when blasted with a shotgun, give up bursts of feathers before flopping to the ground. I'm quite sure I hear someone call loading the launcher "re-ducking." With each new *thunk,* I can't help but think it: "The duck stops here."

A duck dog has what seems like a pretty basic job: Pay attention, notice where the bird lands, go get it, carry it back with the signature "soft" mouth of the retrieving breeds, and hand it over, no nibbles taken out. Hunting with humans is a tweaked version of ancestral dogs' hunting for themselves—a self-preservation turned cooperative behavior that ultimately benefits them more than would grabbing the duck and running for the hills.

When it comes to humans, dogs are masters of the "co-" in "cooperate." But the task is harder and more complex than it may seem. On a real hunt, a dog must ignore a bunch of distractions, including other hunters, other dogs, wild animals, a sore paw or itchy ear, a constant barrage of attractive scents. And she must adapt to all sorts of conditions: fickle weather, gusty wind, mixed terrain, a moody owner. Even in the structured conditions of the trials, it's easy for a dog to lose focus. The best performing dogs are alert and excited but in control: "We want to see drive," one judge tells me, "but controlled drive. A dog whose body gets ahead of its mind will struggle. We need him to think."

It's about *choosing* self-control. I notice that after duck three hit the ground, the owner of a particularly eager dog takes a few extra beats, like calming breaths for the dog, before sending the animal on his way. It is clearly done to help the dog gather his energy into a focused intent, rather than waste it on a wild run. "Way to be patient with him," the judge says to the young handler.

An out-of-control dog will fail at the test as well as in the field. In trials, a dog who rushes before the command or who picks up another scent trail and "switches" birds mid-run is out. A good dog makes a beeline to the mark and "hunts up" the bird using the olfactory smarts dogs have in abundance. If he gets off track and needs "handling," a smart dog pays close attention to the owner back at the line and responds immediately. Dog 17 rounds up all three ducks, no problem.

Then comes the blind test, in which the handler must guide the dog to a fourth bird with whistles and gestures alone. An experienced handler with an attentive animal can zigzag the dog to the mark without saying a word. "Attentive" is the key word here: As I witness over and over during my reporting, for such collaborative enterprises to work, the invisible line between handler and dog must remain taut. Communication is everything. A good duck dog, a *smart* duck dog, is driven and persistent in her efforts, but if she's missing the mark, she'll accept help—even solicit help—from her person. She's adaptable that way.

Which is just what you'd expect of an animal who has learned beautifully how to take advantage of the tools at hand. She's got us on a leash. And though sometimes our narrow thinking can be a hindrance, the truth is that if a dog wants our input, we have something real to give.

CHAPTER TWO

DOG SMART
SCIENCE

More and more these days, scientists are investigating the inner
dog. They're asking questions about canine thinking, feeling,
learning, and behavior that researchers have never asked before. The
intriguing results helped inspire this book.

But why the change in focus? In part, I'd suggest it's about access:
Technologies have come online that enable more sophisticated investigations than before. It also stems from the broader reach powered by the
internet; researchers can now easily engage with large numbers of enthusiastic subjects via keyboard and video, assembling datasets that can tell
truly meaningful stories.

The strongest driver, though, is a transformation in outlook. The idea
that nonhuman animals are entirely "other"—that they have little in the
way of thoughts or feelings, or are glassy-eyed robots running on instinct
alone—is losing its grip. Across the animal kingdom, researchers are
discovering capabilities that force even the hardest-core "human firster"
to acknowledge that our species isn't the only one that can (fill in the blank).

To this point, I ran a quick search. Immediately, a plethora of articles appeared, documenting evidence that magpies act altruistically, crows beat out monkeys in recognizing certain types of patterns, chimps combine screams to create some 400 "words," and octopuses who are particularly annoyed throw things at each other. As for dogs, there's no longer a question as to whether they cooperate, plan, and problem-solve, perform various kinds of math, differentiate between color, size, and type of object—and even understand the concept of zero. (They can.)

The attitude derived from, and driven by, these kinds of findings has given scientists permission to clear away old presumptions about what animals, including dogs, can and can't do. It also allows them to pose questions once considered unnecessary or unanswerable. Consider, for example, the moment in 1995 when the renowned canine researcher Brian Hare disputed the then common conviction that dogs can't follow human pointing gestures. Based on studies indicating that great apes don't do so—and as our closest relatives and the presumed "smartest" animals, their abilities were long the high bar—the assumption was that other animals surely wouldn't or couldn't do it either. As a student, Hare set out to prove them wrong by setting up a simple experiment in his parents' garage. Hiding a biscuit under one of two cups, and controlling for scent clues, he tested whether, when he met the dog's eyes and pointed, the animal would choose the indicated cup. The dog did. The work both proved dogs' gesture-following prowess and launched Hare's career.

Let's also consider the acclaimed animal behaviorist Temple Grandin. Her work to improve the experience of commercial farm animals has shown that when livestock husbandry practices take into account the psychological lives of animals—their sensory experience and sensitivities, their fears and preferences—those animals can be managed in ways that are not only more humane, but also more efficient, less expensive, and less dangerous for the people involved. Her ways of seeing through an animal's eyes, and of working to solve problems based on that animal's point of view, have doubtless influenced dog researchers and trainers to offer the same courtesies to their subjects.

New thinking about the inner animal has enabled other intriguing lines of research that are expanding the list of dogs' capabilities. Few studies have examined whether our pups can be creative—defined loosely as the ability to produce new ideas—but a 2022 citizen science project out of Eckerd College in Florida, drawing trainer participation via a Facebook group, showed off dogs' behavioral fluency, flexibility, and originality. Based on work first done with dolphins and orcas, five dogs were trained to create new behaviors on verbal cue. This meant understanding that each time, the trainer wanted something different from a previously given response, as well as remembering not to repeat their own actions. All five dogs, of different breeds, mixes, and ages, were able to perform non-repeated behaviors on cue more than 70 percent of the time, and three were correct more than 84 percent of the time. It's an ability that could prove extremely useful for working dogs to learn, as many of them face complex problem-solving tasks on the job.

Though I've come to dismiss hierarchies of "intelligent" animals because I no longer think smarts work in such a straight line, I'm clearly comfortable suggesting that no other animal is more embedded in our world, more wholly adapted to our niche, or more deeply lodged in our hearts than *Canis familiaris.* And as attitudes shift about animals in general, the growing acknowledgment of the importance of the human-dog relationship—both as it arose thousands of years ago and as it shapes each species today—is giving scientists reason to investigate the what, why, and how of it all. Questions that once may have languished as curious head-scratchers among dog lovers have piqued the interest of people with scientific know-how and resources, prompting researchers to develop sophisticated studies to answer them. And the topics on the table are fascinating: What's going on in the canine brain? What can we learn about the neural underpinnings of dogs' interactions with us? And what do those underpinnings tell us about the evolution of canid cognition and emotion? Smart people with some very high-tech tools are digging in.

So although I've mostly been interested in what it means for a dog to be dog smart, I'm also interested in what it takes on humanity's part to answer that question—and why we're interested in asking it at all.

The fMRI says ...

Peering over the shoulder of an Auburn University psychology grad student through a window into the imaging room next door, I watch a small black Labrador named Zeus jump up on the long table and lie down on a green mat with just a little coaxing from his handler. His head, wrapped with purple ear-protecting fabric, disappears into the tube. I switch my gaze to the computer monitor in front of us, which offers a view of Zeus's little face poking through the tight halo of the machine like a pimiento stuffed in an olive. He seems relaxed, his tail swishing back and forth against the mat. This is not his first fMRI.

Actually, it is one of many practice sessions for a study that will require four scans. At the moment, Zeus is one of a select few pups at Auburn who is in training to be a go-to animal for fMRI (functional magnetic resonance imaging) studies. I ask my university hosts to let me peek behind the curtain of the smart-dog world, so they usher Zeus in to show off for his curious visitor. He lies still for half a minute, and his trainer uses a clicker and treats to let him know he is doing well. But soon he gets wiggly, then suddenly stands up and turns around, sniffing the mat where his rear end had been. Nope. Can't do that, doggy. Let's try again.

The next time, he stays put for about two minutes as the machine runs, his innermost thoughts represented on-screen as light and dark areas on what looked like the bumpy sides of walnut halves. The picture doesn't tell me *what* the pup is thinking, of course. But it does show where brain activity is concentrated, which speaks volumes to scientists who know brain anatomy much better than I do.

If you really want to begin to understand the dog's mind, you have to get up in there, to where the thoughts, feelings, memories, and perceptions are whirring. Technology is catching up with our desire to know, and today we're well ahead of where we were 20 or even 10 years ago. And it's not just the advances themselves, but also the fact that dogs are allowing us to use the new tech on them in surprising ways. The cooperation of pups like Zeus is opening a window on a whole new world.

The fMRI was invented in the early 1990s, and quickly revolutionized how we think about *our* thoughts. Using radio waves and magnets, an fMRI scan paints a high-resolution picture of the brain and reveals where neurons are active as blood flows in to fuel them. It lets a researcher offer a stimulus to a person (or other living creature) and see where in the brain the information is processed. It's a remarkable tool. But if you've ever undergone an MRI scan, you know that it's a special kind of hell, requiring that you not only remain immobile but do so in, essentially, a coffin, while what sounds like heavy metal pans are banged together around your head at random intervals, with the volume turned up to 11. For decades researchers used an earlier type of MRI (minus the "f") to scan the brains of anesthetized animals only, for anatomical and veterinary studies. But getting the livelier story—that is, to ask questions of a fully conscious pup and watch its brain respond in real time—required convincing a dog to participate voluntarily.

At a number of institutions, including Auburn, Emory University in Atlanta, and Eötvös Loránd University in Hungary, researchers and trainers—two types of experts who typically approach dogs with different mindsets—have partnered to do the remarkable: Get dogs to lie stone still for minutes at a stretch in this tight, unnatural and noisy environment with zero wiggle room. That zero is literal, as any movement renders the expensive, time-consuming scans basically useless. Dogs weren't the first nonhuman species to experience the fMRI; rats, pigeons, and monkeys all had a go for various imaging studies. But dogs can be convinced to do it unrestrained, making for a much kinder, gentler experiment that provides more valid comparisons to human studies.

Emory neuroscientist Gregory Berns had a lot of questions that the fMRI might answer—many of them related to how dogs think and feel about their human companions. The scans would speak for the animals through their neural responses to different stimuli. Using a strategy for comparing the brain structures of dogs and humans called functional homology would offer clues to what it means to think like a dog, to *be* a dog.

With stories of military dogs trained to leap from helicopters on his mind, Berns thought that dogs might also be coaxed into an fMRI tube. So he enlisted the help of Mark Spivak, owner of Comprehensive Pet Therapy (CPT), a dog training company in Atlanta, to figure out how to teach ordinary mutts to be smart and steady subjects. "You don't normally expect a dog to be a concrete statue," Spivak says, "but when Greg asked me, Is this possible to do? I said, absolutely. Then I got in the fMRI myself and 'became the dog,' emotionally and physically, to really think about what we'd need to overcome."

It turned out to be a long list of things. Dogs aren't dummies: None was going to do this scary thing, which included behaviors not entirely in a dog's nature, without a lot of coaxing. It took "extreme patience, baby steps, and lots of food rewards" to finally perfect the fMRI training protocol, Spivak says. "But once we figured out how to manage the challenges, we flew." He relied on a method called chaining, which breaks down a desired behavior into very small steps and teaches it in matching increments with rewards at each step along the way. (This incremental approach is how dogs learn their scenes on TV and in movies, too.) Spivak soon had Berns's own dog, Callie, a feist (a smallish squirrel hunter related to terriers), and McKenzie, a CPT trainer's border collie, climbing a wobbly walkway up to the machine, resting their chins on a specially designed pad, and lying utterly still in the closed-in space despite bursts of noise and vibration from all directions. Callie and McKenzie made history in 2012 as the first dogs to successfully undergo awake fMRI scans. Eventually dozens more joined them.

Dogs are smart enough to learn well by a variety of methods, of course. Others training for the fMRI have used a target stick, which teaches the dog to focus and follow one spot so the person can direct his movements. The model/rival technique has a second person act as Trainee #2, who demonstrates a correct behavior and is rewarded in front of Trainee #1: the dog. Seeing the "rival" win, the dog is more likely to mimic the successful behavior the next time.

Kinder, more dog-forward training has helped connect interesting scientific questions about cognition to the very latest tools that can help investigate them. And those tools, like training methods, are changing as scientists figure out how to make them a better fit for dogs. In 2023, for example, a team out of Austria introduced a new coil, the part of the fMRI equipment that acts as an antenna to receive the radio frequency signal coming from the subject; theirs, K-9 Coils, is tailored for canine anatomy rather than human anatomy, to ensure a scan provides the best information possible for the subject at hand.

The fMRI studies have certainly given scientists a cool, high-tech way to consider a dog's point of view. Dogs lying still in the scanner have helped us better understand how they think about us, their people. For example, their brains link pleasure with their owner's scent and have evolved special areas for both processing faces and recognizing novel words. Also, remarkably, some prefer our praise to a food reward. And so on.

Berns says that because of dogs' comfort with the scanner, "we're closer to understanding what it's like to be a dog than we were 10 years ago." And despite perceptual differences, he says, "in many ways our two species really are more alike than different." That's the case even in one level of variation he didn't expect to find. After scanning more than a hundred animals over the course of his project, Berns says, "it was clear that dogs are as different from one another as we are from each other. You see it in the scans, in the same experiments with different dogs. Even with the rarefied bunch that are MRI dogs, it reminds you that dogs are individuals, and that we have to consider individual response" in assessing any findings that might seem to have broader significance. "There is so much variation, even within a breed, that I will forever be skeptical of 'dogs, or border collies, or X breed, are *fill in the blank*,'" he says.

More dogs, better answers

Documenting that degree of individual variation renders the use of small sample sizes—an issue for many studies, including some mentioned in this book—more significant. A study that includes three or four animals to represent a species with a billion members has some serious limitations.

Fortunately, growing interest in animal cognition has yielded not just better equipment but also bigger pools of dogs. Much bigger. Moving away from studies involving lab-raised animals, whose environs are hardly "natural," many dog cognition centers are recruiting hundreds of "locally grown" subjects (pets!) around the world. The U.S. is a hotbed, but university-based facilities exist in Canada, the U.K., Italy, Australia, Argentina, and Japan, among others.

Bolstering this research is a growing number of online community science projects that tap dog owners—sometimes thousands of them—to submit data on their own pups from afar. Those studies often seek out every iteration of mutt in addition to purebreds, and assess cognition and behavior across the life span. The biggest so far is Darwin's Ark, a multi-project collaboration of the Broad Institute of Harvard and MIT, the University of Massachusetts Chan Medical School, and the International Association of Animal Behavior Consultants. To date, it has amassed data on more than 41,000 pets (and counting) to help answer questions about the interaction of genes and environment. Contrast that with, say, an early 1960s Woods Hole study that made assorted claims about canine early development, socialization, and capacity for connecting with humans based on the experience of a couple dozen beagles born and raised in the lab. In this regard, times certainly have changed for the better!

These larger and more inclusive projects are crucial in part because results from very small studies can lead to far more sweeping conclusions than the limited data truly support—and they're often overhyped by eager university PR staff and equally dog-enthusiastic media outlets. People reading popular coverage of canine science "may end up holding their own animal to standards that are unrealistic," James Serpell, an animal ethicist at the University of Pennsylvania, tells me, "assuming their dog understands more than he does, for example, or is 'more like us' than is true." The larger data sets—and especially the publication of results that defy our anthropomorphic ideas—can help counteract such biases and allow us to see our canine companions as they really are.

Big online projects have their difficulties, of course, from getting non-scientists at home to consistently follow data-capturing procedures to obtaining the funding and human support to review reams of data provided by thousands of fervent dog lovers. Still, the outreach capabilities of the internet have opened access to giant datasets. The value of findings based on several thousand animals or even several hundred versus two dogs or 10? No contest.

CHAPTER THREE

HOW SMART DOGS GET SMARTER

The seeds of dog smarts—in the way we tend to think of intelligence—are always there. As it turns out, growing a genius dog is about cultivating a genius dog, clearing away the weeds. And a little instruction can give a pup the chance to dig deep and show skills we might not have expected he has.

As a group of Italian researchers found while studying dogs' skill in locating sound sources, canine "ability scores" can change significantly during the process of evaluation. Just like human test takers, pups who are familiar with test conditions and get a chance to practice the challenge are likely to better their performance—and research designs that allow for more than one "try" yield a much more accurate picture of canine capabilities.

But not all instruction is equally productive. For service or lap pets alike, I prefer the kind that lets dogs have fun and make choices like the smart animals they are, rather than feel pressured and get punished for doing the "wrong" thing. In fact, research shows very clearly that stress and fear impede learning and performance in all kinds of animals—people and dogs included. Thank goodness, aversive, punishment-based methods are losing followers as more and more trainers suggest that the dogs aren't actually the problem when "acting out" or not learning easily. I heard this a lot during my reporting, and you'll encounter it more than once in these pages: "There are no bad dogs, just bad trainers." (That would be us, folks.)

This perspective, in tandem with the advancing science, is part of that broader change in how we think about animals—a wider acceptance that other beings are cognitively and emotionally complex. And it turns out that incentive-based training simply works better: "There is abundant evidence that dogs trained this way are happier, more engaged, and learn more quickly," James Serpell tells me. "Most dogs are very ready to engage, to do things and look for things, to get involved. They have very active minds." But if we aren't tapping those minds in the best possible way, he continues, we may miss out on whole layers of their intelligence capacities.

The positive reinforcement teaching that desensitizes dogs to the fMRI turns out to be useful beyond brain studies—especially for preparing working dogs for stressful situations. "A dog that holds steady during this 'earthquake in 360 degrees' is a tolerant and confident dog," Mark Spivak says.

These traits specifically are essential for service dogs. The group Canine Companions found their dogs became more capable and achieved higher graduation rates when they taught new behaviors using the fMRI training protocol. "Those dogs not only understood the tasks better and were more competent, but they more reliably performed under difficult circumstances," Spivak says.

Data from a scan can also be useful in evaluating service dog candidates, as when the fMRI indicates a stimulus causes more activity in the caudate nucleus, where high-level functioning including learning and planning occurs, and less in the amygdala, where fear and anxiety originate. Though the proper training for a stint in the scanner doesn't necessarily make a dog smarter, it does help a dog become more tolerant of novelty, pushing the limits of what she'll accept before refusing—it contracts her mental flight distance, if you will. The training, Spivak notes, also creates more adaptable, more reliable working dogs.

That we can partner with dogs for these kinds of studies is an outstanding example of both our own ingenuity in communicating what we want dogs to do, and also dogs' ability to adapt to some wholly unnatural conditions to work with us. But as always, success depends on the dog in question. As U.K.-based trainer Vidhyalakshmi Karthikeyan points out, "Conditions and consequences shape the behavior of every individual dog in a unique way. But the common strength of these animals is their ability to learn under all those different circumstances."

That capacity to learn all manner of things under all manner of circumstances is what allows individual dogs to adapt to their environment—in ways that mirror the species-level adaptability that we've already discussed. With the foundation of a trusting relationship, it seems there's almost nothing a dog can't learn.

The sky's the limit

Ouka (rhymes with "Luke-ah"), an insanely fluffy Samoyed, has learned to fly. Paragliding is hardly a natural activity for a dog, but this one will do just about anything his owner, Shams—who goes by just one name, like his pup—is doing. They live out of a van, traveling around Europe together. And whatever adventure Shams finds for them, Ouka seems game to try.

Ouka was around three years old when Shams adopted him, after two previous owners failed to make it work. "Sammies" may look like stuffed toys, but they tend to be willful, smart, high energy, and in need of mentally and physically demanding occupations. Breed heritage aside, this particular animal required a person willing to put in many hours each day to earn his trust; he was wisely wary after being passed from home to home.

In the Alps, Ouka started out joining Shams on daily runs and hikes. Far from the problem dog he'd been for others, he was "completely chill" with Shams. Together they played, watched sunsets, made friends with other travelers, and wore themselves out paddling rivers and wandering the land. Back at the van, Shams took online dog training courses and then gave Ouka opportunities to learn new skills and solve new problems.

Finally, Shams felt his pup was even ready to join him in paragliding. "Of course, to fly with a dog is not super common," he says without a trace of irony. "So I went step-by-step, first spending time in a place where pilots take off and land, to get him used to the movements, the gliders, the lines."

The dog quickly got comfortable with the human bustle and the large equipment, so Shams borrowed a dog harness from a fellow flier to see if Ouka would wear it. The pup stayed still and didn't try to squirm out of it. They worked up to where he'd approach the harness and step into it on his own. Then came Ouka running with the harness, Ouka running with Shams strapped over him, and finally, Ouka and Shams lifting off for a brief inaugural tandem flight. It took social savvy, immense trust, and athleticism—what educational psychologist Howard Gardner would call kinesthetic intelligence—to leave the ground with grace. "He ran with me down the hill until the glider's wings took over, and we flew for about 10 seconds, then landed," Shams tells me. "He showed no fear or anxiety, did everything right. And when we were done, he ran around excitedly to all the other pilots." Sounds like one proud dog!

In the sky there's no need for instructions. "It's just the whoosh of the wind and a majestic view," Shams says, noting that paragliding is not like parachuting out of a plane or bungee jumping off a bridge: "It is very calm and smooth and relaxing." Shams says that people who have seen Ouka's popular videos online sometimes accuse him of forcing the dog into something dangerous. "Absolutely not," he says. He has always ensured that the dog is choosing to participate—part of the positive training he's committed to—and has learned Ouka's body language for what's OK and what's not. "He communicates very clearly when he doesn't want to do something," Shams says. In this case, man and dog have made the same choice. In the air, Shams wraps his legs around the dog's body below him "so he knows I'm there." Ouka rests his paws on his owner's feet, and they glide. "He trusts me because we have that bond," Shams says.

You have to marvel at the land animal who takes to the sky. Think about Ouka's willingness to forego solid ground beneath his paws, to move so swiftly upward, and to accept a host of wholly unfamiliar sensory experiences, including a view of the world that must come as quite a surprise. Adaptability is truly a *Canis familiaris* superpower, and a dog gliding through the air at 19 miles an hour doesn't need a cape to prove it. Whether the big fluffy dog who flies has any concept of the adventure he's living is impossible to know. But there's no question of the evolutionary history, the multiple intelligences, and the gift for learning that got him up there.

A smart start

Let's go back to the beginning, shall we? Think about how complex and variable the human environment is. Now, drop newborn dogs into that environment (this is where they evolved, after all). From day one, their world is packed with information that can be learned in a host of ways. Puppies are good at social learning from the very start, and not only when their teacher is another dog. Ethologist Claudia Fugazza and colleagues at Eötvös Loránd University in Budapest reported that eight-week-old puppies learned to open a puzzle box with food inside whether another dog (familiar or otherwise) or a person modeled the task, demonstrating their flexibility in social learning. The researchers also found the little pups remembered the how-to for at least an hour.

Now, imagine a new litter of puppies: nine of them with smooth skin under peach fuzz and eyes still tightly shut. Their key senses aren't yet online and won't be for some time. For now, nothing seems to matter except the warmth of their mother's body and the flow of her milk. One might assume there's no sense in exposing these pups to much of anything in these earliest days of life; it's enough that they're getting the nourishment they need to grow their bodies. "Getting smart" can come later.

But why wait? Their minds are already open for business. Trainer Julie Case, founder of the Ultimate Canine, based in Westfield, Indiana, sees an opportunity to begin shaping the pups into the very best and smartest animals they can be—right out of the chute, so to speak. Case, whose team produces therapy, service, police, narcotic sniffing, tracking, and other working dogs, believes you can't start too early. "People mistakenly think that if a dog is still blind and deaf, they're too young for this," she says. "But the brain is developing and grasping everything, even then." That's why, starting on day three of an Ultimate Canine pup's life, she is purposefully handled, tickled, nuzzled, and gently tipped this way and that. She's placed on materials with various textures and exposed to a variety of soft sounds along with a new scent every day.

And in a few weeks, 12 kids might spend a Saturday sitting in a circle, knee to knee, each holding a puppy from the latest Ultimate Canine litter. Case sits among them, reciting instructions like lines from a nursery rhyme: *"Head rubs: 1, 2, 3, 4, 5, 6, 7, 8, 9, and 10. Chin and neck! Chins up. Brusha brusha brusha brusha! Chest time: Scratchie scratchie scratchie scratchie! Now tails: If you're happy and you know it, wag your tail. Choo choo!"* Following along, the kids scratch bellies, kiss noses, wiggle tails, rub gums, blow on faces, softly massage ears, wipe eyes, and squeeze toes. They lift and tilt and flip the pups gently, pass them to the kid on the right, and give them a round of applause.

In those early days, too, the dogs hear louder noises: vacuum cleaners, hair dryers, crying babies, music, and recordings of fireworks (turned down low to start). They're exposed to sudden motions. They crawl over, under, and through small obstacles to get around in their whelping box. Handlers go through the motions of grooming. Every day is an adventure.

It's worth the effort, Case says. Because even before their senses arrive in full force, "they're feeling sensations, vibrations, and their brains are responding. They're receiving signals and creating synapses and making connections. Receptors are firing. Their brains [are] like a sky lit up with stars." And when their senses click on? It's a whole new world.

The idea is to normalize as many stimuli as possible, to reduce the things these dogs will worry about when worrying becomes a thing they do. And so within weeks, these pups will have met 100 new people of all colors and sizes and smells, with beards and noisy jackets and squeaky shoes, with bald heads and flowing skirts and hoodies. And soon they will have taken rides in a wagon through schools, hospitals, and other public places. This offers wonderful stress relief for the people who meet them as well as stimulation for the dogs.

Once they're able to toddle along, the pups experience an array of textures and new noises and problems to solve. They run mini-obstacle courses and fall into baby pools filled with empty plastic bottles (it's loud—trust me). They lie on a mat as strollers, skateboards, wheelchairs, and suitcases roll by within pawing distance, as umbrellas are opened and closed, as tarps and trash bags are whipped through the air. To reach their kibble, they learn to run up tiny ramps or over wobbly bridges, walk over wet towels, metal cage bottoms, and crinkly foil. They meet cats. "We create positive associations with things that might be unpleasant," Case says. Her aim, though, isn't to eradicate all fear—just to shape dogs so that they can recover from it quickly. "If these dogs see a crowd of kids running and screaming in Halloween costumes, sure, their cortisol will go up a little. We don't train away their need for self-preservation!" But the early exposure, she concludes, bumps up the threshold and gives them thicker skin. That means the dog can spend less time and energy being anxious throughout his life, and more time learning and communicating and solving problems.

So, early enrichment not only feeds dogs' intelligence from day one, but it sets them up for a richer, smarter life down the line. About 80 percent of the pups from Ultimate Canine litters enter some type of service work, and some end up being truly exceptional. Case calls those her "Navy SEALs," who go on to become the highest-level working dogs. Breed matters some, she says—DNA does affect where a dog excels naturally and how it handles the unfamiliar, for example—but most important is what the individual dog brings to the table and whether she's had the opportunity to use what's in her head.

Of course, not all of them have what it takes. "You don't come bald to a hair stylist and ask for flowing locks," Case says. "Sometimes people want their dogs to be service dogs and I say, you don't have the dog for that. It's not in them."

On the other hand, one of the working dogs Case trained is well versed in *three languages*. "We ran out of words [in English] and had to keep expanding," she says. Clearly, that dog started with the roots of greatness, and got the nourishment he needed early and often to grow his intelligence.

The more we discover about the nature of dog smarts, and the more we pay attention to how dogs learn best from puppyhood on, the more opportunities we can give them to learn. And what may appear to us to be super-complex and surprising tasks—things that behavioral scientists long assumed dogs simply were not capable of mastering, like assessing quantities, imitating, and correctly interpreting signals from another species—can be mastered rather easily. That is, *if* the training is smart and if it makes sense from a dog's point of view.

Step-by-step: This is better than that

"You have to build your training program from your learner's perspective," U.K.-based trainer Vidhyalakshmi Karthikeyan tells me. "Then you ask yourself, what does the end goal look like and what's the smallest step toward it I can teach?"

Karthikeyan calls this the "layer cake approach," a term I first heard her use at the 2021 Lemonade Conference, an annual trainers' forum. Each "layer"—each behavior or skill—looks nothing like the final goal, she says. But through reinforcements at each increment, you eventually get where you want to go. Breaking down complex tasks into progressive learning stages doesn't mean dogs are dumb, she notes. It's exactly the same way we humans learn: step-by-step. Walking, running, grasping and swinging tools, and focusing on fast-moving objects before giving tennis a go. Counting and mastering basic arithmetic before we tackle algebra. We get there one step at a time, or we are likely to fail. (Don't get me started on finding the value of x in seventh-grade math.) Remember, small step by small step, not in one giant leap, is how Ouka learned to fly.

That method, similar in structure to what other trainers call "chaining," allowed Karthikeyan's dog Beanie to learn a game of multiple choice that appears miraculous. But "it's more logic than magic," she says.

The puzzle-loving lurcher-greyhound mix had to choose from items placed in front of him based on a hierarchy of value that he learned one rule at a time: Toilet paper beats pasta. Pasta has value over any *other* item (a toy, for instance), but if TP is present, TP always wins. She rewarded Beanie based on a schedule that reinforced the hierarchy: "By building up a *huge* bank of wins for the first-choice item," she explains, "that ever important reinforcement history tells the dog *TP is best!* while setting up a slightly less robust reinforcement history for #2 (pasta), making it worth choosing only if TP is missing." And so on.

Karthikeyan also relied on basic behaviors the dog had already mastered, like paying attention to his owner and to items she showed him, using his nose to point, taking his kibble reward, and then readying himself for the next round. All he had to learn were the new rules. Very soon, his owner was speedily swapping out and moving around items and asking Beanie to choose, and every time he would nose the item of highest value relative to the others in the mix.

Beanie's smarts shone in part because the game was designed with his skills and interests in mind, and in part because he wanted to participate. (Not all dogs would.) It was a positive experience, with dual rewards of playing with his human and getting treats. Karthikeyan, in her incremental approach, had fully thought out each training layer, anticipating where the dog might get confused and correcting for potential errors in advance. And her reward system not only incentivized the game, but helped make the rules clear to the dog.

After watching Karthikeyan working with the enthusiastic Beanie, considering his point of view, and building her training from inside his mind, I was pretty sure she could teach the dog to knit—opposable thumbs be damned.

Step-by-step: How many?

Step-by-step, with delicious incentives, is also how a dog might learn to imitate another dog or a human. The games Copy! or Do as I Do are now common in training workshops, and seeing your dog watch you or another dog spin around, then doing it himself on command is a *wow* moment for sure. For him, it's just another series of moves he already knows how to do, put into a new context, that seems to make his owner very excited. Recent research, including work by Fugazza and colleagues, shows that not only can dogs imitate either other dogs or people, but they can generalize the "copy" rule and use it to learn a novel action. They can also do it with time in between the demonstration and the request to copy—a capacity called deferred imitation.

Ken Ramirez, of Karen Pryor Clicker Training, says that dogs are sometimes the most limited by what we assume they can and can't understand. He was convinced early in his career that they were capable of learning to mimic a behavior, even as others in his circle thought it was beyond their ability.

Ramirez was inspired partly by a study in which investigators compared litters of puppies allowed to watch their narcotics-detecting mothers at work versus those not exposed to the behavior. At six months old, the pups who watched learned the tasks more easily than those who didn't. It was a start, and it led Ramirez, and then others, to successfully teach dogs to "Copy!"—or do what the other dog just did.

I ground-truthed it at a workshop led by trainer Pat Miller on her rural property in Maryland. There, I watched participating pups work toward copying their *owners'* moves on the command "Do it!" It started with a behavior each dog already knew how to do, then moved beyond it. As a dog progressed, inching toward the desired mimicry, he was well rewarded. Ultimately, following in their owner's footsteps, the pups quickly learned to walk in a circle, step up on a block and down again, or bow.

Ramirez also trained a dog on quantities while other experts denied it was possible. (He later did controlled studies to convince them.) Coral, his Airedale mix, learned to associate a group of items with the same number of dots on a board. Five socks in a tray? Coral could nose the board with five dots. With socks, balls, rubber bones, Kong toys, disks, and other items visible, Ramirez could even indicate which item he wanted the pup to count: If he waved a ball in the air, she would ignore everything else and just count the balls. Seems simple to us, as we are biologically prone to crunch numbers starting as toddlers. But dogs' cognitive experience with math? It's still a bit of a mystery, but they are capable, as we are, of this kind of quantity matching. Awake fMRI studies suggest that dogs have a dedicated spot in the brain just for mathematics: a "neural mechanism for quantity perception," as humans do. (In fact, it's a characteristic that has likely been conserved across mammalian evolution.)

To be fair, Ramirez tells me, a dog succeeding at this game may not be *counting* exactly. "We are careful not to call it that, because it's tough to prove the dog is mentally pointing at each item and thinking, One, two, three, four." It's very possible the animal is instead "subitizing"—which means judging a (usually small) amount with a quick glance at the whole. "It's like when you roll a die, you don't have to count each dot on the die face," he says. You recognize six dots as an entity. So, in the dog world, the behavior is called "quantity recognition" instead of counting. Whatever you call it, think about your dog, the goofball over there happily licking the filthy bottom of your shoe, and imagine him acing an elementary arithmetic test. It could happen.

Coral even applied the concept of the quantity game to an unfamiliar case. Ramirez asked her "How many?" of an item that was not there. "I was holding my breath, wondering, What would she do with an item that was missing?" he says. "We hadn't trained her to use the blank board." Incredibly, she went right to the empty board that represented "none," and tapped her nose to the target. "It showed she really understood what she was supposed to be doing," Ramirez says, admitting he "was doing backflips inside" at her intelligent choice. (I'll just mention here that scholars who study the history of science tag the idea of "zero"—of thinking of nothing, of absence, as a concept in itself—as one of the watershed moments in human intellectual development. So, go Coral.)

Is it narrow-minded of us to assume that animals other than humans wouldn't understand and assess quantities? Studies of animals in various environments suggest that "numerical competence" helps them keep track of multiple offspring in a litter, exploit food sources, thwart predators and hunt prey, find their way around, and interact socially. Even single-cell bacteria make use of quantitative information through something called "quorum sensing." Through this process, organisms communicate their presence to one another, chemically or otherwise, until a threshold number is reached that drives the group to take action. Ants seem to use a similar strategy when deciding to move their colony.

Wild canids—wolves in particular—have optimal group sizes for hunting different kinds of prey, depending on the fight-back of the animal they're going for. That's one way numbers matter to them. And apparently, numbers also matter to domestic dogs, because there's no doubt Coral knew her quantities. But she had a limit: 14. "She did exceptionally well up to that point, but that's where her ability began to fall apart," Ramirez says.

He hypothesizes that it may have to do with litter size: A canid mom needs to keep tabs on all her pups, and dog litters don't often pass 12 or so pups. "It could help explain the capability, especially in a female dog," he says. But no doubt, some dogs will take to math more readily than others. Herding dogs, for example, do something similar on the job—easily separating out a certain number of sheep on command. The concept of quantity may be relatively easy to master when you're bred to keep track of animals scattered across a field.

Ramirez's broader point: Dogs can learn to do all sorts of "human-only" things if taught in a way that makes sense to them. And they can understand the concept of a game and apply it more broadly. "You see that with hand signals," he observes. "The first time, the dog doesn't have any idea what to do. But once he learns two or three, then he knows the rules, gets the concept, and can learn the next ones, *bang bang bang*, no problem."

Smart moves

Hawkeye is an athlete, a performer with a talent for mastering complex choreography. On cue, the agile pup tears across the grass and suddenly flings himself through the air, Superman-style, toward his owner. He pushes off against her chest—front paws *thump*, back paws *thump*—grabs the disk she's tossed, and hits the ground still running on her other side. At her request, he'll also bounce straight up and down like a pogo stick or jump through her hooped arms like an old-time circus tiger leaping through a ring of fire.

For an animal without wings, Hawkeye seems totally at ease with four feet off the ground. If knowing where your body is in space and how to maneuver it is a form of intelligence, then this dog is a kinesthetic genius. He's also a beautiful little specimen: a border collie–Australian shepherd mix with a painterly coat, mismatched eyes, and a stripe like a wide river down the center of his face that matches the white tip of his tail.

Hawkeye is one of two pup performers I met when I connected with trainer Sara Carson, owner of a company called the Super Collies. Carson and her border collie Hero achieved a bit of celebrity status during their performance on *America's Got Talent* in 2017. They were finalists, and you've never seen Simon Cowell so smiley. Appearances on lots of talk shows followed. Hero is now retired from showbiz, but Carson has other dogs in trick training. When I joined her at Atlanta Dogworks, a boarding and training compound in Ball Ground, Georgia, where she was teaching trick workshops one summer weekend, she had been traveling around the country in her camper van with four of them: Hawkeye, plus a brown-and-white border collie–Aussie mix named Marvel with her own mad skills, and two unruly puppies—another border collie plus a golden retriever still to be trained. There was also a very tolerant cat.

I should say for the record that I came to Carson and her superdogs with a pretty low bar. Because here's how things go with my own dogs when it comes to performing: "Monk, sit. Sit. SIT!" Monk sits. "Good boy. OK, Monk, shake. Monkey, can you shake? Damn it, Monk, SHAKE!" Monk whaps me with his paw. "Good boy." Cheese cube dispensed. Performance complete. Repertoire exhausted. But even someone with superobedient trick-loving dogs—the ones who roll over when "shot" or balance a treat on the nose—would be wowed by how Carson's dogs respond to her and what dog and human accomplish together on the stage.

Yes, Carson's Super Collies happen to belong to a breed renowned for "intelligence." Border collies, which appear repeatedly in this book, are, along with other herding dogs, genetically primed to use their heads to watch and learn. "These breeds are indeed innately smart," Carson says. "But more importantly, what they are is motivated. They want to get it right, and they want to perform." This is true regardless of breed, she continues: "If you find the right motivator, a dog will learn." For her, this has always been a bout of playtime, but an even more important incentive is *doing the thing:* The dogs show visible joy in the performances, especially those involving a Frisbee and spectacular leaps.

The dogs are intensely observant, "obsessively so," Carson says. That's a genetic thing, too: part of what herding dogs are bred to be. "You can really see them thinking, the little wheels turning," and I have to agree. As she and Marvel prepare to demonstrate the good girl's best tricks, Marvel stands at the ready, head tipped slightly to the side, ears aimed at

Carson as she speaks. She's *concentrating, assessing, deciding.* "Deciding whether it's worth it to do what I ask," Carson grumbles. Mostly, it is.

Indeed, "these dogs are the ultimate opportunists," says trainer Greg Tresan. "They are always weighing their options"—he mimes a pair of scales—"deciding, 'Which way is better for *me*?'" Tresan, who has long worked with dogs in the entertainment industry, runs Atlanta Dogworks, where Carson was teaching. He notes that smart dogs "will improvise, trying variations to keep from getting bored—especially if you keep asking them to do the same thing over and over."

But Carson knows how to change it up. As her commands fly—some audible, but many just a flick of the hand or a subtle body movement—Marvel turns in circles, backs up, slithers through her legs as she walks. At "Shy!" she dips her head and puts a paw over her eyes; at "Pray!" she lays her paws on Carson's outstretched arm and ducks her head underneath; at "Ouch!" she holds up a front paw as if she's stepped on a thorn and limps along. As Carson lies on her back with her legs in the air, the pup jumps atop her flexed feet and strikes a pose. She presses her snout to her owner's ear and "whispers" a secret. She sits like the Sphinx and crosses one paw over the other, then reverses. She does a "handstand," then switches to standing on her back legs and hops forward, back, and in circles. Carson makes an "O" with her arms and the dog leaps through, again and again. She flies into her owner's arms for a quick hug before the final move: Together, they bow.

The sheer range of tricks the Super Collies can perform makes you wonder, How the heck does a dog learn to do that? The answer, as usual, is "one step at a time." Like other trainers I met, Carson teaches in increments, sometimes tiny ones, and uses positive reinforcement to keep it going. "Trick training is ALL positive; there's no 'forcing,'" she tells me. "The dogs have to want it."

And want it they do. Carson works with dogs that both need a job and love a game. Her training encourages them "to offer behaviors, to keep trying, to really use the brain," she says. Novelty excites them and pushes them cognitively, so teaching them tricks and acrobatics is both fun and stimulating, giving them confidence to learn the next step. Studies using fMRI have shown that some dogs prefer gushing praise from their person over a food reward. Others really like the treat, though. For best results, Carson says, a trainer must adjust accordingly.

In a cool, sunlit classroom, about a dozen owners and their dogs take up spots in a big circle for Carson's midday class. A mix of breeds is represented, but with few surprises: border collies, Aussies, Labs, a retriever or two. Stereotypes often have a basis in reality, and there is no denying the DNA at work in this group. The Labs are competent but easily distracted by other dogs passing by outside the windows; the golden retriever is utterly enthusiastic (the tail never stops wagging) but slightly inept; the border collies make the quickest progress while the Aussie, intent on her young owner, appears frustrated by the girl, who is making her own mistakes. (It seems that although the dog knows what to do, the instructions are wrong; her audible *chuff* might as well be an eye roll.)

A big takeaway from hanging around Carson: "Dogs, like people, want to succeed!" Those that associate with us, anyway, want the praise, the ball, the treat. They want us to be happy with them. "But to get there, you have to set a dog up for success," she says.

Other trainers told me the same thing. Part of that is seeing through the dogs' eyes and figuring out what they're experiencing, then making adjustments that let the dogs think like dogs, not like people. Which is not always easy for people to do. As I watch Carson's class, I see many mistakes—by the owners. A little boy's rapid-fire repeating of commands clearly confuses his pup, who doesn't know whether to act on one word or three. A woman is so quick to reward her dog that the animal is learning he doesn't have to finish the trick to get the treat. A girl's tight hold on the leash must feel to her dog like a constant correction, which is likely why the dog is timid in her actions and making little progress learning the steps.

It occurs to me that we limit our dogs' ability to learn by doing a poor job as teachers. Remember our mantra—that there are no bad dogs, just bad trainers? (Good for you. Treats all around!) In so many small ways, we unknowingly set the animals up to fail: simple things like inconsistent signals or using terms that sound alike, for example. "'Down' and 'bow' are just too close," Carson says. "Pick something else."

I've often heard from experts that the humans need more training than the canines. It's another way dogs' connection with us affects how they think and perform, and another reason we owe it to them to do better at speaking their language.

Make good choices

More than 100 years ago, a zoologist named Herbert Jennings proposed that even pond scum is capable of making decisions. His lab work showed that the pond-loving protozoan *Stentor roeselii* generates complex and predictable behavioral changes to escape something unpleasant—first bending and contorting, then fanning its cilia at the yuck, and eventually swimming away. The basic capacity for choosing—this essential cognitive act of judging between good for me and bad for me—is present in the simplest of beings.

In fact, studies have shown that various nonhuman animals like to choose and benefit from doing so. Pigeons prefer "free choice" to "forced choice" for the same reward. If given a direct route to food or the choice of more complex maze routes, rats will choose the latter—preferring to pick from several options than to take the one given them. Monkeys, too, like options, even if the forced choice leads to a preferred reward. They also like controlling the order of tasks given to them, opting to choose from tasks they like less, rather than performing preferred tasks in a given order. Being allowed to choose can also boost cognitive performance, motivation, and confidence as well as lower stress levels in captive animals, whereas *not* having choices has the opposite effects.

Dogs are a long evolutionary way from pond scum. They are brainy creatures that learn from experience, just as we do, and make decisions about their behavior based on their experiences, just as we do. "Our brain is evolved to retain experiences and then give them back to us at key moments to improve our decisions next time," says Susan Friedman, a psychology professor at Utah State University.

It works that way for dogs, too. Like us, a dog seeks to control its environment every day through its behavioral choices. According to Friedman, the act of making a choice is in itself reinforcing, whatever the outcome. "When my dog chooses to bring a huge stick into the house, part of his motivation is that he gets to do it, to solve that problem of getting it through the door," she says. "It must be enormously reinforcing to succeed at controlling his world."

So control itself is a primary reinforcer, a reward. We make choices in part because having control over our world feels good and right. We *need* to make choices. It's in our DNA. Like us, dogs and other animals are always making them.

Making decisions and learning from their outcomes help animals build a bigger and better repertoire of ways to affect their environment, Friedman says. Those who can overcome an obstacle on their road to reinforcement—and who can pluck alternative ways forward from their repertoire—*"that's* what intelligence is all about," she explains.

What if a dog exists in a world where its repertoire remains small because there are no challenges, no decisions to make? That's all kinds of missed opportunity. Which is one reason Friedman is very much of the mind that we should give dogs more choice in their lives, allowing them more control over their own destinies. It can be as simple as letting the dog decide between basics: This treat or that one? Walk down the street or up? Play with the Kong or the stuffed toy? A game called You Choose! has even become a training tool—one I saw in use at Pat Miller's workshop and elsewhere. Even if a human is orchestrating the situation and setting up the choices, giving an animal the feeling of control is beneficial, both Friedman and Miller say.

Giving options is beneficial not just in training, but also in health care. Friedman has trained zoo animals and described a case in which a giraffe would make behavioral choices that let it practically give itself an injection, positioning itself in the right spot and pushing back against the syringe of its own volition. Zoo animals are often taught to present a body part on cue or open their mouths wide for an exam. It's all about the animal *wanting* to perform the task, Friedman says. "You teach them a way to say no, but then make sure the reinforcers are stacked so that they choose to do as we ask."

A robust enough reinforcement history makes coercion—force and restraint that can be dangerous for animals and caretakers alike—unnecessary. Meanwhile, an intelligent animal saying no is important data, Friedman explains. "It tells us something is wrong in the environment, or the animal needs more information or better reinforcers. In a sense the dog becomes the trainer, telling us what we can do better."

Assistance Dogs of the West (ADW) in Santa Fe, New Mexico, a working dog training facility, chooses not to focus on lists of client needs and dog attributes. Instead, the trainers will ask different dogs to interact with different people, letting the animals choose whether to engage. If a dog isn't interested in someone, she's allowed to say so, simply by walking away.

"Letting the dog pick her owner and her job lets you go much further with that dog," notes Jill Felice, ADW's founder, during my visit. A pup named Bonnie, for example, "was really looking for *her* person; she was very picky. During an interaction she might seem to be connecting at first, but then she'd put herself in her crate. It meant this [person] wasn't the one," she says. Then one day, "she *chose* him, very definitively. It was a young boy with autism. She seemed fascinated by his unusual speech cadence and was content to sit staring at and listening to him." The partnership proved long-lasting. "If we had pushed her into a relationship, it might not have worked out," Felice says. "We knew to trust she was smart enough to make her own decision."

Thinking about choice reminds me of those childhood years when my parents would order me to practice piano. They didn't try to make it fun or gratifying, so it became just another chore. Proponents of positive styles of training urge us to do better for dogs, to "game-ify" training exercises so that working with us becomes internally reinforcing for our dogs. That way, they can't wait to participate.

All this is in search of what renowned trainer Ian Dunbar calls the "holy grail" of partnering with a dog: "That's when a dog completes an obedience trial or walks happily by the side of his human because there's nothing he'd rather do."

CHAPTER FOUR

WHEN LEARNING MATTERS MOST

Smart pups like Beanie and Coral make brain games look easy, while high-flying dogs like Marvel and Hawkeye have mastered an impressive and entertaining suite of tricks. But there are more high-stakes kinds of learning out there, through which dogs give their humans priceless gifts of greater freedom and safety. It's dog intelligence at work—with real-world, life-changing results.

Let me be your eyes

Guide dogs may be the most familiar icons of the supersmart pups. But what they're doing for their partners with visual impairments isn't exactly what I imagined. Being blind doesn't mean being directionally challenged, necessarily. The human partners of guide dogs explained to me that *they* actually are responsible for mapping out trips. Their dogs learn the way and then lead them safely to their destination, but of course, the animals aren't figuring out a route from the get-go. Yes, dogs can learn the lefts and rights for regular trips, as well as "lead" or even reroute if an obstacle is in the normal path. But it's a little less about canine GPS than I expected.

That's one of many things I learned when I fell in love with little Jesse, the guide dog in training you met at the beginning of this book. (If you didn't read the preface, please check it out now; it may be my favorite bit.) I met Jesse on my second day observing staff and trainers at The Seeing Eye, the oldest and second largest guide dog organization in the country, located on a grassy campus in Morristown, New Jersey. Jesse was not the last dog I would dream of taking home with me from that place; I met impressive pups at every turn.

The Seeing Eye, founded in 1929 and at its current location since 1965, serves an average of 260 people a year, each of whom undergoes a residential course to learn how to work with their guide dog. Of the 500 or so puppies bred there each year, more than 60 percent make it through training to graduate as Seeing Eye dogs.

I went to The Seeing Eye to get a sense of how these pups learn what they learn and do what they do. I've always thought of guide dogs as particularly intelligent working animals, because they don't just learn commands but also sometimes have to make their own decisions about what's best for their person. They have to think ahead where their owner can't—and that takes a special kind of smarts.

However, it's very much a two-way gig. "People think a blind person picks up the lead and says, 'grocery store!' and the dog leads them there," says Dave Johnson, director of instruction and training, as we chat in his office. "It's not like that. The dog needs to focus on the guiding and safety, and on problem solving. It's the person's job to know where to go, how to get there, and so on."

The dogs quickly learn routes to common destinations, of course—but according to Johnson, it's not a magic carpet ride. "It's work for both parties," he says. Senior training manager Tom Pender adds that these dogs are intelligent enough to lose faith if their owner is inconsistent. "You lose a dog's trust by constantly making errors in judgment yourself," he says. "You have to be consistent and mostly right" for your partner to stick by you.

As it happened, a working trip into New York is scheduled during my visit, and I jump at the chance to observe these smart pups in the big city. The team brings a van full of dogs in training, including variously colored Labs, young German shepherds, and a couple of Lab-golden crosses. All are so quiet and well behaved that I almost forget they are stacked in crates behind us during the ride in. Before day's end, each animal will get a speedy, miles-long walk "on harness," plus a couple of subway rides complete with trips through narrow turnstiles and up and down escalators.

On the first go, the escalator into the subway depths proves a scary surprise for most of the pups. "All they can see is a drop-off to the next floor down, so they are quick to refuse," Johnson tells me. Picture a lanky shepherd striding with confidence, then suddenly hunkering down, a clear no to going any farther. The trainer helps him onto the steps where the pup stands stiffly all the way down before taking a graceless leap off near the bottom, feet skidding on the landing. All do better the second time around. They're quick learners about what's truly dangerous, these animals.

Because guide dogs need to learn to press on despite such discomforts, and to ignore all kinds of distractions, it makes perfect sense to familiarize them with the noisy, smelly, crowded, unpredictable, obstacle-strewn environment that is midtown Manhattan on a Tuesday. Think of trying to stay on task with your senses bombarded by odors, noise, and constant motion from all directions. No wonder so many pups flunk out of guide dog school.

But the experience is also a test for the people. By three in the afternoon, we have covered nine miles on foot, which explains why The Seeing Eye trainers get an annual shoe allowance and are mostly under 30 years old. As Pender unharnesses a petite black Lab named Roger to swap him out for the next canine candidate, he says, "You're going to sleep well tonight!"

Thinking he means Roger, now done for the day, I say, "He certainly is!" Pender replies, "I was talking to you."

My exercise with Jesse is about handing off my most relied-upon sense to another being, giving up control, and trusting that creature to be cognitively capable. Here is an animal thinking for both of us, necessarily making crucial choices at speed. Johnson tells me, "Standing still is not really an option for these dogs. You want them making decisions on the move, planning ahead about how to manage a barrier or avoid pedestrians, and making sure not to let their person get into trouble." When the dog is seasoned and good at the job, he explains, "He'll really dig in and take over."

I feel a little of that with Jesse, which is both terrifying and freeing. Certainly, it is all the clearer why the bond between dog and owner is so essential to a pair's success. Because the relationship is indeed a partnership, not just two individuals of different species who happen to be connected by a strap.

"Both of you have to be fully invested for it to work," says Melissa Allman, who has been blind since birth and relied on a cane to assist her until taking The Seeing Eye's course and getting her dog Luna from the organization in 2017. "Sometimes it looks like magic to others, but it's really hard work. I'm not just managing and arguing with myself but with another brain, dealing with another living creature with her own thoughts. The cane was never this challenging!" Despite those challenges, "now that I have Luna, I can say it's one of the most meaningful things I've experienced," she continues. "I'm no longer trapped in a box. Her abilities and our connection have added new dimensions to my life. I'd be lost without her."

Later, I visit Allman in her office at The Seeing Eye, where she works as an advocacy and government relations specialist. As I enter, Luna, a small watchful yellow Lab lying on a dog bed in the corner, lifts her nose for a cursory sniff, then tucks her head between her paws and sighs audibly. Although I have a childlike need to be loved by every dog I meet, I know it isn't appropriate to approach her, and I try not to take the lackluster greeting personally. Guide dogs are necessarily one-person animals, extremely focused on their owner and trained to ignore what doesn't immediately affect the pair of them. Allman keeps a hand on Luna for much of our conversation—possibly reinforcing the "stay" command but also, perhaps, communicating something more subtle, just between them.

"Once you have that connection," says Allman, "everything runs up and down that leash. It's a conversation that's sometimes invisible to others because the dog speaks her language through the harness." I love the way she puts this, and I'm pretty sure I know what she means. At least for a few moments on my short stint with Jesse, I relaxed enough to really feel the dog's tiny adjustments and to "answer" with my own parallel movement. I was told if your arm is in the proper position, you can feel the dog breathing. I wasn't quite there, but close. A seasoned handler naturally, instantly, responds to those subtle cues, making for a smooth ride, as opposed to the frantic shuffle of the uninitiated (like me).

The dog uses another superpower to read her owner's body language, hand signals, and tone of voice. And that's in addition to detecting scents and who knows what other invisible (to us) cues, completing the communication loop.

There's intelligence in this back-and-forth. But "smarts" as we usually think of them don't have to be off the charts in these dogs. Yes, they need to learn commands, to problem-solve, and to bond with their person—all cognitive exercises. "But you don't need to be a rocket scientist in the dog world to be a good guide dog," says Peggy Gibbon, The Seeing Eye's director of canine development. "High willingness plus modest intelligence—really, the confidence to make decisions on the street—is the best combination. You don't want the dog that's always thinking, What's in it for me?" Most important, she says, is that the dog "has the desire not just to work, but to work *with a person.*"

With dogs trained to guide people with visual impairments, though, one special kind of "smart," not necessarily taught to all working dogs, is truly essential. "It's called intelligent disobedience," Dave Johnson tells me. "And it's the backbone, the hallmark of what these animals do."

Do as I say, except sometimes

What intelligent disobedience means: *Do as I say! Except sometimes! And use really good doggy judgment as to when to refuse, because it can be a matter of life and death.*

A Seeing Eye dog must tap into this kind of intelligence, leaning on his own best judgment, or he will fail at his most important task: keeping his person safe. Because if you can't see a car zipping around the corner and your dog can, he darn well better refuse to lead you into the street, regardless of your insistence that it's time to cross.

I see it in action—the training of it, anyway—on the subway platforms, where Oscar, Tom, and two other trainers work their dogs right up to the edge, commanding them to go forward when it would have been dangerous to do so, and then praising the heck out of them for refusing. "It's partly self-preservation," Tom tells me as he tries to coax Roger beyond the safe zone. Roger holds firm, then squirms away from the edge, and gets big praise for his refusal. Once the dog bonds with a person, Tom says, something else kicks in—a real caring and desire to ensure nothing bad happens to their best friend.

And that caring takes the relationship to a new level. Peggy Gibbon points to the power of these dogs' emotional intelligence: "After a year or so, it's not always about the guide work but sometimes just about companionship," she says. "Sometimes that's more important than what they do in harness."

Working on intelligent disobedience and practicing a range of other skills—not just for the dogs, but also for young Seeing Eye staff and the dogs' likely owners—starts back on the less hectic streets of Morristown. Joan Markey, senior manager of instruction and training, takes me out with a young trainer named Brooke, who strides confidently, blindfolded, behind German shepherd Monty, the leather between them. "The hardest thing is to get the dog to look up," Markey tells me as we scurry a few steps behind the working pair. It's more natural for pups to keep their noses low, but a dog needs to gauge the threat of overhanging obstacles to their person. "It takes some teaching, but eventually the dogs have this *ah-ha* moment when they realize what's above—even if it doesn't get in *their* way—also matters," she says.

As we zoom down the street, blindfolded Brooke suddenly slaps a lamppost with her hand, pretending to bump her arm. She stops and so does the dog, and she slaps the pole twice more for emphasis as Monty watches. "We have to be actors, bonking into cars, stumbling at curbs, walking into poles, and making a big deal of it so the dog learns from mistakes," Markey explains. When teaching, the trainer will back up and rewalk a stretch so that the animal gets another try at taking a wider arc around an obstacle or staying farther from an edge. Any inkling of a shift in the right direction merits much rejoicing (and, in response, tail wagging). "Small corrections and big positive reinforcement work wonders," she says.

I notice a Prius up ahead, waiting to turn at the light, and Markey points out it's "one of ours." The near silence of the hybrid electric vehicle makes it a special challenge for dogs. As Brooke and Monty begin to cross, Walt from The Seeing Eye purposefully cuts them off in the car, forcing Monty to stop short despite Brooke's forward command.

As on the subway platform, this is where intelligent disobedience comes in to play. But on this first pass, the car comes awfully close to the training pair. So the driver issues a correction—bonking the pup on the nose from inside the car, wielding a foam cylinder gently but with purpose, before pulling away. "You want the contact associated with the vehicle, as if the dog got bumped by the car," Markey says. "It's how they learn to disobey in the future."

Bite me maybe

Unlike independent-thinking guide dogs, police and military dogs must be capable of absolute, instantaneous obedience in crucial moments, because they have to attack and bite people on command.

I can't help but consider how making this particular request of dogs is the antithesis of the relationship we're meant to have with each other. We've coevolved toward friendship, but here we are teaching these animals to use their predatory and protective urges against us. And, under certain circumstances, they'll happily oblige. What amazes me most is that a "bite dog" is trusted not only to follow a handler's instructions absolutely and to channel that powerful instinct at just the right time, but also to be able to flip a switch and shut it down in an instant. As the bite itself is the reward for dogs trained in this task, just imagine the incredible self-control it requires to quit at exactly the right moment. But during my own encounter, the dog gets his reward.

The bite suit is stiff, smells of dried sweat, and is at least three sizes too big for me. But I shrug into it because I want to know what it's like on the other side of a dog's powerful jaws when he's given the command to attack.

I am at a park in Atlanta on a rainy day, under the cover of a riding pavilion, waiting to meet up with renowned police-dog trainers Mark Leamer and John Bobo, as well as a couple of local K-9 teams. These generous guys, plus two uniformed police officers, have offered to demonstrate what happens when a "bad guy" doesn't follow a K-9 team's instructions. Before they set up the attack scenario, I get to meet Wick, a tall, regal Belgian Malinois with brown-sugar fur, a black mask, and giant, black-rimmed rabbit ears, handled by Officer Brandon Decosse. Energy rolls off the dog. I get no cuddles or kisses when he makes introductory rounds; he is all business and raring to go.

Once suited up, I follow the handler's instructions and stand in a corner of the pavilion on an angle, legs splayed and knees bent slightly for stability, elbow bent and forearm held away from my body like an offering.

I feel my skinny little arm swimming in the sleeve built for an extra-large man, and for a moment I question most of my life decisions, including this one. But it's happening.

I giggle nervously for a moment, but when Officer Decosse and Wick come around the corner into view, the latter pulling so mightily on his leash that the full-size cop, outfitted in 40 extra pounds of gear, is stutter-stepping to stay in control, I feel my legs start to shake. Knowing he is on the job, there is no subtlety in Wick's communication: He barks and snarls, his eyes staring straight into mine. *Ah, shit.* Decosse and Wick pause just shy of me. And then, on command, Wick lunges. Even though I know it's coming, the hit is a shock and the power behind it throws me into the wall. I bounce back into place mainly because I am now attached to Wick, his jaws tightly locked on my arm, teeth buried in the black sleeve. His prey drive is dialed to high: Barking through his bite, he jerks my arm back and forth. The wrenching has my head flopping like a rag doll's, and I know I will have bruising, not to mention a neck ache, despite the padding.

Sensing I've had enough (I think I yelled, "OK, enough!" but it's a bit of a blur), Decosse grabs Wick's collar and follows the script he uses in an on-duty situation—yelling at me to stand still and stop resisting his dog (as if), then commanding Wick to release me. Police-dog commands are typically in German or Dutch, in part because many dogs are imported from Europe and exposed to these languages early on, and in part to make the words distinctive and not easily guessed and used by a non-cop. Plus, there's just more power behind *"Los!"* (German for "loose"), than "Let go!" Still, for some reason, Wick doesn't *los* right away. Decosse tries the verbal command again, to no avail. Finally, he uses his baton to separate Wick's jaws from my arm and set me free.

I've done a lot of potentially dangerous things in the name of reporting—diving with tiger sharks, hunting for cobras, climbing onto small rickety planes in remote parts of the world—and on the face of it, this didn't seem any more or less risky. I expected to have the bolt of fear, the adrenaline rush, and just after, the elation mixed with relief.

But I feel something new in this case that takes me some time to name. It is a sense of betrayal—that a dog would attack *me*, of all people, that he wouldn't see me for the dog lover and all-around animal whisperer I am—and refuse to harm me.

I'm only mildly embarrassed by my severe case of Disney princess syndrome. I want to be that girl who has a magical relationship with animals, the one wild creatures approach when their paws are pierced with thorns, the one at whom they gaze with trust in their eyes. In the dog's case, I fantasized that he'd refuse to attack me because he would sense my goodness and want to befriend me. Commanded to bite, he'd instead lick my face.

And according to Jim Crosby—a former police officer turned veterinary forensics expert and researcher who rehabilitates dogs from fighting rings, hoarding situations, and other tragic contexts—it can be tough to flip the bite switch once dogs connect with humans. "In the military and for police, the hardest thing to teach the dogs is to bite humans, because it goes against the friendships they've developed," he tells me. "Teaching that aggressive contact with humans is OK is harder than any obedience work. Our bond just goes so deep."

In my case, Wick had no second thoughts. He treated me as he would any target, just as he was taught. He even held on longer than instructed, as if to let me know this was no fairy tale. The dog was expertly trained and committed, physically and mentally, to the job he had.

It took me some time to wrap my head around it, but dogs trained to go after a perpetrator—to attack and take that person down to the ground, to potentially mess the person up if he or she isn't complying—aren't *aggressive* dogs, nor are they usually "sharp" (a term used to describe a particular wariness around people that some dogs have, especially among strangers). Wick the Atlanta police dog would never attack unless instructed to, and even then it's really just a game to him. In another context, that dog would completely ignore me or, perhaps, let me pet him if I were invited into his home. As John Bobo explains it, "A police dog on duty is a bad-ass. Off duty he's just a dog. When the blue lights and siren go on, he goes straight into work mode and his connection with you on the job is so intense he knows your heartbeat. But when those lights go off, he's family, playing with your kids."

Knowing the difference, he says, is one mark of an intelligent dog.

Cease and desist

Self-control is an essential part of any intelligent dog's tool kit. At Lackland Air Force Base in Texas, I observed how a dog committed to biting on command learns to hold back when the situation calls for restraint. Dogs of war, like those on police patrol, sometimes have to bite. It's an ugly necessity, and one that nobody on the teams at Lackland takes lightly. Fortunately, a dog rewarded for this behavior in one scenario understands that using his predatory power is context-specific and doesn't do it without permission. "We can't have dogs going around biting everybody they meet," one handler told me. I was glad to hear it. As with all their trained behaviors, the animals know when it's the right move and when it's forbidden. They're smart that way.

The chase-and-bite behavior is rooted in the dog's prey drive, making it especially hard to stop before the chomp. But that's what these dogs must learn to do. The technical term is "controlled aggression," and from the edge of a field at Lackland, I watch a young Malinois named Griffin masterfully demonstrate this ability. This one happens to be male, but female dogs are also trained for "aggressive" military and police duty. (That they go into heat, however, makes them a little less desirable for such work.)

It looks like this: The person with the padded arm first teases the dog with the arm, whipping him into a frenzy, then runs away. By now the pup wants nothing more than to get his teeth into that arm, so when given the command to go after the moving target, he's committed. Ears back and spit flying, he tears across the field in full-on predatory fervor. But just as he is about to land his prey, his handler yells "OUT!" and "SIT!" That dog has to screech to a sudden halt, fighting his deepest instincts to pounce as his prey remains tantalizingly within reach, and sit. He has to forego the natural progression of the chase, as well as the prize, because sometimes the bad guy waves the proverbial white flag and the pursuit is called off.

I've always thought of self-control as a component of intelligence, but hadn't really considered why. Psychologists have an explanation: Self-control is one of the "executive functions"—a set of foundational mental skills used to manage everyday life—and studies in people have found consistent parallels between executive function and scores on general intelligence tests. In fact, high executive function may be a more accurate indicator of success in many areas of life than IQ. That doesn't mean the two always go hand in hand, but often they do. Of course, IQ is a human measure irrelevant to canines, but executive function and general intelligence likely pair up in dogs much as they do in us.

That seems to be true in Griffin: He goes from zero to 60 and back to zero, no problem. He makes it look easy. But I imagine that his drive to complete the attack, and his training to respond instantly to changes directed by his handler, must do battle in his head each time he launches into a chase.

Toy power

Most of us, I hope, have at least one passion in our lives for which we would eschew all else. For the dogs at Lackland, that thing is the snowman-shaped hollow rubber chew toy, usually red (oddly, as dogs are red-green color-blind), with a loop of rope attached. Brand name: Kong.

I'm no stranger to a toy-loving dog. Gretel, the Weimaraner of my teenage years, was wild for her tennis ball. It was her soggy, filthy companion by day and her pacifier by night—she'd lie in her bed and chew it rhythmically, eyes half mast, until she finally drifted off. But never have I seen dogs get as excited over a toy as the Lackland dogs get over the Kong. It replaces the prey their instincts crave. The handlers help things along by really winding up the dogs in preparation for toy time, but Kong appreciation is a whole different ball game. In fact, the only way to easily get a young dog to let go of his Kong is by giving him another Kong. That's part of the training strategy: The trainer will tempt the dog with the second Kong until he releases the first in trade. Eventually, the replacement isn't needed anymore.

But as familiar as the sight of a toy-loving pup may be, it turns out that playing with an object is not really "natural" for a predatory animal. When I meet with Stewart "Doc" Hilliard, a behavioral neuroscientist who has managed Lackland's renowned military working dog breeding program for about 20 years, he points out that object play is sort of a mutated hunting behavior that breeders have tweaked over hundreds of years. And it's an extremely useful tweak: "Because of this propensity to want involvement with an object, I can take an arbitrary item"—he holds his cell phone in the air and wiggles it around—"impart movement to it or put resistance on it, and see how engaged a dog will get."

It never occurred to me that a dog's toy drive would be essential to its military training, but indeed it is, Hilliard says. And it's mostly a hardwired trait: "Dogs either come to us with enough of it or not." Those who do have enough of this particular "right stuff" will learn to do some serious jobs, sniffing out bombs included. In fact, for a military dog, Kong commitment is initially more important than intelligence, though the Lackland dogs seem to have both.

Like many other astute canines, military dogs may need to employ intelligent disobedience. In a life-and-death situation, as bomb detector dogs often are, they may have to use their judgment whether to follow the handler's order or what their own senses are telling them. "These dogs should be obedient to the odor first," Hilliard tells me. "If I'm a handler who has an inkling about where a bomb is hidden, I may lean in that direction, purposefully or not. But if the dog's nose is telling another story, she has to ignore my focus and go with her nose, and do so willfully. If need be, she should push me out of the way."

It's a delicate balance, he says, because these dogs are so well trained to respond to handlers' cues. "They have to learn, 'listen to me but be prepared to ignore me if I'm wrong.'" Because sometimes the dog really is the smartest person in the room.

Please don't tell

As mysterious as their abilities may seem to us, we need to remember that dogs are not infallible sniffers; their noses are not machines. After all, they are thinking, feeling beings, and because of their desire to please us, they may make errors in sniffer tasks.

But errors don't suggest inferior intelligence. A different kind of smarts—the kind that gives dogs a constant read on us, supporting a beneficial interspecies partnership—may sometimes override even the solid messages of the nose.

You may have heard of Clever Hans, a horse whose crowd-pleasing ability to do math on command back in the early 1900s turned out to rely on subtle, unintentional, cues from his owner. His story has become a sort of shorthand among scientists for the need to avoid situations in which investigators could inadvertently influence the results of animal studies.

Dogs are in tune with us, just as Hans was attentive to his owner; they're always watching and learning whether or not we're aware of it. And dog handlers can easily "tell" a dog what to do without meaning to. That's especially important to acknowledge where we rely on dogs to find things that can profoundly affect human lives.

Back in 2010, a UC Davis neurologist named Lisa Lit, who also had experience as a detection-dog trainer, published a powerful study that called into question the impartiality of police K-9 teams. The researchers set up tests in which the dog handlers were told target scents (explosives or drugs) were hidden in four rooms in a church, including in spots marked with scraps of red paper. In truth, the rooms had no target scents at all, though sausages and tennis balls were hidden as decoys.

With nothing to target, there should have been no alerts in any of the rooms. Instead, dogs alerted in all of them, and most often at the places indicated by the red flags—suggesting that the handlers, for whom the markers were meaningful, were somehow influencing the dogs' choices. It's important to note that the aim of the study was neither to question the dogs' detection abilities nor to suggest the officers were dishonest. "Directing" a dog can be entirely unintentional, the authors noted; all it takes is a tiny inadvertent glance, gesture, or nod.

This matters especially when K-9 teams' findings affect what happens next. In most states, a detection dog alerting on your car gives police the right to search inside the vehicle (some police jokingly call the dogs "probable cause on four legs"). This can lead to all kinds of legal troubles for a driver if anything illegal is discovered. In some locales, police even get to decide, based on their own experience with the dog, whether a behavior constitutes a cue. (So: *I know my dog and the way he was staring at the wheel well told me he'd found something.*)

But if the dog's alert is prompted by handler misdirection or misinterpretation, the driver should never be subjected to the search. I observe handlers in training working detection dogs on vehicles at Lackland, and I can see how easy it would be to show your bias, if you have one, by unintentionally overdirecting a dog.

An afternoon of testing is in progress when I approach the long parking lot behind the barracks, where dozens of old vehicles in various states of disrepair squat side by side. Oscar Clayton, the senior military-dog evaluating officer, stands by with a clipboard watching a young airman and a small shepherd on a short but loose leash moving among the vehicles. Clayton is no-nonsense and mildly grumpy as I pester him with questions while we watch what turns out to be a less-than-stellar performance.

It starts out OK. As the handler circles a derelict Ford truck in hastily applied spray paint blue, his hand leads the dog's nose along the lower part of the car, around the door seams, and into the wheel well. He taps the vehicle here and there as they go, encouraging the dog to check high and low. That's all good. But then comes the error: The dog seems to catch a scent at the corner of the front bumper, her head suddenly flicking left. But the handler is looking ahead and keeps moving. As he taps farther down the bumper, the leash tightens and the dog rushes to catch up, abandoning whatever she's almost discovered.

"See that?" Clayton asks me. "The dog was trying to tell him something and he wasn't listening. He should have gone where she wanted to search, let her take him to the scent. The rule is, read your dog. Follow your dog."

Reading a dog, he notes, includes listening for her sniffs to speed up as she aims to pinpoint the source of the scent. Clayton is stone-faced as he ticks boxes and makes notes on the form on his clipboard. For a moment, I have that exam-day feeling in my gut, then a hit of relief that he isn't testing *me*.

Testing is essential to ensure handlers give dogs the right amount of independence and act as attentive, but not pushy, partners. In this case, because the airman is rushing and, perhaps, focused on where he expects the sample to be, he misses out on what the dog has to say. It is easy to imagine the opposite scenario, too: A handler makes assumptions that come through unintentionally and puts pressure on the dog to *find the thing right there*. And the dog, a little confused and wanting to please her handler, ignores her nose and signals, "Found it!"

As a last hurrah at Lackland, my guide takes me to the whelping facility where the military working dog program's own puppies spend their first days. There is just one pup there at the time—an ankle-high four-week-old Malinois, nearly all warm gravy but for his black muzzle and a stripe across his tail. He is the sole survivor of a rough pregnancy, a real fighter, named Warrior, of course.

I cuddle the soft little guy to my neck until he goes for an earring. Then we play tug of war with a chew toy to keep his needle teeth from tearing up my hands. (Malinois fans call puppies "malligators" for that mouthy tendency.) Yes, puppies bite, and maybe it's the context, but I swear this dog is showing off what he can do, and will do, as a grown-up.

"You may take down some bad guys with those teeth someday, little dude," I say to him, extracting my punctured pinkie from his mouth. "You could end up a hero." Or maybe this particular pup won't take to soldiering and will instead find his way to a job that uses his considerable cognitive powers more than his physical ones. His path remains before him, but no matter what, I know he'll get the opportunity to learn all kinds of things from all kinds of people.

Whatever kinds of brightness are inside him will find their way out.

CHAPTER FIVE

WALKING TOGETHER IN DIFFERENT WORLDS

Dogs are clearly primed, both genetically and developmentally, to flourish in environments shaped by humans. They connect with us, and they learn from us. But that doesn't mean they experience our shared environments the same way we do—and not just because they're down on four legs. Dogs gather information about their surroundings in ways that are so different from ours that they occupy, in a sense, a whole other world.

In part, dogs' sensory data-gathering mechanisms differ: The structures of the nose, the mobility of the ears, the sensitivity of the whiskers all matter. But also, the information dogs' brains respond to isn't always the same as what our brains glom on to. So whatever thing your dog does that you think of as inexplicable, weird, gross, or even dumb, consider it *doggish* instead.

And it's crucial to remember that although the dog's nose, tongue, ears, whiskers, and paws gather the data, those data are *understood* by the brain. I suppose this is obvious, but it's not how we tend to think about it.

The brain is where sensory information is collected, sorted, classified, and remembered, and where decisions are made. That's why it's appropriate to think of these systems in terms of sensory intelligence, not merely as sensory receptors. As I've explored the ways dogs' sensory world is unlike ours, I've begun to realize that we are pretty clueless about what a dog's experience is really like. We'll get to the nose shortly. But first, let's consider a few other striking differences between dogs' and humans' sensory lives.

Hear, hear

Neuropsychologist Stanley Coren elegantly wrote that the right side of an 88-key piano would need 52 extra keys to play the highest notes a dog can hear. And the top 24 notes would need to be tuned electronically because even the sharpest-eared humans wouldn't be able to hear them at all.

If you prefer drier stats, humans with perfect hearing can detect frequencies from about 20 to 20,000 hertz (Hz), the core of which roughly lines up with the human voice. Dog hearing starts slightly above ours, around 40 Hz, but they can hear to 65,000 Hz. Their volume sensitivity is four times ours, especially in the high-frequency range. This makes good evolutionary sense for a predator who hunts small mammals by their squeaky distress calls (when there's no kibble in the bowl, at least). And with 18 muscles controlling each earflap, dogs' supercharged ear mobility allows them to triangulate the source of sounds, discerning both the whereabouts of the noisemaker and whether it's coming or going.

So it makes sense that your dog knows your spouse is almost home before wheels hit the driveway—he hears the car when it's still a long way away. Canine hearing sensitivity also explains why some dogs stress out over everyday noises. Not only is a vacuum cleaner just plain loud, but who knows how much it's screaming at Hz above our ears' range? Or how many of our electronic devices put out high-pitched sounds we don't even know are there?

A lot to see here

Like their hearing, dogs' visual system is also tooled for detecting prey. They see well in the low light of dawn and dusk, and their eyes are as much as 20 times more sensitive to motion than ours. That means they spot not just the wiggle of a rabbit's whisker or the pulse of a rat's heartbeat, but also minute yet meaningful changes in our facial expressions and body postures. No wonder they seem to read their owners' minds.

Dogs tend toward nearsightedness—they might not recognize an approaching friend until he's fairly close—and while their visual universe lacks sensitivity to the red and green parts of the color spectrum, they do see blues and yellows and are acutely sensitive to shades of gray. (Think about those exquisitely detailed black-and-white films from cinema's golden age before you feel sorry for "color-blind" dogs!) Canine eyes may even be built for visual capabilities that we don't have at all: Like those of many other animals, their lenses transmit significant amounts of ultraviolet light, wavelengths that human lenses block.

Can touch this

Whiskers are supersensitive sensory tools, and dogs have four sets on their faces. Each whisker follicle has its own blood and nerve supply, and together the bristling hairs can detect changes in airflow as a dog approaches an object well before any contact is made. Their footpads, and the skin between their toes, are also supersensitive. (One overlap with us: Many dogs are ticklish!)

The taste of water

Dogs have significantly fewer taste buds than we do—only around 1,700 to our 9,000. Unlike us, though, they have a patch of taste buds at the back of the throat, which gives them a final warning before they swallow something that tastes potentially harmful. And dogs have special taste buds on the tips of their tongues that let them taste water. As in, the "flavor" of the molecules themselves, not anything dissolved in the drink. Cats also have this ability, though we, of course, do not. Stanley Coren suggests this ability would have evolved "as a way for the body to keep internal fluids in balance after the animal has eaten things that will either result in more urine … or will require more water to adequately process." Smart buds, if I may.

Oh, so sensitive

All told, it's no wonder our dogs are so miserable when they have to wear an Elizabethan collar after an injury or a veterinary procedure. That "cone of shame" we laugh about must flub up their sensory experience: disrupting airflow and therefore smells, walling off peripheral vision, blocking or amplifying sounds, and keeping them from their natural "nosing" behavior. I suppose it's a sign of dogs' faith in humanity that they mostly tolerate this indignity.

Along with smell, which we'll explore in the next chapter, these are the familiar senses we all learned about in elementary school. The list of five, which dates back to Aristotle, is nevertheless ridiculously limited, and misses a great deal about how living beings from trees to terriers experience their environment.

These days, scientists recognize a wealth of sensory systems, of varying degrees of functional significance, in different organisms. Some are thought to be common to mammals, or even to vertebrates in general, so it's safe to assume they play a role in how dogs perceive the world. They include the ability to sense time via a "body clock," and to anticipate weather and seasonal changes signaled by electromagnetic impulses "in the air." Recent research has even uncovered a whole new (to us) sense in dogs: the ability to smell weak thermal radiation of the sort emitted by a small prey animal, for example. (Think of it this way: Cold nose, warm mouse; the difference directs the pounce.) Bottom line: Dogs' sensory intelligence gives them access to rooms in our shared house that we've never entered—ones we can't even visualize.

In considering dogs' distinctive sensory abilities, I wondered about one in particular: Are they really the miraculous wayfinders we celebrate in books and movies? Are their brains tooled with a doggy GPS? How do some wayward pups find their way home and some stay utterly lost?

Lost and found

Waits (named for gravel-voiced musician Tom Waits) was a big yellow Korean Jindo—a soulful and nearly unflappable beast we adopted from our county shelter. His new life included regular visits to our cabin in the central Virginia woods. When we were there, Waits was allowed to roam off leash. Driven by Jindo guardian genes, he would patrol the property each morning and return an hour later. "Waits is back," we'd say when we heard him headbutt the door. And he always was.

Then one day Monk took advantage of a not-quite-closed door to streak out after a deer, and Waits followed. Two hours later, Monk came back wet, smelly, and alone. Waits had never run off before, and we spent hours until sundown shouting his name through the woods, calling neighbors, and hanging posters in local establishments. We even draped some of my husband's sweaty clothes at various points to serve as scent beacons.

We took comfort in knowing that Jindos are renowned for their excellent homing instincts. In one famous story from the breed's native island, a family sold a young girl's adored pet for much needed cash, and the five-year-old dog spent seven months walking more than 180 miles to return to her beloved human.

But apparently Waits didn't get his ancestors' "directional intelligence" gene. When we finally got a call that he'd been spotted, two days after he'd trotted off, he was eight miles away from where he'd started. We brought the bedraggled, dehydrated pup home, where he took a long drink, went to his bed, and didn't move for 48 hours.

An aptitude for wayfinding might have helped Waits get home sooner, but your average homed pup, who's more likely to ride in a car than wander the countryside, doesn't have much chance to develop the ability. Perhaps it's a helpful skill for sled dogs—but even traversing snowy wilds, a human is always the primary navigator. In *Dog Behaviour, Cognition, and Evolution*, Hungarian ethologist Ádám Miklósi declares that the incredible journeys we read about in the local news are outliers: Most lost dogs stay lost unless a human happens to find them and get them home.

A dog who does make it back from a walkabout likely uses scent maps: Being able to backtrack even several miles is not miraculous for a dog that has rich odors—a freshly composted garden, the scent of a familiar human—as guideposts along the way. Dogs can also be trained to "track"—using their nose to reverse an outbound trip—or "scout," which requires blazing a new trail and risking wrong turns. But there aren't many formal studies of the long-distance return in dogs; some that do exist suggest that a dog with an exceptional emotional bond with his person is more likely to find the right path home.

Recent research also suggests that magnetoreception helps account for the masters of wayfinding among dogs. A team from the Czech University of Life Sciences strapped GPS collars on 27 hunting dogs of 10 breeds and set them free in the woods. After more than 600 trials, they reported that dogs who didn't use the same path out and back began their return trips with a short "compass run"—65 feet along the north-south geomagnetic axis. It didn't matter in which direction home actually lay; the exercise appeared to sync the dogs' mental map with the magnetic compass, helped them find the right heading, and significantly improved their homing efficiency.

It's possible that the selective breeding of those hunting dogs may have given them a genetic leg up in this task. The ability to tap and use navigational intelligence is clearly variable, as Waits's wanderings demonstrated. Miklósi advises that "miraculous homecomings based on navigation in an unknown terrain are not to be *expected* from dogs" (emphasis mine). That doesn't mean miraculous homecomings aren't possible. (Speaking as someone who gets lost in her own neighborhood, any directional intelligence a dog displays has me beat.)

But of all the sensory experiences a dog may have, the one most radically different from our own must be the canine sense of smell. The ways dogs capture, analyze, and respond to odor molecules is so important to them that I'll give canine olfactory intelligence its own pages, just ahead.

But before we dig into that snoot-first sensory superpower, let's pause for a point that is relevant throughout this book. As evolutionary biologist Marc Bekoff likes to say, "There is no *the* dog." Dogs vary hugely by environment and circumstance, by genetics and stage of life. They're individuals, each with a personality and moods, with delights and annoyances, with things they excel at and things they struggle with. Where I write that "there's evidence dogs can do X" or "dogs aren't known to understand Y," I am setting aside this truth to try and get at the essential doggishness all pups seem to share.

CHAPTER SIX

NOSE SMART

D ogs are nose thinkers. Therefore, it would make sense that when-
ever they demonstrate an especially impressive show of intelligence, their mighty sense of smell is probably at the heart of it. The
astounding canine snout leads dogs through life in ways we can barely
grasp: It measures space and tells time; it identifies friends and analyzes
danger; it pinpoints opportunity. A top-notch sniffer can find the past
deep in the dirt, follow the merest swipe of a human hand, and even
smell the future on a breeze blowing toward her from a place she hasn't
yet reached.

That's why over millennia, we've turned to dogs to help us find things
that are hard to spot or even invisible to our own eyes. It's amazing to
consider: This very moment, a variety of dogs are sniffing for the tiniest
endangered species. Invasive plants. Toxins in the environment. Missing
elders. Human remains. Bedbugs. Bombs. Drugs. Gas leaks. Gluten.
Epilepsy. Diabetes. COVID-19. Cancer.

To dogs, of course, there's nothing remarkable about their nose. It's
just a tool (albeit their primary one) for perceiving their environment.
And make no mistake: Though canine scent-collecting anatomy is

impressive, what goes on in the brain is even more so. Dogs recognize, sort, categorize, and respond to odors using cognitive skills, including memory, discrimination, evaluation, and choice. The olfactory intelligence their ancestors needed to survive in a smelly world—to track down food, find a healthy mate, tell friend from foe—is alive and well in their descendants today.

Our own sense of smell works well enough for human purposes. But dogs need more of everything we've got—five times more olfactory cells, 1,200 genes coding for those olfactory cells compared to our 800, and more space in the brain dedicated to smell. A dog's olfactory bulb—the brain structure that reads the neural emails coming from cells in the nasal cavity—and the associated tissue is substantially larger than ours. Smell is dogs' most evolved sense, and their most utilized.

As a visual species, we tend to put smell on the back burner—even asking our nose-wise dogs to respond to us mostly with their eyes *(Look at me! Where's your yellow ball?)*. Those of us with sight receive and process information through our eyes first—the light of the morning sky, the face of a beloved, the alignment of words on this page—and these things drive us most directly in our day-to-day lives. Though dogs may miss the streaks of pink in the sunset, they catch scented messages on the breeze that we'll never know are there. In a sense, we and our pups live parallel lives, experiencing sometimes dramatically different aspects of the same world. It's easy to forget as we walk beside our canine partners. We'd be wise to keep it in mind.

Watching my own dogs using their noses, I've wondered what it would be like to move through life so sensitive to the bombardment of smelly molecules. With some 300 million scent receptors compared to our meager five or six million, I imagine it as a constant rapid-fire experience: *Kapow, kapow, kapow! Smell this! Smell this! Smell this!*—which would help explain a pup's stubborn insistence on sniffing as we tug and tug and tug on the leash.

But aren't we humans similarly pelted by visual signals? After all, streams of data constantly rush along our visual pathways, and yet our brains dismiss enough of the clutter to let us function. A dog's sense of smell does this, too: His brain amplifies one scent at a time, making it possible to pull out specific data points from a snootful. In addition, to really smell something, dogs need to actively pull volatile airborne particles into the nose, which explains the nostril wiggles when they are intent on a scent. Accessing and analyzing smells heavily informs many of a dog's behavioral choices.

With that in mind, Monk's walks have become miniature research expeditions for me: a time to consider all the fine details he has to rummage through and what they might mean. Monk is my most dedicated nose thinker, so "walk" is a bit of a misnomer. We're really out for a sniff. Or at least he is. (Mostly I'm just the other end of the leash, as Patricia McConnell so brilliantly put it in her book of the same name.)

When Monk is on a serious sniffing mission, our progress is slow. Head down, nostrils twitching, he'll give a robust clump of grass an examination worthy of a crime lab crew—each blade sniffed along its full length. Then a tangle of pale, dry veg gets the once-over. There may be snorting involved. Though I've heard that the cold changes a dog's experience of odors, Monk's olfactory acuity seems on point even during winter outings. Scientists don't yet know if falling temperatures alter the odorants themselves or the dog's nose function. Or both. Another mystery!

Suddenly Monk will dip into a roll, doing a quick shimmy on his back before I can intervene. But when I put my nose to his fur and take a tentative whiff, I get nothing. Deeper inhale, still nothing notable to *my* nose. So what's the appeal of that particular spot? Did something die there a month ago? Pee there last week? Lie down there last night? What's the takeaway?

Then there's poop. Sometimes worth Monk's time, sometimes not. How does he decide? On our left is an impressive pile, but we're walking on by. Does he recognize it as something he sniffed on a previous walk, and figure he's gleaned all he can from it? I don't leave his poop behind, but if I did, would he check it out the next day or ignore its familiar messages? When he puts his nose so close to the source that I cringe, what story does it tell? We aren't sure of all the details, but we do know that animal leavings contain multitudes, from data on reproductive readiness, stress levels, and health status to clues about available resources and maps of where the pooper has recently traveled. An odor's slowly fading strength also functions as a time stamp. With each stinky pile, Monk becomes more fully informed.

As a human, I'm more of a "sidestep the scat" type of creature. Any investigating I do is strictly visual: Looks like cat poop! Looks like a bird met its demise by feline! I try to keep my nose out of it. In her acclaimed book *Inside of a Dog*, Barnard College researcher Alexandra Horowitz imagines pups experiencing the scent, not of poop, but of a rose—stem, leaves, and petals, fresh, bruised, and wilting. It's a beautifully written observation that celebrates dogs using smell with the same exquisite sensitivity by which we use sight.

But dogs do more than just passively "see" with their noses. Monk's sniffing reminds me of how I plow through my online news feed—reading some items in detail, skimming others, ignoring the rest completely. What captures my attention, or his, is quite idiosyncratic and may vary considerably from day to day.

Speaking with Horowitz about how transformative it would be to live in a "smell universe" got me thinking about time from a dog's point of view. "Smells don't arrive with the same predictability as light on our eyes," she says, "which makes a dog's sense of the present moment different from ours. Smelling the floor might tell my dog something about what happened here earlier, while sniffing the air might tell her something about the future—about someone who is coming whose smell arrives before the person does."

That nose clock gives dogs yet another way of encountering the world that is mostly out of our reach. I've said it before and I'll say it again: Dogs are different.

Scent and sensibility

Scent is so crucial to dogs that it may even be the key to their recognition of themselves. We've long considered having "self-awareness" as a defining component of intelligence, and scientists have always used a visual test to assess it in other creatures.

The setup: If you paint a colored dot on an animal's fur and let her look in a mirror, does she investigate the mark? If so, does she touch it directly on her body—recognizing that the mirror image is *her* reflection—or by touching the mirror, suggesting that she believes what is in the mirror is separate from her?

This test was first tried in 1970—on chimps, who "passed"—and since then on many other animals. Children pass it at around age two; dolphins, Asian elephants, and Eurasian magpies have also "gotten it." Not dogs. They look *at* a mirror and can use it to see what's behind them, but they don't appear to use it to "see" themselves. Dog owners may have observed a version of this: Fido bristling and barking at the pup in the mirror as if at an intruder. This failure to recognize a reflection as "self" has long been peddled as proof that dogs aren't self-aware.

But some researchers, questioning whether a visual task is the right test for a nose-wise species, have sought an approach that makes more sense for a dog. Evolutionary biologist Marc Bekoff, for one, played around with "yellow snow," testing his dog Jethro's interest in his own urine versus that of other dogs. Remember that among other information, urine reveals social standing and reproductive receptivity in the canine world; often, dogs will add their own stream of data to a pee-laden spot. Whether they're joining a neighborhood conversation, blunting another dog's signals as a status move, or both, no one is quite sure. But, however it's read, urine is a major media outlet in a dog's smell universe.

When Bekoff moved Jethro's pee sample to a new spot, the dog paid it little mind and quickly moved on to investigate other dogs' leavings instead. Horowitz took the idea into the lab, designing an "olfactory mirror test" that let a dog sniff its own natural urine and an altered version of that urine. She, too, found that dogs seemed to "know themselves," showing more curiosity about the modified urine than about their regular pee scent.

The point here is twofold: If self-awareness is a true mark of intelligence, then dogs have demonstrated that they are truly intelligent. Second, if we must make comparisons, we need to consider the perspective of dogs—an odd mark on the fur has no significance, while smelly pee is packed with valuable data!—and design our tests around their superpowers, rather than ours. In investigating dogs, we need to be more dog smart. It's something to work on as we try to better understand dog olfaction.

On that note, and before we go further with the nose, I want to mention another case in which a more dog smart approach could boost the value of research outcomes. Clinical animal-behavior specialist Daniel Mills and his team at the University of Lincoln in the U.K. point out that oft cited studies of dogs' emotional reactions to human faces may be missing the mark because they focus strictly on facial clues, not taking body language into account. "Dogs attend more to the body than the head of human and dog figures," the authors write in a 2021 paper—a difference between our species that supports a shift in methodology if we are to truly understand what's going on in the canine mind. No doubt scientists can find many other such cases in the research sphere if they begin looking for them.

But for now, back to the sense of smell. One thing we know for sure: Dogs can detect substances at concentrations so low that we should bow our noses in humble deference. In *The Other End of the Leash,* Patricia McConnell writes, "Human scent from fingers brushing glass left for two weeks outdoors or four weeks indoors is still a beacon to a dog on the trail. So is one quarter-billionths of a gram of sweat left on the ground by an average man's footstep."

How acute is a canine's olfactory intelligence when it comes to barely-there scents? How low can they go? Paul Waggoner, co-director of the Canine Performance Sciences program at Auburn University's College of

Veterinary Medicine in Alabama, has been trying to tease out that thresh-old using a microwave-size box called a Trace Vapor Generator (I silently named it "the brain"). This equipment allows users to adjust the intensity of odor from a compound. It was designed at the U.S. Naval Research Laboratory to generate well-controlled concentrations of explosives and narcotics, which dogs are also good at detecting, and to test (human-made) instruments built to perceive those scents. At Auburn, it's been modified to release vapor through a duct into an observation room where a dog can sniff the research smell du jour through a funnel in the wall.

As with all such studies, the dogs have to be trained to "look for" the particular scent and then let researchers know if they find it. I am invited to watch a few rounds, so I sit outside the small "sniff room" and peek through the observation glass.

For each round, a dog waits in a crate that opens into the testing space. Once Waggoner adjusts the vapor and sends it streaming through the tube, the doggy door opens, letting the dog rush to the funnel and sniff. If she catches the scent in question, she sits at the cone. If not, she uses her nose to bump a "touch stick" located in the middle of the room, on her way back to her crate. Each test takes just seconds to complete.

We've all heard the mind-blowing claims: A dog can detect a single drop of blood in three Olympic-size swimming pools' worth of water, or some variation on the theme. Indeed, studies have proven canines can sense some substances at concentrations as low as parts per *trillion*. But here, with the most recent iteration of the vapor-generating technology, the Auburn dogs are being offered much weaker doses than that. And they are telling the researchers, *Yep, I can smell that.*

Glory, a superfriendly yellow Lab still learning the game, who gives me a kiss after completing her turns, seems to forget what she is supposed to do on her first run. She sniffs the funnel, then turns around. She walks to the lever and sits next to it. She looks around, waiting for instructions. Someone calls her back to the crate for another try.

The next time, she remembers the rules. With the scent set to 100 parts per billion, she sniffs, sits at the cone to signal "yes," and then returns to her crate. Waggoner dials the machine down to 10 parts per billion for the next run. Glory catches the scent that time, too. This is considered easy practice. "Ultimately, the dogs may be better than the machine," the researcher tells me. "What we can say at this point is they can detect scent *at least as low as* 500 parts per *quadrillion*."

Later, I try to wrap my head around that number, and fail. What does a quadrillion even mean, other than a number with 15 zeros after it? It appears we're still a long way from the true threshold of dogs' ability. The field remains a scientific frontier much like deep space and the deep ocean: It's exciting, enigmatic, and will require new tools and technologies for full exploration.

In the case of sniffer dogs, even as they are trained to use their olfactory intelligence for a task, scientists don't always know exactly what the animals are cuing in on to do the job. So, it looks like we'll have to wait to get a grip on their detection acumen. It's another case where human smarts need to catch up to dog smarts. Point: Dog.

How the nose knows

If you pay close attention to your dog's nose when he's intent on a scent, you'll see it do that cute little wiggle and hear the staccato beats of its work. As a tool, a dog's nose is a triumph of natural selection: a complex set of cogs and wheels we rarely think about.

When a dog inhales, the air can follow two possible routes—one for plain old breathing, and the other for olfaction. During intense exploration or tracking, the rapid *sniff sniff sniff*—up to around 200 times a minute compared with about 30 times a minute for a dog on a stroll—takes in extra air and rushes volatile particles into the system. The action creates tiny wind currents on exhales to help the inhales along. Then, within the nasal tissue, a maze of receptor sites awaits, tooled with tiny hairs that snag and hold scent molecules as they whistle by.

Our two nostrils always work in tandem, but a dog's can work independently, further boosting his access to scents. Nostril mobility helps the pup know where a smell is coming from, and a wet nose, dampened by a thin layer of secreted mucus plus saliva, picks up scent better than a dry one. And though human nostrils have to manage both inhalations and exhalations through the same door, a dog taking in new air can, with a twitch of muscles, push old air down deep or release it through slits in the sides of the nose: an elegant solution to the "too many smells" problem.

Not only do dogs have hundreds of millions more odor-detecting neurons than we do, but their olfactory epithelium—the sheet of tissue that converts odor molecules into neural signals that brains interpret as smells—is also a complex labyrinth of turns, folds, and bumps compared to our single flat sheet. Dogs also have a working vomeronasal organ (VNO), a sac packed with additional receptors that sits atop the roof of the mouth and picks up chemical cues called pheromones from incoming air and when the dog licks its nose. When a dog sniffs something message-laden like urine of a female in heat, he seems to "eat" the scent— a behavior that draws more odor molecules to the VNO. What lands there is thought to affect social and reproductive behavior.

Olfactory performance is sensitive to humidity and barometric pressure, inflammation, nasal dehydration, excess mucus, exposure to toxins and pharmaceuticals—and of course, the effects of diet, aging, and disease. A dog can experience olfactory fatigue or "nose blindness," like us, finding herself temporarily unable to distinguish a particular odor after smelling it too much. Thresholds vary across individual dogs. This desensitization occurs to free up the nervous system to respond to new smells that might be important: a smart move for a nose thinker. The gut microbiome may even affect sensitivity to scent. So do training methods; how and how often a dog is exposed to an odor of (our) interest can change his ability to distinguish it from others.

So dogs' nose intelligence depends on a great many factors, many of which are in their handlers' control. And in supporting our dogs' natural olfactory talents, we can boost the superpower that arguably has the greatest value to both species. Because canine nose smarts are most readily used on smells naturally relevant to them, especially those important to their own survival, getting dogs to turn their noses to what *we* find interesting or important requires training.

In this, dogs are not so different from us. After all, don't we have to train our eyes when we are looking for something in particular? Think radiologists, bird-watchers, shell hunters, word search aficionados—even a guy scanning for his friends at a crowded concert. It takes effort and a largely subconscious training of the senses to block out the visual chaos and let that "search image" guide us. A predator trying to spot cryptic prey in the trees or the weakest gazelle in the herd uses the same principle. Once that image clicks into place, and the brain becomes sensitized to the specific characteristics we're looking for, suddenly, that thing comes into focus. It's there. And there. *And there!*

Dogs learn to zero in on a scent or scent variation and to poke at it, or bark at it, or stare it down. Studies have shown that training has a significant effect on both behavior and skill. For one thing, the animals do better finding a target odor in a new context if their first exposure to it was in a mix of scents, rather than by itself. Also, with practice, dogs learn to learn, learn to search, and become more sensitive to the smells in question. The latter has a physiological component: Olfactory receptors are continuously renewed, along with their olfactory sensory neurons. And—another aspect of the superpower—the number of receptors for a particular odor increases the more that odor is sniffed. That's an evolutionary wow, no?

These kinds of details matter: Detection dogs who have only trained on small samples of a scent—say, that of TNT—may miss a large cache because the "bigger" scent is very different, and potentially overwhelming. The animals may not recognize it as something they've smelled before because, in a way, they haven't. "You have to be explicit in training if you want the dogs to find both a little or a lot," canine researcher Nathaniel Hall tells me.

It's a phenomenon familiar from our own olfactory experience: Some chemicals smell radically different to us at different concentrations. Indole, for example, is an organic compound found in cooked Brussels sprouts, fragrant flowers, and our bodies. It's emitted both during sex and after death, and let's just say a little dab'll do ya. In small concentrations, the scent is floral, sexy, and sweet: Indole is a key component of the smell of jasmine, and an important ingredient in perfumery. As it becomes more concentrated, it starts to smell rotten. And a heavy dose smells, well, like shit. Literally.

Some dogs are so well built for scent that it's a wonder they bother with vision at all. The most infamous sniffer, the bloodhound, already has a generously sized snout, droopy ears that fan scented air into the nose, and a perpetual strand of drool that grabs additional scent for the VNO to process. Bloodhounds also have the highest number of olfactory receptors among breeds, having been bred to sniff and to be independent about it. Head down, nose to the task.

Chasing scents is part of the natural repertoire of animals that hunt to survive—or used to hunt, before humans started pouring kibble into bowls. But neither anatomy nor pedigree determine a dog's olfactory prowess for certain. Dog olfaction expert and best-selling author Cat Warren tells me that although the bloodhound has a long history of sniffing and has earned plenty of fame for its nose achievements, many breeds and even more individuals are just as masterful at tracking and trailing. Breed reputations aside, olfactory intelligence doesn't draw clear lines, she says. Individual dogs' temperaments matter, and these can be vastly different no matter who their mom and dad may be—just as in people.

Many other factors play a role. Consider opportunity. Doesn't giving someone the chance to learn and nurture a skill sometimes propel them forward against all expectations? In assessing members of our own species, we get so caught up in assumptions based on, say, family history or economic status or physical "type" that we can lose sight of the potential that lies in all of us to succeed.

We do this to dogs, too. In a small study at Arizona State University's Canine Science Collaboratory, Nathaniel Hall, who has since moved to Texas Tech, and his colleagues compared the untrained sniffing performance of German shepherds, a breed commonly used for detection work, to that of pugs—whose pushed-in faces and labored mouth breathing make them seem less than optimal for the job. Greyhounds were also included in the study, but generally failed to participate. (That doesn't mean they aren't nose smart: Their interests and abilities simply run in a different direction.)

The challenge was to find fragrant anise samples in a box of equally fragrant pine shavings. The result was a complete surprise: Even as the target odor was diluted, the pugs excelled at finding it. The shepherds, who happen to have the largest olfactory mucus membrane among all breeds? Not so much. This suggested to the authors something we know is true of people: Regardless of anatomy (and certainly reputation), opportunity and strong commitment can produce excellence. "The pugs were just really into sniffing," says Hall, "and we see sniffing as an important marker of a dog's engagement in an activity."

So, the pugs were fully engaged. And though sensitivity to the scent was important, as was the pugs' interesting ability to switch from mouth to nose breathing as needed, their "olfactory motivation," as Hall puts it, helped put them well ahead of their longer-snouted cousins.

Factors like agility, stamina, size, distractibility, and independence all matter in deciding which dog's olfactory intelligence will shine brightest. And the job at hand also plays an important role. Police dogs need to be intimidating and big enough to take down bad guys, so putting pugs on patrol isn't likely to produce optimal outcomes. But the loaf-size pups might be just as capable of, and perhaps more committed to, the nose work that large dogs are typically called on to perform.

Olfactory intelligence, then, is not just about sensitivity. It's about a whole slew of factors that don't automatically seem relevant but are. So if you consider how dogs—regardless of breed—think, remember, and learn, and then apply those lessons in training, you can help enhance sniffer-dog performance.

Bad guys and good dogs

Back in Alabama, what the scientists are learning about cognition and behavior at Auburn University's canine science center has given them an edge in developing "Auburn dogs," their own line of Labradors bred and trained for serious sniffer work. Most of these pups are sold to organizations, including the New York Police Department, Amtrak, the Transportation Security Administration, and Disney, for security work, including explosives detection.

One Auburn pup in training gets to show me his protective sniffer smarts in action. A wide stretch of walkway fronting the university's student center stands in for an airport terminal, and I play a would-be terrorist with a bomb. In reality, the "bomb" is just a small sample of smokeless powder, a substance often used in improvised explosive devices (IEDs), packed into a leg of pantyhose and hidden under my shirt. The expectation: The dog will catch the smokeless powder scent as we cross paths and will turn and follow me, ignoring all the other people going by. I walk slowly from one end of the block while a handler comes from the other direction with a black Lab named Jumbo, an Auburn Vapor Wake detection dog being trained to react to bombs on the move. Out of the corner of my eye, I see dog and handler pass me, and then Jumbo pulls to the left and changes direction to come after me. Sensing him closing in, I slow and peek over my shoulder. Jumbo is there, dropping into a sit at my back. *He's got me.*

Research that teases apart various aspects of dogs' olfactory intelligence has revealed many details about how it develops. These include the fact that pups who don't practice for a while are more likely to forget *how to search* than to forget a particular scent; that they remember dozens of scents for at least a year while continuing to learn new ones; and, if findings concur with work by others, that service dogs who are less "mothered" as puppies tend to be more independent and more willing to explore than coddled ones, their boldness suggesting a greater likelihood of success as adult detection dogs. "What is consistent is that dogs' noses are always active, and an olfactory stimulant is always going to be behaviorally and psychologically more relevant to them than to us," Hall explains. "Rarely do you go into a room and start sniffing. But that's the default dog behavior, very intertwined with all that they do. It highlights the importance of this sensory domain in dogs' understanding of their world."

And as it turns out, if a chemist can identify an odorant molecule—even if humans can't smell it at all and regardless of its source or its relevance to a dog's life—the animal can learn to find it. And that lets dogs help people solve some very serious human problems.

For instance, the materials used in digital memory devices—including even the micro-est micro SD cards—give off molecules that canines can track. A coating is applied to components of circuit boards to help them shed heat, and another is used on removable media, neither of which smells like anything to the human nose. In a world where criminals of all sorts leave electronic traces of their bad behavior, a dog participating in a warrant search may find the hidden-away laptops, hard drives, cell phones, or memory cards that make a prosecutor's case.

Dogs have been sticking their noses into such evidence since a black Lab named Selma hit the electronic-storage-device beat with Connecticut State Police in 2013. Having flunked out of New York's Guiding Eyes for the Blind, the exuberant pup found her true calling as the first electronics-detection dog—that is, once a forensic lab chemist figured out there were scents to be detected at all.

Selma, along with a yellow Lab named Thoreau (who later joined the Rhode Island State Police), mastered the telltale aromas of both large and small amounts of the coating compounds so that no size device or collection of them would escape her e-smart nose. Over the years, she worked more than a hundred cases, primarily against child pornographers but also murderers and hackers. This dedicated investigator died of natural causes in 2022, but other electronics-sniffing dogs continue to turn up even the most cleverly disguised thumb drives and most deeply buried micro-discs. Often, these nose-smart dogs find crucial evidence that human investigators missed—and often, quite quickly.

Let's give a special nod to a dog named Kozak, a yellow Lab who works for the Wisconsin Department of Justice. This pup not only helps put the worst criminals out of commission by finding electronic evidence of crimes against children, but also sticks around afterward to comfort kids who've been victimized during what can be a long and difficult legal process. Olfactory intelligence *and* emotional intelligence wrapped up in one furry, brown-eyed package. It's a beautiful thing.

CHAPTER SEVEN

POOPER SNOOPERS

It's no secret that dogs find feces fascinating. They're hardly shy about it. Julianne Ubigau of the organization Conservation Canines, who recently started her own detection company, FieldLab, depends on that stinky allure to help scientists track, assess, and protect endangered species. Inside her freezer, you'll find plastic bags containing fecal samples from wolf, coyote, wolverine, puma, jaguar, cougar, short-tailed weasel, pocket mouse, black bear, grizzly bear, whale, owl, and goshawk. There are also bullfrog eggs at various stages of development, whole bullfrogs, a strand of caulking laden with toxic chemicals, a tangle of animal hair pulled from a barbed wire fence, a chunk of Douglas fir, and some garlic mustard plant.

A stockpile of scat and other stinky stuff is a key tool of the trade when your dog is one of the Conservation Canines at the University of Washington's Center for Conservation Biology. Ubigau's loving, ball-obsessed black Lab, Jasper, knows each sample by smell, along with even more exotic aromas like anteater, sea cucumber, and pangolin, and will happily point to any of them where he finds them out in the world (especially if there's toy time in it for him at the end).

Ubigau got Jasper as a one-year-old rescue pup with serious separation anxiety and behavioral issues. Unlike many working dog programs, Conservation Canines doesn't rely on a particular breed of dog. Team members visit shelters to assess animals, seeking those that are first and foremost excited to work and play. "Toy *obsessed*," in fact, Ubigau says.

The drive and energy to *do something* is the most desirable trait for many working dogs. Problem-solving ability and related "smarts" come next, and they are usually there, ripe for development. Ubigau's dog Sampson, also a black Lab, was one of Conservation Canines' top-notch sniffers, "an insatiable worker," she says, with olfactory intelligence almost on par with his energy. He kept working with great enthusiasm to age 16. When Sampson died, Ubigau took in Jasper to continue the work. As dogs are individuals, "It's taken a little time to get his confidence up," she says. "If Jasper finds something, he looks at *me*. Sampson would look at *the ball*. He knew he was right. He didn't have to ask."

But watching Jasper lumber ahead of us in a rugged area of the Central Cascades, tail spinning and nose to the ground, he seems to me fully zoomed in to his task. He is on the hunt for wolf scat, the fresher the better. Other animal poops might also be useful for filling in the details of the ecosystem's membership—the area supports cougars, coyotes, bears, bobcats, and lynx, among others—but wolf is the target.

In a collaboration between the University of Washington and the state's Department of Fish and Wildlife, Conservation Canines dog-handler teams have been surveying mountainous sections of the northeastern part of the state since 2015. Ubigau and Jasper have been tracking wolf recolonization and movements in the Teanaway area, in part for the ecological data—how the predators are faring, what they're eating, how they're affecting other species' ranges and food resources—and in part to help wildlife managers prepare for the animals' growing presence where livestock are plentiful and farmers are worried about their animals becoming wolf prey.

Regarding Jasper's proficiency at this job, Ubigau says something that echoes what I'd heard from military dog handlers: You actually don't want a *superobedient* dog. She says this as we rush to keep up with the ebullient Jasper on the wooded trail. "Yes to following a simple order," she says. "But if he's sticking by the heel position, always looking at his handler, asking for permission to do the next thing, that's not good." She pauses, considering. "We need the dog to be a little more wild, freer to explore and take the space he needs to problem-solve on his own. Even if you're instructing him on some level, you want him to turn back to his instincts and to trust them. That's why we're working with dogs—because they have a kind of intelligence we don't have."

Jasper ignores cow patties, which are plopped all over the place. It would be a long day if he were alerting on every pie. Instead, he gets excited only when he comes across leavings containing fur and bone. "Can you show me?" Ubigau asks the dog each time he sits near something he's decided is noteworthy. He can, gesturing to the sample with his snout so his handler can put her eyes on what his nose knows.

Some of Jasper's cues lead to many-days-old scats, not terribly useful. But he also locates a couple that are larger and fresher and potentially interesting to Ubigau, who squats, dons gloves, and bags a sample, shoving it deep into her backpack for later. The barely-there scats win Jasper a "good boy" and a few quick scratches. A top-notch pile means happy praise, a game of fetch, and some downtime to chew his toy on his own. I've heard about that smart, dog-focused strategy from other trainers, too: You need to build up a reward hierarchy that matches the value of the targets, so the dog learns to seek out the highest-value scent and will choose it over any other.

Just how specific a conservation detector dog can be is phenomenal— that they know an endangered Pacific pocket mouse from its various mouse cousins, an endangered Jemez Mountains salamander from a nearly identical species. "Every time we start a study, we ask ourselves, what do we want the dog to find and what should he exclude?" says Ubigau. "So, for example, we can train him on the swift fox and have him ignore all other kinds of fox."

But the pups can also generalize to a remarkable degree. With so many different scents packed into a single scat (depending on exactly what meal produced the poop), along with all the other individual details that scat records, the handlers train on a variety of samples, even from the same individual animal, to make sure the dogs are exposed to as many variations as possible. From there, "somehow the dogs sort through it all and come up with the common denominator," she explains. "We don't know what the difference is in one case or the commonality in another. But their noses can pick it apart."

Tracking scents with a nose-smart dog "is like exploring with a borrowed superpower," Ubigau likes to say. "Having that added sensory apparatus makes me more attentive to my surroundings. I'm a better, smarter investigator because of him." And you can really see a detector dog processing, thinking, parsing through the background scents, and putting the information together, she says. "The way they perceive the world is so different and complex that we may never fully understand it. I'm constantly in awe of them."

When Jasper isn't searching for poop, you might find him leading his handler around the University District area of Seattle in search of toxic polychlorinated biphenyls (PCBs). PCBs were long used in many commercial and industrial materials, but their production was banned in the U.S. in the late 1970s as their carcinogenic effects became clear. That doesn't mean they're gone from the environment, though; they can, unfortunately, hang around for decades. And though PCBs seem odorless to us, dogs can smell them. That's why Jasper and Ubigau work with Seattle Public Utilities and with local companies searching for PCBs persisting in buildings, waterways, and soils. Identifying where they are can help spur remediation activities both on campus and in the broader Seattle region.

On a warm Sunday afternoon Jasper is happy to show off his olfactory smarts in an urban setting. Architecturally questionable buildings from the 1970s seem to grab his nose most readily. He stands on his hind legs to sniff high on wall faces; he attacks corners, seams, and window wells with his snout and offers clear cues to Ubigau that they're hot. "It's in the caulking, for example," she says, pointing to old rubbery strands exactly where Jasper's nose had gone wild. The toxic stuff, it occurs to me, is one of many scents dogs can easily track that are totally irrelevant to them in any natural context. Only because we ask them to notice do they attach importance to them. For the record, regular testing and limited time on this task protect Jasper from overexposure to the cancer-causing chemicals.

Jasper and other Conservation Canines are also becoming versed in the smells of global crime at the Port of Seattle, where shipping containers may contain illegal wildlife and other contraband from abroad. Especially at a time when "supply chain disruption" has had real effects on consumers, coming up with an efficient way to detect illegal items in cargo containers without having to pull containers out of line, break security seals, and slow commerce promises a big advance in efforts to fight illegal trade, along with slowing the spread of invasive species and potentially devastating plant and animal diseases.

In response, biologist Sam Wasser, longtime director of Conservation Canines, had the idea of sampling the air from inside the containers via their vents—literally sucking air out, much as a dog's nose would, through a removable canister lined with a cotton pad. The pad can then be presented to a dog trained on the odor of the material of concern, from highly valuable timber to elephant ivory to live pangolins. Wasser pioneered the broader conservation work back in 1997, realizing that dogs' olfactory intelligence could make the job of finding endangered wildlife much faster and easier.

Spending time with Jasper and Ubigau, I couldn't help but be wowed by their connection—their melding of thought and movement—which is absolutely part of their success. After Jasper would work an area (whether in the mountains or in town), running circles around us, his owner would call him back for a rest. With his tongue halfway to the ground, he'd lean against her legs and pant while she'd rub his head. In a few minutes he'd settle, let out a deeper breath—a big sigh—and only then would Ubigau send him back to work.

I watched Ubigau wait patiently for that breath that signaled Jasper's readiness. I saw in her a sensitivity to the dog's body language that was very powerful, and his eyes showed trust when he looked to her for guidance. They'd learned each other's languages, which gave each of them access to the intelligence of the other rather profoundly. The social smarts, the masterful silent communication, clearly went both ways.

In my reporting I came across a number of groups making great strides in conservation-related sniffer-dog work: Seattle-based Rogue Detection Teams has former shelter dogs like Lady, Duo, and Hugo doing carnivore surveys and sniffing out rare and endangered species across the country. Working Dogs for Conservation depends on smart anti-poaching pups like Chai, Earl, and Rudi to find stashes of ivory and rhino horn, bushmeat and skins, plus traps, guns, and ammunition, in national parks across Africa. And New Zealand's Department of Conservation has dozens of dogs tracking both invasive predators like rats and feral cats and endangered native animals with names like kākāpō, takahē, whio, pāteke, and kea. Elsewhere, detection dogs are learning to pinpoint crude oil on beaches—even distinguishing between naturally occurring "tar balls" of weathered oil and fresher spilled crude oils as deep as three feet under the sand surface. They're also sniffing out leaks in buried pipelines, bedbugs in hotel rooms, and invasive pests destroying grape plants in vineyards.

The latter skill has attracted the attention of the U.S. Department of Agriculture, which recently funded scientists at Texas Tech and Virginia Tech to evaluate the full capacity of dogs to assist in targeting the most devastating and costly pests and diseases in the agricultural industry. With losses to vineyards at an estimated $300 million a year from just two invaders—powdery mildew and the spotted lanternfly—smart noses attached to smart dogs will be a welcome and extremely valuable addition to the tool kit.

Nathaniel Hall, who heads up the Texas Tech lab and field studies to quantify dogs' abilities in this arena, says that since beginning this project, he's gotten a lot of calls from people in different industries looking to tap the dogs' olfactory smarts. "They'll say, 'We have this agricultural disease or problem but it's hard for us to pinpoint it. Do you think dogs could help find it?' And the answer is yes: There's a long list of things that could potentially be applicable here. We've just scratched the surface."

Mission (almost) impossible

Have I mentioned that conservation sniffer-dog noses are sensitive enough to track the scat of even the tiniest endangered species—from quarter-ounce Pacific pocket mice in Southern California meadows to caterpillars of silverspot butterflies in the mountains of Oregon—which produce poops roughly the size of rice grains and poppy seeds, respectively? Well, they are. But at least those micro-droppings fall on dry land and tend to stay put. Perhaps the most extraordinary show of olfactory acumen in the conservation world comes from pups who sniff out the poops of whales at sea.

Despite being protected under U.S. federal, Washington State, and Canadian law, the orcas that make up Puget Sound's Southern Resident killer whale population are in trouble; their numbers in 2023 have fallen to a low of fewer than 75 animals in family groups known as the J, K, and L pods. The causes of their desperate decline are a mixed bag: Persistent organic pollutants contaminate the waters they swim in and the food they eat; underwater noise from commercial shipping and recreational and military activities interferes with critical intraspecies communications; and the salmon they depend on for food have suffered their own major declines. Toxicants, stress, and poor nutrition have combined to devastating effect on the reproductive success of adults and the survival of calves. To keep these glorious animals from disappearing entirely, scientists need to monitor as many members of the population as possible.

But tracking the health of individual orcas over their 30- to 50-year-plus life span may be one of conservation's heftiest challenges. These marine mammals can reach more than 20 feet in length and weigh upwards of five tons. Repeatedly chasing and restraining them for health assessments would be dangerous and grueling for both species, not to mention logistically beastly. Even periodically darting the animals from a boat to snag a tissue sample is a Herculean (and costly) endeavor.

Fortunately, whales poop. And poop is packed with health data, giving the scientists an alternative source of information—*if* they can find and scoop the stuff before it sinks, which it does shortly after being released. And because individuals of the endangered orca pods spend less than a tenth of their time at the water surface and don't necessarily poop daily—well, you do the math. In sum, orca poop is a hot commodity.

The scat samples that are collected contain data on what and how much an animal is eating, whether it is or has been pregnant, whether and how severely it is stressed—as much info as can be found in whale tissues. Poop also gives scientists a noninvasive way to read the animals' medical and dietary records.

But even just spotting scat on the sea surface is difficult. Ripples and tides, reflections, currents, wind, and the vastness of the place all work against even the most dedicated human pooper scooper. It's like finding needles in a haystack, I'm told, but with both the haystack and the needles constantly moving. That's where a little pup named Eba comes in.

"See that? See her nose working there? She's onto something," says Deborah Giles (just "Giles" to her friends and students), science and research director of Wild Orca, a nonprofit based in Friday Harbor on San Juan Island. I'm out on Wild Orca's boat with the scientist, her husband, Jim, at the helm, and Eba.

We've motored into the Salish Sea, a wet border zone between the U.S. and Canada. The pup, leashed and wearing a bright orange safety harness, stands on the gray carpeted deck with her front paws up on the gunwale, her small nose wiggling. Giles already put sunblock (unscented, of course) on that sensitive snout, and on the pup's pink-skinned belly, too.

Eba lowers her head out and over water, then crab-walks along the edge to a new spot and does the same. There's something out there, she seems to be telling us. Reports from shore say orcas from J pod have been around here all morning. Finally, we humans spy what Eba has been smelling: a mother and calf to the southeast and a solo adult to the north. With an audible *whoosh,* they both exhale a fountain of sea spray, curling sleek black-and-white bodies above the surface before flipping up flukes for a dive. Though scientific researchers have special permission to get a bit closer than tour boats are allowed, we remain at least 300 yards away from the animals to avoid stressing them out.

Against the majesty of these powerful whales, Eba is just a morsel of a dog, a mixed-up batch of breeds that likely includes pit bull, corgi, and perhaps Jack Russell terrier. She's also an absolute love who was happily cozying up to me within moments of our meeting. Giles and Jim inherited her from Giles's sister, and shortly after taking her in, Giles started training her to be a whale dog—first on land and then using a floating container on the water—specializing in the smells of the Southern Resident killer whales.

The dog found her first J pod poop sample on her second day on the job, leading Giles and Jim directly to it with her own special "tells." Those clues include a gradually accelerating tail wag that suggests the first whiff of scent followed by whimpers and movements along the bow as she tries to zoom in. The behaviors get more obvious as the boat nears the target and lessen with a wrong turn. The wind can make it tricky to track the source, but Eba stays on it. "We do a lot of zigzagging," Giles says. "I often feel she's the trainer. She's smart enough to know what she's doing: It's me who has to learn her subtle cues."

Once poops are scooped, Giles ships them to a San Diego lab for a workup. Technicians check hormone levels for clues about nutrition, stress, and pregnancies, and test for environmental contaminants like

DDT, PCBs, and microplastics. They also screen for parasites and fungi and test for antibiotics, and can tease out what the whales are eating, how much, and even which river their prey comes from. "Each sample holds the answers to so many different questions," Giles says.

In particular, the researcher wants to know why so many of the Southern Resident females are struggling with reproduction. "We've found that almost 70 percent of females getting pregnant are miscarrying or losing their calf soon after birth," she says. And 30 percent of the miscarriages are happening late in pregnancy, meaning the mothers were heavily invested physically and emotionally in the offspring when they died. During one research season, Giles and others observed a female known as J35 carrying her dead calf for 17 days, refusing to eat as she mourned her loss; it hit hard, and spurred Giles on. "We need to do everything we can to figure this out," she says.

And they're gathering insights along with feces. Eba's olfactory smarts let her smell a sample as small as *a single milliliter* and up to a mile away if the conditions are right. Thanks to her superpower, the organization has already learned, for example, that the whales are most distressed by boat traffic when they're already stressed by starvation. Eba's directions on such outings will ultimately help wildlife managers plan strategies to support the future of J pod in these waters.

Watching Eba on the job, I recall Cat Warren talking about cadaver-detection dogs working on water: "Being on a boat takes a lot away from a dog, which must rely entirely on the humans as their legs," she told me. It's a 3D experience for them, with the currents, wind, and scent cone. "The dog doesn't get to use his whole body. He has a smaller stage and needs escalating signals and a new vocabulary so he can give the captain instructions."

Giles tells me that when Eba finds poop, she gets super animated. She vibrates. When the sample is finally scooped and brought aboard, she even gets a close-up sniff as part of her reward, plus lots of praise and her ultimate prize, a game of tug with one of her favorite rope toys. The team brings not just toys but also a poop sample to share with Eba just in case none is found, so she has a "win" no matter what. Gotta keep up morale.

I sniff a sample of J pod poop in a jar and it isn't what I expect at all. It's grassy—like mildly sour seaweed—though Eba doesn't alert on decaying seaweed when a mass floats by (or to any other marine mammal poop), so she's clearly more nose smart than I am. No surprise. Anyway, it smells nothing like the foul pile Eba herself drops after we return to shore.

Wasser has said that dogs find water-based poop some 500 percent more efficiently than people working alone. A black Lab mix named Tucker was the first to chase whale poop, and the rescue pup helped locate most of the 348 fecal samples from 79 individual orcas that a seven-year-long research campaign collected and analyzed. Tucker retired in 2017, living out his final years with his longtime handler, Liz Seely. The world's first orca-conservation dog passed away in 2020—but Eba and Giles are carrying on the fight for the welfare of the whales.

CHAPTER EIGHT

THE SCENTS
OF A HUMAN

Humans and dogs have been companions for millennia. We matter
to them, and our scents matter to them, too. Studies suggest that
pet dogs have distinct mental representations of each of their beloved
people based on individual aromas. In other words, if Monk was allowed
to sniff my dirty shirt and then was sent to find me, he would expect it
to be *me* waiting at the other end of the trail.

So, dogs can be great human trackers. We make it easier for them to
follow us by leaving long-lasting traces of ourselves floating in the air and
caught in the crevices—our footprints, our fingerprints, and so on. A
human entering an enclosed space, even just for a moment, can't help but
leave a mark—and we don't have to be doused in perfumes, deodorants,
or aftershaves to do so. We shed minute flakes of skin called "'rafts' that
follow us like smoke from a moving cigarette," according to
Patricia McConnell.

We leave a trail of scent behind with each stride: Trained dogs can smell
the travel direction of a person who passed by an hour ago working with

just five footsteps. It's a remarkable talent, but dogs don't generally go around on their own pinpointing lost seniors or ancient burial mounds without instructions to do so. To dogs, "lost" or "ancient" adds no special significance to a scent; smells tell them other sorts of stories.

Whatever the odor source, a dog will cast back and forth searching for the "edge" of the scent in question, then sniff her way toward its strongest point of concentration. The whole smelly area is often described as a "scent cone," but I've come to understand that the cloud of odor is not so neatly defined as that term suggests. Fluid dynamics tells us that forces like buoyancy, temperature differentials, and gravity turn a neat theoretical cone into a shape-shifting plume. The terminology matters because it helps explain why even a proficient detector dog may lose a scent or seem erratic in trying to follow it.

The width and concentration of the plume reveals an odor's age; additionally, wind and time disperse and therefore weaken a scent. But as much as possible, once a sniffer dog finds a hot scent, she will stay with it to the source. "The problem for dogs usually isn't finding the scent," Cat Warren says, "it's sorting out the multitude of scents that are there already."

This means, of course, enlisting that doggy brain to conduct a slew of cognitive exercises that go well beyond data gathering; they involve recognizing, remembering, and ignoring what's not relevant at the moment. The work requires consideration and judgment. In other words, intelligence.

Dogs have been detecting humans by our scents as long as we've coexisted, and they've been doing it *for us* for ages. Certainly, the stories go back a long way: More than two centuries ago, Bavarian officials caught murderer Andreas Bichel after a dog led his master to the bodies of Bichel's victims. A fourth-century B.C. king used dogs to sniff out his enemies hiding in the mountains. More recently, dogs successfully located mass graves dating from World War II through the conflicts in the Balkans in the 1990s. Even literature gives a nod: Sometime around 2,700 years ago, the Greek poet Homer created an homage to dogs' special way of knowing us in the faithful canine Argos, the only creature to recognize his master Odysseus when the king returned to Ithaca—visually unrecognizable but apparently smelling the same—after an epic 19-year-long journey home from the Trojan War.

Snoot of hope

When I was in Borneo not long ago, reporting a story about one of the island's last intact lowland rainforests, I got hopelessly lost. I'd gone deep into the wilderness with a photographer and a local assistant, and while they set up camera traps, I ventured off on my own in search of a view. I'd be back soon, I told them before heading up a steep slope behind us. But coming back down the mountain, I unintentionally left the trail. Two hours later, as I trudged in seeming circles through knee-deep mud, I realized I'd totally lost my bearings and had no idea which way to go. I finally stopped wandering, sat on a rock, and waited.

I felt more foolish than fearful. I wasn't in *real* danger (orangutans don't eat humans) and I knew my colleagues would come looking for me. Within an hour, I heard someone *hoooing* off in the distance (the signal primate researchers use to find one another in the forest); I followed the sound, *hoooing* in reply, and eventually made it back to where I'd started, much humbler than when I'd left. And yes, I'd been waaaay off track.

But the experience made me wonder, What would it be like to be lost in a wild place *without* a lifeline? Maybe no one knows where you went and then you get sick or catch a leg between rocks, or you get trapped under a fallen tree or inside the terrifying mass of an avalanche. You can't do anything but wait, pray if you're the praying type, and hope.

That's where a nose-smart detection dog can really make your day. If you're lucky, your ordeal will end with what I like to call the bark of promise—*Woof! Woof! We're on your scent!*—followed by a superhero nose poking between the rocks or through the snowbank—the snoot of hope.

The bark of promise!

The snoot of hope!

In search of promise and hope, I meet six-year-old Angie, a boxer with a special knack for finding living people. Angie and her housemate Darwin—also a boxer—belong to Alex Collier, a trainer who works with noted canine behavior expert Mark Spivak's Comprehensive Pet Therapy, based in Atlanta. Both pups are certified as level 3 trailing experts by the Georgia K9 Tactical Tracker Team, and, handled by Collier, they volunteer for both live-person search and rescue and cadaver work.

Collier invites me out to observe Angie in tracking mode, having enlisted her father to "get lost" in service of the exercise. With Angie still in the car, Dad heads off into the Atlanta-area forest preserve, leaving behind a sweatshirt he'd been wearing all morning. He takes a circuitous route unknown to his daughter to ensure she can't inadvertently "guide" the dog in the right direction. He doubles back now and then and winds through the trees to turn his line of scent into a confusing scribble, using a phone app to map his exact moves.

We wait more than half an hour before Collier, Angie, and I move to the top of the trail. Collier puts her dad's sweatshirt in front of Angie's nose and says, "Find it!" The pup leaps up and starts the search, a very long, loose leash giving her independence.

Boxers are long-legged and a bit goofy in their gait, but Angie's *nose* leads us today—off the trail, through thick brush, up and over hills, and across a stream and back. A few times she heads one way, stops with her nose wiggling in the air, then turns and chooses another heading. That's natural, as a scent morphs and moves: A dog may lose it for a time and shift direction to rediscover its edge. But "Angie is a bit of an overthinker," Collier tells me. "She's more prone to hesitate and think it over than some dogs. Give her time, though, and she'll nail it."

Indeed, as Angie untangles her target's route, the pup seems to become more and more confident, moving faster and meandering less. And 33 minutes after we started, she spots the man she is sniffing for—sitting on a boulder with a book in his lap—and races to him, dropping into a sit at his feet. Collier, running up behind her, quickly rewards the dog verbally and with the toss of a ball. With the job complete, Angie also is allowed to fully greet Collier's dad, which she does on two legs, with terrific enthusiasm.

When we compare the maps on the cell phones of the lost and the finder, the overlap is remarkable. The dog team covered more total ground than Dad did, but the lines tell us over and over that Angie found and followed the right track. In a few cases, we can see where Collier's father deliberately went out of his way to challenge Angie's skills—taking her up and around and back—and where she did an outstanding job sticking with the smell that followed him. If this had been a real emergency, the dog's olfactory smarts would have gotten a lost man home in time for dinner.

In this case, Angie's target was known to her, and perhaps that helped her to track him down more easily. But as we know from dogs finding hikers lost deep in wilderness, these animals are just as capable of trailing complete strangers, and with only a quick exposure to their scent. With more than half a million missing persons reported across the U.S. in an average year, the need for help in finding the lost is great, and dogs are ready to turn their snouts to our service.

Human odor studies suggest many compounds are involved in the way we smell, not all of which scientists have identified. If handled items are involved in a scenario, those items may carry blended scents—human and otherwise. All told, it is difficult to know for sure what exactly the dogs are smelling and responding to, case by case. And yet, respond they do. Given an individual's scent to locate, the best tracking dogs will parse it out from among the many smells they encounter, latch on, and focus in until they succeed.

Time and again, dogs have amazed with their ability to detect people over impressive distances despite disturbed or contaminated samples and scenes, or time passed since the scent was laid down. It's why detection dogs have been formally investigating crime for more than 120 years. As for sniffing out the human dead, that became an official job for trained working dogs in the 1970s. Training dogs on narcotics began a little earlier, and on explosives earlier still, as the British Army deployed dogs to find land mines during WWII. Snout-smart canines have proven able to solve puzzles going way back in time, finding scent where it would seem it couldn't possibly remain.

Body and odor

I can't help it: I'm fascinated by the whole cadaver-sniffing dog world. I will shield my eyes from a pileup on the highway and from the too-real violence on TV and in film, but describe how a body rots after death or tell stories of dogs nosing their way to that body, and I'm all in. Dogs have, in fact, become essential to solving "scented" crimes, as have the trainers willing to dig into the unpleasantries of death to get their dogs ready for the job.

The latter is not for the queasy. For the very best education of their animals, trainers of cadaver dogs (often called HRD dogs, for "human remains detection") will seek out samples of real human tissue—leftovers from processed crime scenes, when possible. In part, that's because the ingredient list and proportions of volatile organic compounds (VOCs) rising from a dead human are subtly or dramatically different from those of other dead animals a trainer might drag in for practice. A dog working a crime scene in search of human remains must be smart enough to know the difference, or he's likely to alert on every bird carcass and deer bone in the woods. He also needs to make the most of his olfactory intelligence, selectively ignoring hundreds of scents from the surrounding environment. Whatever the details of the scene, he faces an olfactory onslaught to puzzle through.

Further complicating a detection dog's experience, the human body makes 427 VOCs as it breaks down, and different chemicals dominate the blend depending on whether the corpse is above- or belowground.

Concentrations of the ingredients in the "death cocktail" (including hydrocarbons, aldehydes, ketones, nitrogen-heavy compounds, sulfides, and organic acids) wax and wane with decomposition, making for an ever changing scent. To help prepare young body-dogs-to-be for the variation, commercial scents also vary: One company offers recently dead, decomposed, and drowning victim blends, for example. But experts say they don't perfectly mimic the real odors or reflect the whole timeline of decomposition.

The evolving nature of the scent of the dead is a huge challenge for trainers, and a reason some take their dogs to "body farms"—forensic anthropology research facilities that place donated corpses at different stages of natural breakdown in outdoor settings. Such environs ensure that the pup's nose encounters enough entries in the corpse odor catalog that the animal can find what he's searching for, and that he'll know it when he smells it.

No matter how well a killer scrubbed a scene or how weather-beaten the burial ground, a good sniffer dog can uncover the truth of what happened where. Many a floor, from old wooden planks to newly poured concrete, has been ripped up on the say-so of a sniffer dog—not to mention all the gardens destroyed in search of remains. Just 15 milligrams of human tissue are needed to lead to canine certainty: Think a chip of bone, smear of blood, strand of hair, bit of tooth, sliver of fingernail. Weather, water, and time may severely degrade samples, but if anything's left to find, the dog's nose will know. So, neither a cleaned-up nor a chaotic crime scene is likely to thwart detection.

That's certainly impressive. But then there's this: Dogs can also detect the dead and buried a hundred years later. Two hundred years later. Maybe even a thousand years after they're gone.

Time of death

Fletch leaps down from the back of the SUV and takes off across a field. He crisscrosses the landscape, gobbling up acres with long strides. His mostly black tail in a constant wag, he stops briefly at a high point on the bluff to gaze out over the river before returning to his romp.

A small pack of humans follows behind the exuberant dog, including Fletch's owner, Suzi Goodhope, Dawn Lawrence of the National Forest Service, Jeffrey Shanks from the National Park Service, and me. Since 2017 Lawrence and Shanks have worked with Goodhope and her dogs—Fletch now, and earlier another talented pup named Shiraz—to locate the remains of dozens of people who died here at Fort Gadsden, Florida, more than 200 years ago.

On July 27, 1816, a U.S. Navy gunboat fired on the fort along Florida's Apalachicola River, striking an ammunition shed and blowing the entire place to smithereens. Killed in the blast were some 270 men, women, and children. The destroyed citadel had protected the largest free Black colony in the country, made up of former enslaved people from Spanish Florida and escapees from Louisiana, Georgia, the Creek Nation, the Mississippi Territory, and the Carolinas who'd fought alongside British forces during the War of 1812 in exchange for the promise of continued freedom. At its peak, the community had some 1,000 members; most of those still on-site in 1816 died in the explosion or soon after it from their injuries. But what happened to their remains has remained a mystery for more than two centuries.

The broader area, Prospect Bluff Historic Sites, had been closed to the public for restoration since Hurricane Michael tore through in 2018. But on a warm fall day, we are allowed past the locked gate to visit the now peaceful 16-acre fort. Bookended by the lower Apalachicola River and Apalachicola National Forest, the site is gently hilly, scruffy with tall grasses, and punctuated by stands of slash and longleaf pines and occasional majestic oaks and cypresses. An open area just above the river is the perfect place for Fletch to stretch his legs after the long car ride, before it's time for his nose to go to work.

Fletch is a Belgian Malinois, Goodhope's breed of choice both as a pet—"not for everyone," she warns, referring to the dog's incredible strength and independent streak—and for the work they do. He has all the power and intensity that the breed promises and was initially intended for the protection-dog sport called schutzhund. I find that hard to imagine: In the first minute of our first meeting, he puts his considerable weight against my legs and looks up at me with a tongue-lolling grin, then shoves his snout into my palms asking for a rubdown. (I comply, as I always do.) When his original placement didn't work out, Goodhope took him, with plans to train him as a cadaver dog instead. She's had to address some bad behavior—Fletch is a destroyer of packages, hand-knit scarves, and gate locks—but he's proven quite proficient at finding the dead.

It's become clear in recent years that the dogs who work with law enforcement to locate contemporary corpses can be trained to dig their noses into the deep past, sniffing out tiny amounts of centuries- or even millennia-old human remains—even when looters or developers have heavily degraded burial sites. Handlers in the U.S. have been working dogs at Native American and Civil War sites for decades, for example, while in a careful study conducted at an ancient necropolis at Drvišica, Croatia, and published in 2019, dogs alerted on tombs *from the Iron Age*—which starts around 1500 B.C., considerably older than experts believed possible. And if that's not enough to make eastern European canines proud, recently, in a village in the Hradec Králové region of the Czech Republic, a pup named Monty—without prompting—dug up Bronze Age artifacts while out on a walk. Artifacts 3,000 years old. On a walk. Like it was nothing.

As is true of sniffer dogs of all sorts, canines who find what's left of the dead do it for love of the game. Sad and sinister backstories are lost on them. "Find the body," no matter the context, just means good fun. Such games suit Fletch perfectly: He's a big kid in a dog suit, a bit of a goof. Elegant—have you seen a Malinois?—but a goof just the same. "He lives life to the fullest no matter what he's doing," his owner says.

Goodhope tells me that her dog Shiraz was of the same breed but smaller, with a beautiful, expressive face. Shiraz died at age 12 and happily worked nearly to her last days. A lace doily of a dog, she would tiptoe through the grass as if taking care to keep her feet clean. Even her alert was prissy: She would do a gentle sit—unlike Fletch's abrupt butt drop (though on this day I notice him hovering his rear to avoid prickly briars). When Shiraz moved quickly, she floated. And she would gently take and then savor a treat, unlike Fletch who, Goodhope says, "attacks it like a great white shark, and it is gone in milliseconds." Shiraz was a show dog in her first life, a title not generally favored in the working dog world. "Show dogs are thought to be only pretty with little else to recommend them," Goodhope says. "Shiraz was the antithesis of this old adage."

Shiraz learned quickly and was a willing partner in every task. More reserved than Fletch, she seemed older and wiser than her years. In the field, she'd go straight to work—no rocketing around first as Fletch does. And when on task, "Shiraz was unstoppable, circling a scent like a shark," Shanks recalls.

As a result, she had some remarkable finds. Most famously, in 2013, Goodhope brought the dog to a site in the Florida Panhandle, where Shanks had been searching for years for a Native American burial mound referenced in historic documents. Within an hour Shiraz had zeroed in on human remains, which turned out to be a single pinkie toe bone buried more than three feet deep that radiocarbon-dated to A.D. 670. That's more than 1,300 years ago, for those (like me) who need help with math. "Not too shabby," Goodhope says of that discovery. And Shanks, looking reverent: "That find! That find was something else!"

Normally, when working a site, Goodhope will run a dog in a thorough grid pattern, with Shanks or Lawrence mapping and marking spots they will investigate further with ground-penetrating radar. Colored flags poking up here and there across the site mark where dogs had indicated on past visits.

Our day out is less methodical: We focus on areas that have been sniffed before so I can observe the dog's response. We hike away from the river, with Shanks and Lawrence pointing out key locations: *The edge of the fort was here, the explosion started there, a village cemetery seems to end about here.* Fletch frolics. Goodhope has a collection of animal bones she uses in training, so her dogs learn to distinguish between the scent of human remains and other creatures' aromas. While we wander, she collects a skull and a few ribs from something long dead—probably a possum—to add to her stash.

In a shady spot under tree cover, Goodhope points to a slight depression in the ground that's fleshy with plant life. "Bet you that's a grave," she says. Called slumps, such sunken areas give themselves away not just by the indentation but also by their fertility, she explains. Something from below has nourished that patch of soil; in a sense it's now a memorial garden. I start to see them all around us, disappearing into the brush. It's hard to avoid walking on them, and I whisper my apologies to the dead.

To demonstrate the nose work, Goodhope calls Fletch over and sweeps her arm over the slumps. "Find Hoffa," she barks, her command for "get to work," and for a little while he does just that, nose in the air, then to the grass, his breathing a staccato snuffing as he moves over a sunken spot. It doesn't take long before he looks up at Goodhope and drops into a sit, the cue that means *"I smell death here."*

Fletch gets gentle verbal praise for that sit, and encouragement to "find more." But it is far from the celebration I've seen when other sniffer dogs do their job. That's because during a real search, there's no quick way to confirm a dog has marked a legitimate spot. "I can't risk rewarding him for a mistake," Goodhope explains—in part because the dog would get mixed messages about what to respond to, and "because I don't want him to start faking it, giving me false alerts." Dogs are smart, she says, and they'll figure out how to get what they want without working for it—a refrain I've heard from handlers everywhere.

As Giles does for whale-sniffer Eba, on workdays without discoveries Goodhope might set up a problem later that gives the dog a win and a reward, "to end their work session on a good note," she says. Without positive feedback, the drive to do the work diminishes in dogs, just as in people. She also does training runs on "blanks"—no scent—so the dogs learn that finding nothing can also be valuable.

Either way, a cadaver dog has to work now to get paid later. That means his job takes not just immense olfactory intelligence, but also a very special kind of trust that his reward is forthcoming. "Hard to imagine there's 200-plus years of history right here, with so many human stories that nobody has told," says Lawrence. "We're lucky to have Fletch as a tool in that telling." Along with ground-penetrating radar, land surveys, historical texts, and sometimes soil tests or excavations, she says, "The dogs help us fill in the narrative."

Fletch gives us one more clear indication. This time, when told to "find Hoffa," he zeroes in on a vine-choked stump; the rest of the tree probably snapped off during Hurricane Michael. Goodhope isn't surprised by the cue. She explains that human remains, or their scent, can get pulled into a tree through the roots. The actual bones might not be directly under-neath, but some part of the person is now woven into the tree's fabric, and the dog knows it. The idea is pure poetry to me, and I imagine the oaks and cypress and pines around us threaded through with the essence of lost villagers, living dogs howling in their honor.

We end the day on that tree stump alert—a good note—which means some rough-and-tumble play with a tug toy for the very good boy. But outside of the two "finds" that bookend our visit to the fort, Fletch was not very keen to work, for the most part. Even I could tell he was off his game, easily distracted, and more focused on chewing grass and scratching itches than working. Goodhope was hard-pressed to send him into intense search mode for more than a minute or two, and I could sense she was frustrated, even embarrassed that her supersniffer wasn't showing off his superpowers.

But for me, this "off" behavior is the perfect reminder that a detection dog, no matter how important the job and how intelligent his nose, is still a dog. He's not a robot, and he's allowed to have a bad day—especially when asked to abandon his normal routines, hop into a crate and a car he's not used to, set out with people he doesn't know, and then perform regardless of environmental conditions that might not be ideal for the job. "It's true, sometimes you need to go over the day from the dog's perspective," Goodhope says, "and you can find an explanation for whatever's going on."

Several factors can interfere with a cadaver dog's work. Wind and air temperature too high and too low can reduce the dog's ability to locate scent. Humidity, terrain, and soil type all affect performance. But environment is just one piece; emotion is another. Not only is Fletch expected to work well on a day when his regular routine is out of whack, but Goodhope also admits she was nervous that morning, wanting Fletch to perform and worried that I'd think she oversold his abilities if he didn't. "He's very in tune with me, and probably picked up on my anxiety," she says. "His behaviors—eating grass, losing focus—were certainly indicative of a stressed-out dog." Here were emotional intelligence and the dog-human bond showing just how powerful they are.

Another possibility? Like a weary writer staring at a blank screen, Fletch just wasn't in the mood. Even a dog can decide, *Nah. Just don't have it in me today. Please stop telling me what to do.*

CHAPTER NINE

SICKNESS STINKS

Illness makes us smelly. Of course, we're all smelly all the time, and it's nothing to be ashamed of. Like other creatures, humans are vessels of fluids and gases and cellular activities that produce odors, many of them outside of our olfactory range (thank goodness). But some of those smells can be indicators of bacterial or viral infection, parasitic infestation, or a bodily function gone somehow awry. That's because diseases change the body's metabolic processes and generate odorant molecules as by-products.

It's old news that odors accompany illness: The Greek physician Hippocrates, born in the fifth century B.C., wrote that doctors' "nostrils indicate much and well in fever patients." Before and since, many other afflictions have been known by smell. For example, fruity urine and breath are familiar signs of diabetes; scarlet fever, pneumonia, and tuberculosis cause foul breath; typhoid fever causes the body to smell like fresh-baked bread; many cancers cause a rotten smell in the affected area; and malaria alters body odor in ways that make humans more attractive to mosquitoes.

There's even a condition called maple syrup urine disease, the scent of which recalls a drenched stack of pancakes, as long as you don't think too much about the source of the fragrance.

Historically, odors were among the best disease markers available, and physicians relied on them to make diagnoses. Today scientists can connect very specific chemistries to the odors of some of the most dreadful diseases—and like doctors, scent-wise dogs know sickness when they smell it.

That includes the smell of lung cancer, the leading cause of cancer deaths worldwide. Dogs can detect the presence of even the earliest stage of lung cancer just by sniffing breath samples from patients, according to researchers at Taiwan's Kaohsiung Chang Gung Memorial Hospital and colleagues. Reporting in early 2023, the investigators determined that the diagnostic accuracy of their research pups was unaffected by cancer stage or type, or by the location of the tumor mass. "Even in stage 1A lung cancer," they write, "well-trained dogs can have a diagnostic rate of 100%."

For lung cancer, early detection is literally the difference between life and death. By the time obvious lung cancer symptoms appear, curative surgery is typically impossible and even the most aggressive drug and radiation treatments can only slow the cruel progression of the disease. More than half of people diagnosed with lung cancer die within a year.

But scientists at Mount Sinai Medical Center in New York have found that lung cancer patients diagnosed in an early stage of the disease have a 20-year survival rate of 80 percent—astonishing compared to the 18.6 percent average five-year survival rate for all patients with lung cancer. Existing early detection methods involve costly specialized equipment like CT scanners and mass spectrometers, inaccessible to much of the world's population. The Taiwan researchers concluded that nose-wise dogs could change that: "Using sniffer dogs to screen early lung cancer may have good clinical and economic benefits," they write. Snoot of hope, indeed.

The insistent *boop*

It's remarkable: Scents of illness may be wafting from ailing bodies well before perceptible symptoms or lab tests offer warnings, and dogs are impressively capable of detecting such traces. Also remarkable is how hard some dogs work to communicate their findings to humans who may have no clue anything is wrong.

Tangle, a russet-coated cocker spaniel, found one such person. The pup started by making a big mistake, or so it seemed. Over and over, while sniffing jars of urine in search of a sample donated by a patient with bladder cancer, the dog cued on a sample from a supposedly healthy volunteer. Working as part of a study aimed at proving that dogs can detect bladder cancer by smell, Tangle was insistent: The pee in that jar was positive. It turned out the dog was right. It's just that the patient who had donated the sample had kidney cancer, not bladder cancer. The urine sample, which had been marked as a healthy control for the study, did contain cancer cells. Because of the dog's insistence, the man followed up, was diagnosed, and got treatment soon after.

The study took place through a U.K. nonprofit called Medical Detection Dogs (MDD), founded by dog trainer Claire Guest and her partners to study the canine ability to "diagnose" a variety of diseases by scent. Ironically, just as she was coming to understand the extent of dogs' capabilities, Guest had her own very personal encounter with the canine olfactory superpower.

Shortly before establishing MDD, Guest had acquired a fox red Labrador named Daisy—a "gentle, placid, beautiful, loyal, and amazing friend" and one of her "soul mates," she writes in her book, *Daisy's Gift*. She began training Daisy to take part in cancer-detection studies. Then, over the course of two weeks, the dog repeatedly became agitated and nosed at her owner's breast. At first Guest dismissed the behavior as a quirk, but the dog persisted with the "boops." "My colleague noticed and asked one day, have you upset Daisy? She's acting strangely and giving you funny looks!" Guest told me. Guest did a self-exam and discovered a tiny lump, which turned out to be a benign cyst near the breast surface. But in the same area deeper down, a rare cancer lurked—one that's extremely difficult to diagnose.

"When I got the biopsy results, I was thinking, Oh my god, this happened to me!" she said. "With all my understanding and belief in the dogs' abilities, I didn't even realize what Daisy had been trying to tell me. What she was *desperate* to tell me!"

Guest was successfully treated, and gives Daisy credit for saving her life. Adding further intrigue to the story, Daisy had been trained to detect bladder cancer, so like Tangle's, her warning to Guest relied on her ability to generalize from one cancer to another in one of those persistent mysteries of dogs' olfactory intelligence.

Scientists aren't sure what commonality exists in the scents of different cancers; our most sensitive and high-tech tests often suggest they have nothing in common. And yet, dogs' noses know. In some respects, somehow, to them, cancer is cancer. Daisy ultimately became one of MDD's "supersniffers," consistently hitting around 93 percent accuracy in cancer-detecting training exercises.

Superscreeners

Even with all the research exploring the capabilities of disease-sniffer dogs, scientists are still investigating what dogs are responding to. That's not just true for diseases: Cadaver-dog trainers and others told me the same thing. What's clear is that the animals have noses and brains sensitive and intelligent enough to detect illnesses that humans need complex diagnostic equipment and often unpleasant procedures to find.

Case in point: colon cancer screening. Have you had a colonoscopy? It's certainly the most effective way to peer into the gut in search of bits that shouldn't be there, which is extremely important. But without getting into details, let's just say it makes for a crappy two days of your life. The best noninvasive alternative so far is a fecal occult blood test—just a poop schmear, no prep and no scope—but sensitivity to colorectal neoplasia is simply not as good as colonoscopy. Not bad, but for a potentially fatal cancer needing early detection, not good enough.

Compare that to a study at Japan's Kyushu University of dogs who were given both breath and stool samples of patients—some with colorectal cancer, some without. Snout sensitivity to the whiff of neoplasia on the breath? Ninety-one percent. Given a little poop to sniff, the pups' diagnostic accuracy went up to 97 percent. And yet, mainstream medicine is a long way from embracing detection dogs' natural superpower and acknowledging that they can be as smart as some of our lab tests, and maybe even smarter. For the gut, at least for the foreseeable future, our choices will likely remain pooping in a cup or taking a scope up the wazoo. Me, I'd rather ask a dog to do what he's inclined to do anyway—sniff my butt. Wouldn't you?

Medical detection dogs aren't just friendlier than your average diagnostic test, either. They're more adaptable. As we've already heard from a pack of trainers, once a pup learns *how to learn* to copy a behavior, solve a problem, or answer a question, she can master different forms of a challenge at speed, as sniffer dogs showed during the COVID-19 pandemic.

Passengers arriving at Finland's Helsinki-Vantaa International Airport in late 2020 and early 2021 met canines working the crowds. It's one of the busiest airports in Europe, and even during the height of pandemic lockdowns, four to five million travelers a year were passing through its gates. The pups were trained olfactory investigators who usually used their snouts and smarts to detect illicit drugs, dangerous cargoes, and even cancer. But the global health crisis had them nosing about for something then even more pressing: SARS-CoV-2. Dogs proved to be at least as accurate as the standard laboratory tests at finding positive cases and ruling out negative ones, with sensitivity consistently reported well above 90 percent. Remarkably, they also showed themselves capable of both generalizing—ignoring differences among viral mutations and signaling the presence of any version of the disease—and of discriminating among variants, depending on what their humans asked them to do. Whether presented with skin swabs, sweat samples, or even dirty socks, trained detection dogs assessed in Europe, the U.K., and the U.S. excelled at distinguishing those infected from those clear.

Progress against Parkinson's

Though lab tests for COVID-19 were developed at top scientific speed, many devastating illnesses remain frustratingly difficult to diagnose with certainty. Parkinson's disease is one of them, affecting more than 10 million people around the world, with some 60,000 new patients in the U.S. alone each year. It damages dopamine-producing neurons in the brain, and in addition to the tremors and other motor function problems for which it is best known, can cause sleep disruption, depression, lost sense of smell, constipation, cognitive decline, and other symptoms that are often blamed on a wide range of other conditions. The pathology can begin a decade before severe symptoms like tremors point to the true cause, by which time a lot of irreversible damage to the brain is already done. Knowing they've got Parkinson's at its earliest stages would allow people to better prepare for, manage, and even slow the effects of the disease. But a definitive early test for this scourge has long eluded doctors.

In 2015, a Scottish nurse named Joy Milne, whose husband suffered from Parkinson's, asked researcher Tilo Kunath why doctors weren't using smell as a diagnostic tool. Milne has hereditary hyperosmia, a rare condition that gives her an extremely sensitive nose. She had noticed years before that her husband had developed a musky odor that got caught in his shirts—a smell she later recognized in rooms where support groups of Parkinson's patients gathered. Her suggestion to Kunath eventually led to research into the unique scent of Parkinson's, which scientists believe is related to chemical changes in the sebum (skin oils) of people with active disease.

If Milne could detect it, "well, duh … dogs." That's what Lisa Holt thought when she first heard about Milne's special ability from a friend,

Nancy Jones, whose once dynamic husband had become debilitated by Parkinson's. As a professional canine detection trainer, Holt quickly saw that applying canine olfactory intelligence to this terrible disease could be life-changing for millions. Within months she and Jones launched an all-volunteer, self-funded research project to determine whether dogs could indeed smell something specific related to the disease—perhaps the same scent that Joy Milne had detected. They could. Holt founded the nonprofit PADs for Parkinson's in hopes of making the most of dogs' olfactory gift.

As is often the case with alert dogs, those nose smart enough to sniff out Parkinson's defy typecasting. "We have dogs from mini-schnauzer to mastiff, and from pup to veteran," says Holt when I visit PADs at the organization's office on San Juan Island, Washington. One of the original PADs canines is a black standard poodle named Mia who sniffed her first Parkinson's sample in 2016. She's now 10 years old and still on the job. Some members of the detection team are rescues, like basset hound Bubba; some have legal paper–size pedigrees like Bendy, an Italian Lagotto Romagnolo whose breed was created for truffle hunting; some came with a hand-scrawled FREE DOG sign. Their nose drive, plus their "independent working behavior," sets them apart, Holt says.

Her top dogs include a Hungarian vizsla named Hudson who "loves his work so much he tries to outrun his nose." Holt describes a moment when Hudson's sniffing was so vigorous that he stopped on the "hot" sample and "literally flipped, ass over teakettle," she says. A deeply committed Pomeranian named Shugga sometimes attends training sessions wearing a tutu. Another sniffer, a papillon named Tessa, once slipped out of her owner's car at the Friday Harbor fairgrounds where a carnival swallowed the pup in chaos. The owner searched frantically among the thrill rides and snack stalls to no avail. Finally, she reached the far end of the fairgrounds, where the PADs training building stands, and there the eager little papillon was. "This dog was just sitting there at the PADs entry patiently waiting to go in to do her job," Holt says.

For years physicians caring for patients who may have Parkinson's would send samples to Holt and the PADs pups for aid with diagnosis. At the time of my visit, 18 trained and experienced Parkinson's sniffers were on call, and at least 10 of them worked on every sample. It was a small-scale effort then, but the potential to help people before the disease tightens its grip on their lives held incredible promise.

Others agreed, and in 2023 PADs, with papers in the works on its scientific findings, joined forces with Nosaïs, a nonprofit research department within the National Veterinary School (NEVA) of Maison-Alfort, France, on a campus where the detection work has room to stretch its legs.

That promise is why then 47-year-old Sarah Winter turned to the dogs, after a panoply of bodily changes that might seem unrelated rang a bell in her head. First, her sense of smell faded. Then she had severe cramps in her feet, developed patches of flaky skin, and experienced muscle stiffness and vocal fatigue. As a social worker who had spent much of her career working with patients with neurological disorders including Parkinson's, Sarah realized something was truly wrong as the odd episodes accumulated. "But if I wasn't already immersed in the world of Parkinson's," she says, "I might not have pursued it further."

Sarah was familiar with PADs through her work, and once she met the criteria for Holt's project, she packed up her sample shirt for the dogs. Holt reached out soon after with the results: Nine out of 10 pups responded yes to the scent. Sarah is the youngest person so far in whom the dogs have detected Parkinson's, which is a useful data point because scientists don't yet know when in the course of the disease the body's odor changes.

"The dogs have spoken," she tells me, and she considers their voices a real piece of evidence toward a definitive diagnosis. With no motor impairment, her disease is considered "prodromal," and she doesn't yet meet the clinical criteria for Parkinson's. That's made it challenging to get her doctors on board; even just getting a referral to PADs took some doing. Until mainstream medicine accepts the dogs as valid tools, she says, their value won't be fully realized. And any remaining doubters should know that a follow-up test—a skin biopsy that the medical establishment trusts—concurred with the dog's findings.

Sarah turned to a researcher and physician of integrative medicine named Laurie Mischley, who is studying the lifestyle and nutrition of people whose Parkinson's has been slow to progress. The dogs gave her momentum, she says, pressing her to get the skin biopsy. "I trust the dogs, and because of them I took the next steps," she tells me. Working with Mischley, she's changed up her nutrition and exercise regime, based on Mischley's findings that these factors matter to the progression of symptoms. In addition, as she found huge gaps in the health care system related to prodromal patients, she pursued a position with the company that did the skin biopsy to confirm her disease, "to have a seat at the table. I wanted to meet the people who are fired up about finding neuroprotective treatments for people who haven't experienced enough disease progression for a clear diagnosis," she says. Now, she is poised to help shape things like standards of care and legal protections for patients like her, and get whatever research and technology arises to those who need it most. "The dogs set it all in motion," she asserts.

Holt points out that early diagnoses through the dogs' noses could also lead scientists to start identifying triggers of the disease. "And by following the disease upstream," she says, "you may find its source." In time, she hopes, "there will be a cure, and we won't need the dogs' help anymore."

CHAPTER TEN

THE WHIFF
THAT WARNS

Detecting disease by the scent is something dogs have been doing for a long time. Their ability to form special partnerships with humans also creates opportunities for us to have their support in managing the impacts of those diseases—especially the chronic ones. That means putting not just their olfactory talents to work, but also their communicative and emotional smarts. Because in so many cases, they seem truly to care about what happens to us.

A nose for sweets

Typically, a dog caught with his nose in the garbage is a bad dog. But on the day Armstrong rifled around with his snout in a trash can stuffed with paper towels and pulled out a particular one for inspection, Mark Ruefenacht was astounded and lavished praise on the pup. "That's when I knew we really had something," he tells me. That towel had been used by Jeannie Hickey, then a diabetes nurse who also has type 1 diabetes herself. She blotted her sweaty brow during a low-blood-sugar event, marked the towel with a tiny X, and gave it to Ruefenacht.

Ruefenacht had been working for several years to prove that his dog could detect his own low-blood-sugar scent, and Armstrong had become quite proficient at it. But what about someone else's scent? Was there a commonality across people with diabetes, and would the dog have the olfactory smarts to zero in on it? The answer was yes, easily: On that day, Armstrong pulled the correct towel without hesitation. It appeared that if anyone with diabetes became hypoglycemic, Armstrong would be able to tell them so.

Ruefenacht was first inspired to test dogs' noses against diabetes when he had a seizure related to a hypoglycemic episode in the presence of a dog he was fostering. The animal was attentive and seemed upset during the event, which got the man thinking. Knowing that work was going on with canines sniffing out cancer cells, Ruefenacht wondered if the dog had responded not just to the outward signs of the seizure, but also to a scent he gave off before it happened. He and Hickey worked with Armstrong and a chocolate Lab named Danielle, discovering that the animals could detect hypoglycemia and hyperglycemia in samples of both saliva and sweat from people with diabetes.

High blood sugar gives itself away by a buildup of ketones in the blood that make the breath smell fruity. The dog-detectable scent of low blood sugar may come from the chemical isoprene, a common organic compound in our exhalations that can double in volume during a hypoglycemic event.

In 2004, Ruefenacht founded Dogs4Diabetics, a nonprofit organization that opened the door to a whole new industry of at-home medical assistance dogs. Diabetes-sniffing dogs today can smell both sugar extremes with impressive accuracy and well before any other technology sends a warning.

Clearly, there is olfactory intelligence in the dogs' ability to smell any disease, the scent of which may come from just a few molecules among millions. But Ruefenacht pointed to another kind of smarts in the animals who work so closely with their people. "When a dog starts to realize that what he's doing is an important job, something clicks, and changes how he thinks," he says. That's when behaviors become decisions, rather than just trained responses to designated stimuli. The connection between person and pup seems to affect the urgency the dog feels about the health anomaly she's responding to. With time together, she becomes invested in her person in a whole new way; there's not just a scent there, but a scent that means someone she cares about is in trouble.

A family rescued

Bob Collett has had type 1 diabetes for most of his 60-plus years. Early in his married life, his wife, Marie, would wake up five times a night to check her husband's blood sugar, to keep him from having a potentially deadly episode before morning. When his sugar would careen out of balance during the day, Bob would suddenly act drunk or confused and sometimes rude, so the couple and their son became insular. "We had no life," Marie tells me. "None at all."

As I chat on Zoom with the Colletts, who are sitting in their living room in the U.K., I can see a big, square-headed yellow Lab–golden retriever mix on the rug next to Bob—and though the dog doesn't make a move or a sound during our call, he is a real presence in the room. The family lives on a farm with a menagerie, but this dog, like no other animal, has a hold on their hearts. Because not only has Mack protected Bob's life over and over, he's also given the whole family back a life they'd given up on ever having again.

Both Bob and Marie admit it: When they first heard about Medical Detection Dogs (MDD), they were skeptical that an animal could do what no medication or technology had done to help them. But they applied to MDD anyway, out of desperation. Finally, a dog became available that MDD staff thought would be a good match for Bob and family. "He came for the weekend, as a test, and he never left," Bob says.

Any remaining skepticism about the dog's abilities vanished shortly after his arrival: With a hard stare at Bob, the dog gave his first alert a half hour into the "visit," even though he hadn't yet trained on Bob's scent. Normally, if a dog is going to be placed with a client, MDD begins methodically exposing the animal to clothing worn during hypo- and hyperglycemic episodes and praising the dog for responding to them. Mack skipped that step and went right to work. "I said, Bob, he's alerting, check your blood sugar. And *bang*, Mack was right!" Marie says.

Once Mack was fully accustomed to Bob's smell, he began alerting well before his owner's sugar measurably rose or dropped, acting as a (very) early warning system. And he doesn't back off until he's sure his owner is safe. "He'll get restless and stay that way until my sugar level comes down to a certain number," Bob says.

Mack sticks close to Bob most of the time, but if they're in separate rooms, the dog will check in periodically, going to Bob and sniffing the air before returning to his bed or activity elsewhere once he's satisfied all is well. At night he does the same, and if he doesn't like what he smells, he'll nudge Bob awake. If Bob doesn't respond, Mack goes around to Marie's side of the bed and puts his nose in her face. For his efforts, Mack gets excellent care and a lot of love, plenty of his favorite treats (cream cheese cubes are especially appreciated), boisterous praise for doing his job well (a little song and dance is sometimes warranted), and daily "off" time to just be a dog—swimming, hiking, and playing with toys.

Since the dog came to their rescue, the Colletts say, Bob requires much less insulin, has put on weight, and feels immensely better. As an invaluable bonus, in helping Bob keep his sugar from spiking, Mack also appears to be helping preserve Bob's remaining sight, which was declining precipitously before the dog joined the household—a common and devastating effect of uncontrolled diabetes.

Beyond being a daily lifesaver and sight-saver, what Mack means to the Collett family is hard to put into words. It's not just about the physical; his presence and the improved lifestyle he allows have transformed Bob's mental health and Marie's, too. Before Mack came, Bob and Marie's son, who has autism, was often the one to find his father in crisis: "Daddy is lying down in the garden again," he would tell his mother. He would worry aloud that his dad was going to die, but no longer. "Looking back now," Marie says, "I'm not sure how we coped all those years before Mack saved us."

I find that kind of appreciation for dogs' noses and heart smarts in so many households during my reporting. And though I know that detection dogs catch human smells that save lives, the stories continue to amaze me. For example, did you know a seizure has a scent? Neither did I. Neither, in fact, did Ed Crane until he brought home a dog who told him so.

A life restored

Ed Crane can't tell you what he ate for dinner last night. Or for breakfast this morning. Surgery to control severe epileptic seizures that began plaguing him at age 30 impaired his brain's ability to make short-term memories. Scribbled reminders and patient family members do the work his brain can no longer do. The surgery did help reduce the number and severity of Crane's episodes—he doesn't have the most severe sort of seizures anymore—but tweaking his left temporal lobe wasn't a cure by any means. The day we spoke, he'd already had two partial seizures and he'd have more that afternoon and night.

Still, Crane has swapped a narrow sliver of a life for a much wider, fuller one, thanks to a series of seizure alert dogs. Crane has had three of these very intelligent canines since 2003, and not a single seizure-related fall or injury during all those years. That's a huge impact. According to the World Health Organization, the risk of premature death in people with epilepsy is three times higher than in the general population, and those deaths are most often caused by falls and other seizure-related accidents.

A black Lab named Charity was Crane's first helper, a "companion dog" from Canine Partners for Life (CPL) to whom he came home after his surgery. On day one, she warned him of an oncoming seizure 20 minutes before it began. "I laid down on the floor and she waited the seizure out by my side," Crane wrote to me. "It was a new beginning for me."

When Charity died in 2011, "my life took a step backward. That in-between time is really hard, especially not having that warning system." But soon CPL provided Alepo, a cream-color Lab assistance dog—intelligent, adaptable, confident, polite, and always happy to work, Crane says. For six years, the two were best friends, and Alepo kept him safe. "He was completely accurate and reliable. He wasn't satisfied until I'd lie down so he could place his front legs across my waist, and he wouldn't let me up until my seizure was entirely over." The dog would lick his face as a sign that all was well again.

Alepo "retired" in 2018 and still lives with Crane, his time on duty done. Zern, a sturdy Lab with a smooth coat the color of buttermilk and deep brown eyes that seem to see into your soul, is now on the clock. I get a glimpse of Zern, lying next to Crane, during our video call. He is wearing his harness, ready to accompany Crane wherever he needs to go. The dog also helps with balance, among other things, and so stays very close to his person. "I went from hell to where I am today: restored, traveling, getting up and speaking, living my life," Crane says. "Because of these remarkable dogs, I'm no longer a prisoner to my disability."

Canine Partners for Life, the Cochranville, Pennsylvania–based nonprofit that has supplied Crane with his canine lifelines, has a small breeding program producing mostly golden retrievers, Labs, standard poodles, and smooth collies; they also take in mixed breeds from rescues and other organizations. Pups' abilities and temperament are assessed early on to see if they're inclined to do a job. About a third to half of CPL's dogs end up as seizure alert dogs. And here's what's most remarkable: "We don't *train* seizure alert dogs," says Program Director Deb Bauer. "We find the ones that do it naturally." Most of their dogs are capable of sensing a seizure, she says, but only some act on it automatically. These are the dogs whose behavior is reinforced, over and over and over, so they'll continue to respond without fail.

To find out which dogs lean toward alert work, the CPL team exposes the dogs to both clothing potential clients have worn during seizures and the people themselves, observing each dog's reactions. Even without ever encountering a seizure before, "we've had dogs come in from another room to alert," Bauer says. "Others have been sound asleep and suddenly wake up alerting."

In many cases, she continues, "it doesn't matter if the dog knows the person or not. It doesn't matter if he's even said hello. If there's an episode coming, he's going to tell us, hey, something isn't right." Then, "Once we know a dog alerts, we can quickly pinpoint what the behavior is and how far in advance they do it," she explains. Any training related to alerting is really just encouragement to keep using the intelligence already empowering them to act, teaching the dog that performing specific behavior in that context is good, whether by praise or affection or playtime.

Stories go back decades of dogs predicting human seizures—signaling the coming event with attention-getting behaviors like hard stares, whines, nudging, and pawing. And they do it as long as 90 minutes before an episode. How? Evidence points to dogs using their olfactory sensitivity and judgment to respond to VOCs emitted before and during an epileptic event—as with many other diseases. Research has indeed confirmed pre-seizure VOCs, and trained dogs can clearly discriminate between seizure and non-seizure odors in the same patient.

But as Bauer is well aware, the untrained also find the scent meaningful. In a small study a few years ago, Neil Powell of Queen's University Belfast and colleagues found that pet dogs exposed to samples of seizure-associated sweat that appeared to come from their owners reacted to them significantly more than to control samples. "Why this odor evokes attention seeking we don't know," Powell says. "But our survey suggests the best-performing dogs have the most intimate relationship with the owner. So, that affiliation is meaningful."

Scent may not even be the whole story. Some scientists believe dogs are sensitive to electromagnetic changes and may also be responding to minute variations in the body's electromagnetic field as a seizure approaches. (Extra electrical activity in the brain precedes such episodes.) If true, it's yet another form of sensory intelligence we humans lack that may affect how dogs "see" and respond to us, their sensorially limited companions. "There are likely multiple things going on," Bauer says. The obvious would be an odor, or a subtle change in the person's behavior. "But perhaps also their balance is off, or their voice might change—a dog will pick up on that, too. They are so much smarter than we give them credit for: They are looking at the whole picture, and it only takes a tiny change in that picture to tell them something is going to happen."

Many of CPL's dogs alert to multiple conditions, including other seizure disorders, blood-sugar highs and lows, migraines, cardiac issues. And they'll naturally offer different alert behaviors for different problems, which comes in very handy for clients who have both diabetes and epilepsy, for example. It's essential to distinguish between a seizure warning and a hyperglycemia alert to respond appropriately, and the dog is smart enough to make it clear which one he means.

The human-dog relationship goes beyond the health care services the pups perform. Years into their partnership, Crane says Zern's emotional intelligence has grown and added another layer of value to his assistance. "The dog gets me. He is always paying attention, looking, facing me. He helps me battle depression, which is part of any disability like mine." It's the simple things, he explains: "I'll be in agony and he comes over and puts his head in my lap, or he sits close and puts his head against mine and licks me. It may sound small, but it can make a huge difference to how I'm feeling that moment or that day. And he does that for me *every* day."

CHAPTER ELEVEN

BORN TO BOND

Is it fair to say that dogs are the most *people-smart* animals on Earth? I believe it is. What distinguishes a dog even more than her super snout is that she wants *you* to know what she knows. Bark, howl, hip-check, paw-thwack: Your pup wants to share, to make a connection, and this is perhaps her species' pièce de résistance: a social intelligence adapted and applied to humankind. That *Canis familiaris*'s social smarts began crossing species lines millennia ago—that dogs were willing and able to bond beyond dogdom—has resulted in a profound and beautiful inter-species friendship.

I call my pup Monk my Oxytocin Dog. I gave him the nickname after learning that when a person and a dog gaze into each other's eyes, both can experience a spike in oxytocin. The more bonded the two are, the bigger the effect. This particular hormone acts as a neurotransmitter, a chemical messenger in the brain related to, among other things, empathy and relationship building. When your pup celebrates wildly upon your return from the store, oxytocin is underpinning that happy dance.

And along with the associated hormone prolactin, the rise in oxytocin might even cause him to shed a tear: A recent study out of Azabu University in Japan showed that dogs separated from their owners for several hours may indeed well up during the reunion. Whether this is a purely physiological phenomenon endorsed by natural selection—tear-prone pups might elicit more care than dry-eyed ones, and so have higher survival rates—or if dogs actually "feel the love" and are weeping with joy, nobody's quite sure yet.

Anyway, Monk and I have a little ritual for when I'm feeling a bit blue. He'll be sitting at the top of the stairs, and I'll stand with him pressed between my knees. I lean forward and rub the front of his neck, where his fur is ridiculously soft. Perhaps my scent tells him how I'm feeling, or maybe he's just reveling in my touch, but he always tilts his head way back and looks up at me with his rich-brown eyes in a way that feels like love. A gentle chin lick is usually offered (his tongue, my chin). And as we connect, for a moment all is calm and life is good.

Many of us lean on a dog for this special feeling, whether you call it a chemical rush or unconditional love. And for thousands of years, since dogs (mostly) gave up their wild ways and made themselves at home in human-dominated settings, we've come to depend on them for a kind of support that simply wouldn't be possible had they not evolved by our sides. Because not only has our bond affected how dogs think, learn, and problem-solve, it's also helped shape how they feel—including how they feel about us. Individuals vary, of course, but many dogs use a powerful emotional intelligence to relate to us and read us and respond to our emotional needs.

Such social abilities are rooted in physiology, notes Clive Wynne in *Dog Is Love:* "Dogs' affinity for humans originates from deep within their brain, and their neural activity can even determine how much they care about us," he observes. "It may not be a stretch to say that dogs are built for affection." When Wynne and I speak, he quickly gets to the heart of the matter. "To have this being who wants to hang out with us, who makes a massive fuss over friends and family, who barks when a stranger approaches but has a cry of loving anticipation for someone whose footfall she recognizes, it's just marvelous," he says. "If I was a religious man, I would say the dog is a gift from the gods."

As a human, I'm naturally tempted to linger here, contemplating how *we* fit into the canine relationship-skills picture. But let's be patient and first address social intelligence in dogs—as it pertains to other dogs. After all, the *intra*species relationship is the most essential one for any species' survival: If dogs didn't socialize with other dogs, soon there would be no dogs at all.

That kind of intelligence is on obvious display when dogs communicate with one another; if we give them our rapt attention, the immense complexity of their conversations becomes clear. Canine body language alone seems a full-service vernacular packed with subtleties. Brilliant examples of social smarts pop up in the rough-and-tumble of play, when dogs speak volumes in the dip of a tail or the lift of a paw—all the while building up the experience and brainpower to ensure they read incoming signals correctly and are ready for anything.

Smart play

When I was a kid, my brother, Adam, and I played a game we called "You Gotta Gimme a Chance!" It was a race. The object was to be the first to run into the living room and jump on Dad, who stretched out on the living room floor, no doubt bracing for an elbow to the eye or knee to the groin. The round started in the back room of the apartment. On three, we wrestled our way through the doorway, each trying to stop the other from getting through. There was a lot of yelling. Whoever broke away first tore down the hall into the living room and leaped onto poor prone Dad. Kid #2 would pounce too, despite coming in second. It was our version of *Hop on Pop*. Being younger, smaller, and slower, I almost always lost. That's when I would start fake crying and yell at Adam, "You gotta gimme a chance!" And usually, on the next round, he did. Apparently, it was fun for all of us, even Dad, who was always a "get down on our level" kind of father and reveled in having his two bony kids vying roughly to be in his arms.

Thinking back, I can now see more of what was going on beneath the surface of our games. Beyond simply having a good time, we were strategizing, competing over a resource, bonding with family members, reading each other's intentions and emotions, learning about rules and trust and fairness (and emotional manipulation), and (sometimes) practicing empathy. We were growing our social intelligence. Our brains were changing, building new circuits and wiring up the areas where problem-solving and emotional regulation are done.

Dog play offers many parallels to ours. What on the surface may seem like just a mouthy wrestling match is, experts say, a building block of cognitive, social, and emotional skills for our pups. Dogs—especially those living with humans—play more than most mammals, and continue to devote lots of time and energy to play as adults, which is unusual as well.

My own pair, Monk and Geddy, are not timid players. When they're both in the mood, things rev up quickly from play-bow to a high-throttle match. They'll growl and bark and wrestle and bite, sometimes with mouths wide in a sort of "just kidding" way, other times with gnashing teeth, flying spittle, and whipping heads. Monk's postures and body slams appear quite strategic: My husband, a national champion wrestler back in the day, marvels at the smaller black dog's ability to fight from below (not the choice position) and at familiar moves like the "single leg snatch"—using his mouth to grab and yank one of Geddy's legs to get him on the ground.

Dogs don't all play the same way. Only Monk gets the "zoomies," for instance. (This is when a dog suddenly gallops around, often doing a big speedy loop or two, with energy that seems to come out of nowhere and fizzle just as quickly.) Geddy waits patiently for him to come back but doesn't participate. Zoomies actually suggest stress as often as they do exuberance, I've learned. I hope that's not the case for Monk, but it's certainly possible, given our dogs' power relationship. Monk is also more prone to sneak attacks, coming at Geddy from a crouch or a hiding spot. Both, though, honor a time-out: Panting, within reach but agreeing not to engage, they rest. And then, with a new bow or a sudden start, one announces that the next round has begun. The other joins in, or says *Nah* by walking away, and the game ends without incident.

When I took courses in animal behavior years ago, we were taught that the purpose of rough play is to give young animals a low-stakes way to practice skills needed for hunting and fighting. Though playful animals certainly try out behaviors they'll use in adulthood, some scientists say their antics are less about rehearsal and more about social brain development. "Play is brain food," Marc Bekoff tells me. Even for adults like Monk and Geddy, play is fulfilling, and it keeps the social wheels greased. It's a platform for physical exercise and for practicing problem-solving and intraspecies communication. Plus, they clearly love it.

Inside of a Dog author Alexandra Horowitz tells me that studying dog play transformed how she thought about the dog's world. For her research on the subject, she spent many hours with eyes glued to videos of dogs playing, going over them frame by frame, noting even the tiniest behavioral changes second by second. "The interaction looked completely different in this very slow-motion rendering," she says. "When I looked at how one dog used the other dog's attention in deciding whether and how to communicate—Should I use a play signal? How do I get his attention and what do I say to him once I have it?—I found it was actually a complicated dance that took each other's thoughts into account in a high-speed way." If one dog in a play pair was distracted, she could see just how quickly the other adjusted to get the game back on track.

Bekoff agrees that this kind of exchange seems to be evidence that animals can think about mental states—their own and that of another—as part of their social intelligence. Researchers call it having a theory of mind. "If I ask you to play and you say yes, I have an idea of what you're thinking and feeling and vice versa," he says. "There are long sequences of beliefs and goals" in that exchange, in part to do with certain behavior patterns both parties expect. "When we parse it all out, there seems to be some theory of mind going on."

So perhaps it's not surprising that a peek into the minds of the rough-and-tumblers turns up some fascinating cognitive gymnastics, with genes flipping on and off, and neurons firing, connecting, and rewiring the brain. According to the late Jaak Panksepp, a neuroscientist and psycho-biologist at Washington State University who studied play in rats, play is a highly conserved activity, evolutionarily speaking, lighting up the whole neocortex and causing lasting neuronal changes. The activity is essential to building "prosocial brains," he said, meaning brains tooled to let animals navigate social groups.

Claudia Fugazza and her colleagues at Eötvös Loránd University report that supersmart dogs—specifically the "gifted word learners" in their Genius Dog Challenge—are also the *most* playful. We know that in humans, play helps create flexible skills used for innovative thinking and problem-solving. So an association between play and smarts in another intelligent animal makes sense.

Social play also lets animals test boundaries and "train for the unex-pected," says Bekoff. Deliberately trading off control lets them grow their repertoire of physical and emotional responses to whatever position they find themselves in, whether underdog or top dog. More powerful players need to learn self-control to avoid overpowering a weaker partner and ruining the game, for one thing. Through these interactions, the animals learn that *fair* play is smart play, as it helps them form solid social bonds that can be lifesaving later on.

This dynamic is often on display at the dog park: Socially intelligent players sustain the game, get the benefits of exercise, and solidify rela-tionships; dogs who "cheat" or who simply aren't responding appropri-ately to cues from other players are likely to get into fights or be shunned by the group. It's true in the wild, too: From field observations of juvenile coyotes, Bekoff reported that those who didn't play fairly more commonly left the group and were up to four times more likely to die young than their rule-following counterparts.

"Hidden in the frivolity is a language of play that includes honesty, empathy, and cooperation," Bekoff says in an interview with *Current Biology*. Dogs at play perform a "kaleidoscope of actions," he says, including invitation and clarification, warning, and apology; they also deal with a lot of unpredictability. They make mistakes, and the most socially astute ones learn from them, even "apologizing" if their signals are crossed (which is more than we humans do a lot of the time).

In any social interaction, mistakes can cause things to go awry. Here's where dogs smartly employ whatever signals they need to reestablish peace. Clear messaging is socially intelligent messaging. Growls, for example, are extremely variable, context specific, and packed with meaning. Changes in timing, pitch, and volume can adjust the message fairly dramatically. In a study published in *Animal Behavior* in 2010 under the title "This bone is mine: Affective and referential aspects of dogs' growls," researchers found that play-growls had their own acoustic signature compared with agonistic growls, and food-guarding growls were different from those emitted during a "threatening stranger" situation and deterred other dogs from snagging a seemingly unattended bone accordingly.

The sound of a growl, and the intent behind it, then, both matter a lot. An effective "back off" signal is an essential part of the vocabulary of an animal for whom an injury can lead to disabling infection or even death. Have you ever noticed how stoic dogs can be when in pain? That's a survival mechanism: In the wild, weakness is its own signal, and predators are exceptional at detecting it. If possible, avoiding the fight before it starts is the best choice.

Furry-body language

Try wiggling your ears. Any luck? Except for somebody's grandpa, few humans have that muscular control. But dogs have it. And their mobile ears speak loudly about mood, stress, energy level. Ears held high on the head suggest an alert dog who might even point the ears toward something interesting. Ears up and forward signal aggression. Ears pulled back show friendliness, while ears pulled *way* back say "I'm scared" or "I submit." Both floppy and naturally upright ears have a lot to say to other dogs.

A dog also speaks with the position of her jaw and lips, where her whiskers are pointing, and whether her teeth are showing. A relaxed mouth with teeth peeking through only incidentally suggests friendliness. A fearful dog might keep her mouth closed but stick out her tongue or lick her lips; if she pulls back her lips into a "grin," she's signaling submission. Flared whiskers suggest arousal. An "agonistic pucker" that shows the teeth with mouth open and lips curled back and maybe a side of growling means a conflict going on, with potential for aggression. (That message, at least, we recognize!) And plenty of other facial positions each signify a specific intention.

The eyes, too, express. "Canids use face to face, direct eye contact judiciously," writes Barbara Handelman in *Canine Behavior: A Photo Illustrated Handbook*—a great resource, by the way, for those wishing to learn Doggish. A meeting of the eyes speaks with power, so it has to be done just right. Dogs need to translate hard eyes, soft eyes, squinty eyes, even "whale" eyes. That last one usually occurs when dogs are stressed or threatening—it's when the skin across the top of the head goes taut, stretching the eyelids away from the eye and exposing the whites. But the whites might also show just because a pup is straining to see something in her field of peripheral vision—no stress involved. Dogs need to know the difference.

Even the way canids breathe in certain contexts may convey meaning, as was discovered during a study of African wild dogs in which the animals sneezed—or as the study authors write, performed "audible rapid nasal exhalations"—to vote on pack movement. The authors reported that "rallies never failed when a dominant ... individual initiated and there were at least three sneezes, whereas rallies initiated by lower ranking individuals required a minimum of 10 sneezes to achieve the same level of success." A 2022 study by researchers including Horowitz indicates that dogs perform a "play pant" that is mostly absent during periods of training and rest. "These vocalizations mostly co-occurred with play behaviors (e.g., play bow) or tickling and cuddling," the authors write. They call it a potential "laughter equivalent," and consider it a meaningful non-speech-like vocalization that deserves further study.

Then there's the eloquence of dogs' other end. Canines may have no more expressive appendage than the tail, and it tells all manner of stories—not all wags are happy wags!—in the context of postures, utterances, eye and lip positions, and so on. We're all no doubt familiar with the simplest words in the tail's vocabulary—the goofy wag of happiness and the tail tuck of apprehension.

But observe more closely: Fast wags, slow wags, high wags, low wags, floppy wags, stiff wags—all of these, and their various Seussian-sounding combinations, are part of the language of dogs. Even the *direction* of tail wagging sends a message. Happy stimuli seem to cause more right-side wagging, whereas negativity pulls wags to the left.

Breaking the signals down even further, the *quadrant* of a wag appears to have meaning, and research suggests dogs can detect asymmetries in other dogs' tail moves and glean from them data on what that dog is feeling. (Wow, right?) Combined with other signals, a dog reading wags can make an educated decision about what to do next: Sniff? Play? Fight? Flee? Tail wags are often affiliative—my favorite, and the most reliably friendly, is the relaxed circular wag, at its most adorable when performed while the dog is running toward you in greeting. But don't be fooled: "Tail wagging is a context-specific behavior, which signals excitability or stimulation, such as friendliness/confidence, anxiousness/nervousness and even a threat of aggressive behavior," writes behavior expert James Serpell.

That said, it's not surprising that interfering with dog-dog conversations can create problems. I never thought of one form of interference as an issue before embarking on this book: Guide dogs for the blind are trained to *not* react to other dogs when they're working, and this seems to make them more vulnerable to attacks.

A survey undertaken by The Seeing Eye revealed that 44 percent of guide dog teams have been attacked by other dogs, while cases of aggressive interference are reported as affecting 83 percent of teams. That's a lot. Most often these incidents take place on the sidewalk or street, where, say, two pet dogs on leashes might normally eye and sniff each other, perhaps exchange growls, but stop short of a fight because they can communicate enough to de-escalate the situation. But the guide dog's trained nonresponsiveness means she may miss cues that she would otherwise react to—and another dog, wary of being ignored, may attack out of confusion or fear.

To turn dogs into our helpers, then, we may be inadvertently stifling a critical component of their intraspecies social skills. I'm not arguing against training dogs to work as guide dogs by any means. But it's important for all of us dog walkers to realize that working dogs are necessarily "silent" among their kind, and that silence can have unintended consequences.

A plea for awareness – and kindness

Because we're talking about ways we may interfere with the normal channels of canine communication, I'm going to climb up on a soapbox for just a moment if I may. When we alter a dog's anatomy for a desired look, or to match a show-ring standard, we can disrupt or even silence that animal's natural voice.

Ears and tails, the most commonly altered parts, are used to calm intraspecies aggression, among many other essential conversations. "Cropping"—surgically modifying the outer ears to be permanently erect and forward-facing, which requires cutting the ears and then "training" the cartilage into position with painful stretching and taping—makes a dog appear aggressive to other dogs. The practice also largely immobilizes the ears, so that the dog cannot move them to help detect and locate sounds. The tail's role in dog communication, meanwhile, "has been seriously underestimated," according to a 2018 study by David J. Mellor

of Massey University in New Zealand, and "docking" the tail—a euphe-
mism for amputation—"can markedly impede unambiguous interactions
between different dogs and between dogs and people. These interactions
include the expression of … emotions, moods and intentions that are of
daily significance for dog welfare."

The American Veterinary Medical Association opposes these procedures
when performed for purely cosmetic purposes and encourages removal
of cropped ears and docked tails from breed standards. "Surgical amputation of the dog's tail," reads the association's policy statement, "produces
behaviors indicative of acute pain," and such suffering when pups are very
young "may permanently alter the normal development of the central
nervous system." Tail docking was banned in the U.K. in 2007 and has
been banned or highly restricted in most European countries as well as
in Australia, Israel, and South Africa, among others.

I'm reminded of Gretel, the Weimaraner my family had when I was a
teen. Fortunately, the breed standard for these elegant, energetic pups
calls for natural ears, but not so the tail. And because Gretel was to be a
show dog, her long tail had to go. I remember her tiny cast, and later
giggling at the way her little gray stump vibrated rather than wagged. But
now I realize that such elective alterations chip away at animals' ability
to exercise their social intelligence—to express themselves, and to respond
to the communications of others. They deserve better from us: We're
supposed to be their friends.

Gretel, I'm so sorry.

CHAPTER TWELVE

CANINE NETWORKING

When allowed to "speak" with all their natural tools, dogs tend to be ready and willing to banter with us—and with lots of other animals as well. In recent studies, including one by Eötvös Loránd University, ethologists have used electroencephalogram (EEG) leads attached to dogs' heads to noninvasively read brain waves. Findings suggest that dogs very quickly learn the differences among the vocalizations of different species. Whichever language is spoken, dogs often offer themselves as interspecies playmates.

My *Unlikely Friendships* series is chock-full of *Canis familiaris*—I even did a special edition just on dogs. Their willingness to connect with other creatures and their skill at doing so, whether with us or with cats, goats, chickens, dolphins, even tortoises, is remarkable and says a lot about the reach of their social smarts. Granted, their lives both in households and on farms with many other animal residents may afford them more opportunities to pal around with more diverse companions than many other species. And with their basic needs met, homed dogs may have the luxury of putting energy into such nonessential relationships. But whatever the backstory, dogs do have a special way about them when it comes to social interactions. Again and again on Fido's report card: *Plays well with others.*

At home in a busy species intersection

Carla King is the kind of woman who gets a sheep for Mother's Day and couldn't be happier. She has been a shepherdess throughout her adult life, always with herding dogs by her side. I contact King in hopes of seeing what herding dogs do for a living and learning about the kinds of intelligence that play into the choreography of their days. "Come early," she tells me, preferring to work the dogs while the grass is dewy and the air still cool.

On a sunny April morning, King greets me without fanfare at the edge of her Davidsonville, Maryland, farm. Her four pups are quiet but restless as we approach their kennel just up the hill from King's house. She's been smitten with border collies since watching them herd cattle on a neighbor's dairy farm as a kid, she tells me. "I have no patience for dogs that aren't as smart and sensitive as these."

She lets the aptly named Trim out for the first demonstration. The two-and-a-half-year-old female is black-backed and white-bellied, black-eyed and white-nosed, and has that feather duster tail that border collies wear so well. She gives me a cursory knee sniff before turning to her owner, all about her human and the work to come (I don't even get a full wag).

We move together toward the gate to the field, and Trim stays glued to King's leg, crouched and vibrating all over. Her posture and movements have an almost sheepish (if I may) quality—as if she's apologizing in advance for any errors she might make. A good herding dog wants so badly to do the job just right. I'm taken with how hyperaware the dog is of King, eyes on every move and gesture, as if an invisible line tethers them together.

Herding is modified hunting behavior with a gentler outcome. Herding dogs are as intensely connected to their charges as hunting dogs are to their intended quarry, and the series of engagement behaviors is the same: eye, stalk, chase. But a herder's job stops short of the pounce-and-kill that a hunter enjoys.

The border collie is literally born into this career, tooled with highly instinctive behavior genetically reinforced through selective breeding since the late 19th century. Spun from a long line of "shepherd's dogs" out of Great Britain and Ireland, modern working border collies typically have a stunning work ethic and do the job with heart, soul, and intelligence in many forms. They aren't the only ones, of course. Kelpies from Australia are lithe pups derived from Scottish smooth collies, while huntaways from New Zealand are a carefully curated mix—likely, of collies, Labs, rottweilers, setters, and harriers.

Both kelpies and huntaways are popular and extremely smart herders. Huntaways were first bred in the early 1900s to handle the particular climate and terrain of New Zealand's large farms, where shepherds lose sight of dogs and dogs lose sight of sheep. Whereas collies' silence would make it hard for shepherds to keep track of their movements, huntaways bark—deeply, loudly, and near constantly—to control the flock and keep in touch with the boss.

Just because "herding dog" is in an animal's formal description doesn't mean he's going to thrive at it, of course. "You expose a dog to sheep and see what it offers you," says King, of how to pick a winner. Some give you nothing. No matter how smart the breeding plan and how well conserved the genes, a so-called herder may or may not have the temperament or desire to round up the flock. That's because, as we've already seen many times throughout this book, dogs are individuals with diverse proclivities, not machines with a manufacturer's guarantee.

And getting the most "intelligent" dog for the job matters, just as an effective farm dog can be worth more than five times the amount invested in her over her lifetime, according to some estimates. A good herder can make himself known at an early age, proving to be smart at "reading" both shepherd and sheep, often from a great distance. Then comes the learning part, the dog precisely mastering the language he will share with his human—a combination of word, song, and dance.

Dance? Indeed. When King trains a young dog, she speaks to him with her body as much as her voice. In a sort of no-touch tango, she leads, stepping toward the pup to put on pressure, stepping back to release it, urging him this way and that with small changes in position. Her body leans, and the dog responds as if pressed by the block of air between them. Words and whistles—some standard among shepherds, some King's own variations—accompany the moves, and there is meaning not just in the sounds themselves but also in the shepherd's tone, how rapidly she repeats a sound, and the rise and fall of each note. Once a collie masters the dual languages of movement and sound, King can ask him to do just about anything, and he will keep trying until he gets her approval.

As impressive as the connection between dog and human is, let's not forget that another animal is in this mix that also receives the dog's attention. And despite their notorious barnyard stare, sheep are not dumb animals by any measure. They bring their own intentions, their own defenses, their own flight distance; and any flock can have rogue players. So the dog, already attending to his human, is also reading every jostle and shift of the flock as a whole, keeping an eye out for individuals trying to escape or just *thinking* of doing so, and adjusting to protect himself from any animal choosing to fight the power. A foot-stomping sheep is a potentially dangerous sheep, as the antipredator behavior often precedes a nasty headbutting.

The handler, too, needs to be smart about the livestock, also reading behaviors well enough to give the dog appropriate instructions and corrections. As a guide to livestock working dogs out of Oregon State University puts it, "Successful handlers strive to understand *at least half of what their dogs know*" (emphasis mine). "It's a very busy intersection," King says of the trio of species. It takes the dog's natural smarts—interspecies social intelligence and fluency in multiple languages—along with a powerful canine commitment, to keep traffic flowing in all directions.

In training, King tells me, there is no "punishment" for mistakes—just verbal discouragement, "asking them to think it through and try again." Herding dogs are always assessing and walking the razor's edge of other animals' flight distance and tolerance. If they step over that line, the sheep (or cattle or other livestock) will scatter and flee. Research has also shown that a herding dog in the wrong position can stress the sheep, sending their cortisol levels higher, which can lead to poorer meat quality and reduced wool production. The smartest dog, from the owner's perspective, is the one who aims to do the job either embedded within the flock or at a great distance from it. Both positions are apparently less upsetting to the sheep than is a dog running next to them.

Making decisions on the fly and correcting an unsuccessful move in an instant are key parts of a herder's repertoire. When King sends Trim out to show me what she's got, I can't help but think what she's got is telepathy. Some of King's commands are uttered so softly I wonder whether the pup hears a thing. There are big sounds as well, including whistles with a burst of power behind them. I ask King how many whistle variations there are. "Oh good lord," comes the reply. She demonstrates four or five. And then, "Awaaaaaayyy," she calls, and Trim takes off flying, head and tail tucked, her path a smooth, wide arc that seems to mimic the drawn-out word.

Once the dog is positioned behind the herd, King choreographs and conducts from afar using sound, again, to direct the shape and speed of Trim's movements. A stretched-out whistle tells Trim to go wide, which she does. Quick staccato whistles boost her pace; soft whistles slow her down. The latter are just wisps of sound, but the dog catches them on the breeze, somehow.

For a minute they are all out of sight at the back of the field. Then comes movement from behind a hill, the dog flanking the herd. Two dozen–plus sheep move en masse, with one very small speedy dog running the show. As they approach, King whistles and calls, and the dog drops to her belly and waits for instructions. Then she stalks slyly on a new angle, gathering stray sheep back into the flock.

Trim is utterly tuned in, knowing when to fly, when to tiptoe, and when to push the sheep homeward. The flock nearly tramples us as Trim finally delivers the tight bundle to her shepherdess. "That'll do, Trim," King says, and offers a quick scratch and an "Atta girl" to the panting pup, who, open-mouthed, leans against her legs, bubblegum pink tongue dangling. Mild praise is all King offers and apparently all Trim needs. No toy is tossed or treat flung. "For these dogs, the reward is doing the work," I'm told.

Being a good herding dog doesn't take away from an individual's other skills and smarts. The dog can be just as emotionally intelligent back at home as any other, for example, and many border collies are excellent solvers of less woolly problems. The Genius Dog Challenge project in Hungary, assessing pups' ability to learn the names of items, was heavily populated by this breed, for instance, before the researchers actively sought a more diverse mix. King tells me that the poorest workers often make the best pets, because those individuals aren't always searching for something to do beyond hanging around with a human.

King and her pups clearly have a solid relationship, but I notice she doesn't use baby talk or overly large gestures of affection toward them. She doesn't believe in the lovey-dovey stuff, she says: "It takes them away from the work, and that is what they are meant to be doing."

Which appears to be just fine with her dogs, because nothing seems more important to them than completing the job. Their cognitive focus is on interspecies communication—and getting the sheep into the barn. It's the way of herders who are herders through and through.

Is it language? Does it matter?

"Our dogs are brilliant at perceiving the slightest movement we make, and they assume that each tiny motion has meaning," Patricia McConnell points out in *The Other End of the Leash*. And though we're obsessing about the words we're using, she writes, "our dogs are watching us for the subtle visual signals they use to communicate to one another."

Part of being "dog fluent," as Marc Bekoff suggests we try to become, would be to take this into account. Our babbling is mere background to the signals our dogs really care about—our glances, gestures, body language, body aromas. They may search for something familiar in the sounds we make: The Hungarian study of gifted word learners suggests the adorable head tilt some do when spoken to is a sign of a smart pup working hard to find meaning. But we are communicating in other languages they understand all the time without realizing it, and what we "say" matters to them very much.

Still, despite clear evidence for intra- and interspecies communication happening throughout the natural world, scientists have long debated whether nonhuman animals can be said to have "true" language. Arguers get into the weeds about what defines "language" and whether one component or another of human language is represented in other species' communication systems. It's all very human-centric because, of course, language is one of those abilities that *seems* to set us apart from the mere beasts around us.

"We have to keep justifying our 'We're #1' T-shirts," Stanley Coren tells me. And so we keep coming up with abilities that we're sure must make us unique. For a while it was tool use. But apes use leaves as rain hats, otters use rocks to crack open shellfish, and dolphins have been seen wrapping their snouts in sea sponge for protection when foraging on sharp-shelled prey. Octopuses build shelters with found items, and both chimps and crows fashion twig tools that they use to probe tree holes for insect larvae snacks—to name just a few of my favorite smart animal moves.

Nope, tool use doesn't set us apart after all. "So humans had to move the goalpost," says Coren. "And we made language that new goal." But as we pay closer and closer attention to our animal cousins, that one is fading, too.

Evolution works by building on good ideas. Our wonderfully flexible language abilities confer a huge survival advantage on us, and it makes no sense to suppose that this extremely complex physiological and cognitive system sprung up out of nothing. Logic—and the evidence of every other highly evolved system—suggests that human language has its roots in something simpler. "If we look hard enough," writes Coren in *How to Speak Dog,* "we will find a continuous series of stages that lead to our own form of language ability. These early language abilities will not appear full-blown, but the precursors should first make their appearance in the communication patterns of other animals—such as dogs. The logical expectation is that the 'language' of dogs will be a lot simpler than the language of people, but that same logic suggests that there will be a language of dogs."

And Coren isn't alone in his thinking. More than a decade ago, Constantine Slobodchikoff (Con for short), an animal behaviorist at Northern Arizona University who has long studied animal communication, proposed a new theory of language he called the Discourse System, which, as he describes in his book *Chasing Doctor Doolittle,* "takes language off its ethereal cloud as some sort of angelic gift granted only to humans, and places it back where it belongs: as part and parcel of a functioning physiological and structural system, a system common to many species." Sure, human language is immensely intricate, and it has vast reach in how it shapes our thinking and allows us to not just express ourselves but also to enter the past or travel to the future, to narrate truth or spin fiction. It's special, but not entirely unique.

"The evidence of language in other species is overwhelming," Slobodchikoff tells me. It's especially obvious in cases where animals need to share intricate information to thrive in their niche. Though detractors argue that nonhuman communication is solely instinctive, Slobodchikoff explains there's plenty of evidence that many animals "intentionally communicate with each other, deliberately selecting the best signals in their repertoire to transmit a lot of information about the world around them and often using their signals to influence others."

Slobodchikoff's research on prairie dogs uncovered vocal signals within the colony that are mind-blowingly precise, seemingly grammatical, and clearly context-dependent. Not only will one animal warn the rest that a threat is approaching, he says, "but it will indicate that the threat is a *tall human walking quickly wearing a blue shirt and carrying a gun*. It can be that specific." And if something novel needs mentioning, he says, "they have a store of descriptive labels in their brains" that they will put together in a new way to get their point across.

Chipmunks are similarly precise in their chatter, researchers have shown, as the pitch of their calls lets family members know whether a predator is coming by land or by sky. Plenty of other species are known to converse in awesome detail, from honeybees giving their sisters excellent directions to a food source by waggle dancing the flight path, to elephants sending low-frequency rumbles miles through the earth when discussing plans to meet up.

Coren says that in barks and growls and whines and huffs, dogs have syntax and grammar and the ability to decode sequences. Tone and volume, too, have meaning. For instance, a rising bark with a "breath growl" is an invitation to play, he says. Switch them around and you've got a dog saying something like, "back off, you're bugging me." As an aside, wolves produce just a single type of bark—an agonistic one—compared with dogs' varied and context-specific woofs that even we humans can recognize as distinct.

That dogs find meaning based on the order of utterances certainly suggests a simple form of syntax. Much of dog language is subtle, and no raised hair, hard stare, or tucked tail goes unnoticed. As we saw in the last chapter, they "talk" with everything they've got—every posture, huff, and scent tells a story. Whole body communication, for dogs, is intelligent communication. A pressed-back ear, a curled lip, a stream of urine. Whale eyes, a raised paw, a stiff tail. Howl, bark, whimper, growl. There's meaning in all of it, and when put together, the possibilities seem endless.

To the human uneducated in Doggish, of course, the combinations can seem confounding, even contradictory. But another dog will know what's what. That includes chatter at frequencies we can't hear; researchers of these pup whispers hypothesize that "ultra-high fundamental frequencies function to allow private, 'tête-à-tête' communication between members of social groups."

Parlez-vous Doggish? *Non?*

During a family trip to France years ago, I proudly wielded my high school French at every opportunity. My dad and brother would look to me when it came time to ask for a price, find a bathroom, or order lunch. One afternoon in a café I "conversed" with our waiter at some length. After he walked away scribbling on his notepad, my father asked, "Did you order fries?" And I replied, "I might have."

The outcome of miscommunication in that case was small potatoes. (Literally. The waiter brought something resembling hash, with not a single *pomme frite* on the plate.) But uncertainty in using another's language can have serious outcomes when a person and a dog are interacting—as I learned recently when a neighbor treated my dog Geddy's protective stance and mistrustful bark as an invitation to play, and almost ended up with a bite on the hand.

I mentioned this story at a workshop led by trainer and author Pat Miller, who agreed that it's an all-too-common problem. When she invites a client to let their "reactive" dog off leash, she says, "often the client is nervous, worried *I'm* going to get bitten. But I know a cautious dog approaching to sniff is *not* inviting me to reach out and pet him, contrary to what many people think. I can see he's not being affiliative. His eyes are hard, his body is tense. But people miss these cues all the time."

In part, these misfires occur because our two species are simply very different beasts. That may seem obvious, but stop for a minute and think how unalike primates and canids are in how they navigate the world, cope with stress, and communicate. Being a full-time primate, I've interacted with many dogs in ways that gave them pause—reaching a hand over a wary dog's head to pet it, thinking a stroke will ease its fears, for example. And what about the hug? Primates hug. Dogs aren't naturally huggers, and many of those who hold still while we embrace them may be simply tolerating us to make us happy (that interspecies social intelligence at work). Remember being told to let great-aunt Marge with the mustache kiss your cheek when you were seven years old? I suspect for some dogs, we are great-aunt Marge.

Of course, tolerance is relative, dogs are individuals, and each dog has its own limits. "Really, it's amazing our dogs don't eat our children," Coren likes to say. (He said it to me, and then I heard him say it in a TED Talk). "Kids do all the wrong things—make eye contact, offer a toothy smile, run at the dog with arms out and fingers like teeth in their faces. It's all threatening behavior." Thank goodness, the vast majority of dogs are smart enough to learn the difference between an aggressive animal and a naive, excited small human.

The blunders of youth aside, it's a great failure on our part as (adult) humans that so few of us try to learn the language of dogs. Bekoff is adamant on this point: "Dogs are constantly telling us what they want and how they feel," he says. "And while we ask our dogs to learn our vocabulary and understand our meaning, few people bother to become Dog fluent." Others call it "speaking dog" or "speaking Doggish." Whatever name you give it, it's a worthwhile aim if we are to become as socially intelligent as our canine friends.

For my part, I've been working really hard at this new language—harder than I ever did in French class. As I've spent more and more time watching and interacting closely with dogs, I've been impressed at how nuanced and complex their conversations are as they bounce between vocalizations and the sign language of postures and facial expressions. The language of dogs serves its users perfectly well in conveying essential information, mostly to each other. But also to us if we're smart enough to catch on.

Dogs converse with intention about the same things we do: their wants and needs, their social relationships, and their emotional states. But how they do it is all their own; even with real effort, it's not always easy to follow along. For example, a squinty look from a dog could mean "I'm not a threat," or it could mean "I'm definitely a threat." Or (depending on the degree of tension in the facial muscles) a squint could be a sign of pain. Other dogs know the difference, but for us it's not so obvious.

"We all know the signs of imminent danger between two dogs, right?" McConnell observes in a blog post. "Immobile stiff bodies, direct eye contact, round eyes. Except when dogs are playing and then the exact same postures and expressions are nothing but pauses between frolics."

Failed translations no doubt occur in dogdom, but its inhabitants know how to autocorrect. We, on the other hand, may struggle mightily to redirect in a timely fashion. When we misinterpret or ignore what dogs are saying in Doggish, our failure can put both people and dogs at risk.

One frightening for instance came from a Denver news show that was celebrating the rescue of an Argentinian mastiff from an icy lake with a live on-air segment. In the studio, sandwiched tightly between the owner, the firefighter who saved the dog, and the news anchor, the dog endured the human chatter and the anchor's vigorous head petting for a time before "suddenly" lunging and biting the newswoman in the face.

I put quotes around "suddenly" because, according to dog aggression expert Jim Crosby, the smart student of dog behavior who examines the full segment closely, as he did, will conclude that the bite was not at all surprising. It seemed to happen in an instant, but "in the minutes and seconds before the bite, you can see the small but clear messages that dog is sending," Crosby says. The animal is stiff all over and staring ahead, not engaging in a friendly way, certainly not soliciting attention.

"He's saying, I'm uncomfortable, I don't know this place or these strange people, I don't like these hot bright lights and I had a really bad day yesterday," Crosby observes. So when the chatty anchor leans fully into his space, "his head goes back, his eyes tighten, his teeth show, and then he snaps. It was a controlled snap—he could have taken her face off. But it was avoidable. The humans just weren't paying attention."

Such misreads on our part have real consequences for dogs. Many are put down for lesser transgressions than the TV studio snap. Rehabbing and rehoming dogs that have bitten people is costly. With so many pups who haven't harmed anyone needing attention and homes, biters often lose—even if the bite was, for a dog, the obvious next step in a failed interspecies communication.

Crosby trains police officers to read canine body language so they can walk safely into situations where a dog is present. He wrote the handbook on it, in fact, in hopes of reducing situations in which pet dogs are shot unnecessarily. "If officers learn what a dog is 'saying' and how not to present themselves as a threat," he tells me, "most of the time the dog will give them the benefit of the doubt."

That body language, he continues, "is sometimes very fast and subtle. It can be a body posture or where they're looking—even a tiny eye move to the side after eye contact has a tiny message." Of course, it can also be decidedly unsubtle: a throaty growl, a meaty bark, something that even a clueless human can't miss. Though it seemed the news anchor received no audible warning, "the dog was transmitting concrete information about his mental state, asking her to back up," Crosby says. "It's high-level communication—well beyond barking for a bone." The dog was acting socially intelligent, in Doggish. The people were oblivious in any language.

Here's where we need to step back and observe our own behavior through canine eyes. That mastiff had no exit from an uncomfortable situation—he was literally surrounded—and though the woman petting and gazing into his eyes meant to be friendly, let's put ourselves in the dog's place. Though reaching out to touch is a deeply rooted social behavior for us primates, dogs just don't do things that way. In fact, a "paw over" is a precursor to "standing over" in canine ethology, notes McConnell, usually done in the context of establishing or reinforcing a social hierarchy. So the woman's hand on the dog was one of many mistakes she made.

If there's a big takeaway here, it's that understanding a dog's language requires that we use our own intelligence *and* our full attention. We need to look not at a single signal, but at the context and the combinations of signals that dogs so cleverly employ. As Crosby writes in his 2023 doctoral dissertation, "… a dog does what makes sense to it. In the dog's perspective, its behavior is appropriate for the situation. The critical issue is that, to understand the *dog's view* of a situation" (emphasis his).

Meeting Odin

I was deep into my research for this book when I met a dog named Odin, a mountain cur with some 70 pounds of muscle wrapped in a dark brindle coat. He'd been labeled "unadoptable" by the shelter where his original owners left him; when my friends Margaret and Trevor took him in as a foster, he was edgy and growly, not to mention terrified.

The story goes that his former family knew little about the breed; they'd expected Odin to be an undemanding house dog content in a small space with nothing much to do. But mountain curs are bred to work. They are hunters deep in their genes—masters at treeing small animals or baying big ones—and great farm dogs. Lazing around unemployed is not in their DNA. Odin's stay at the shelter didn't help. Confined to a kennel, bombarded by the sounds and smells of other stressed animals, he was utterly unsure of himself. No wonder he was moody.

What he really needed was a job, Odin's foster turned owner told me. Though the dog was intimidating at first and didn't let anyone touch him, Margaret and Trevor were determined to bring him around. They gave him a loving home and a half-acre property to patrol. Once the young dog realized he had open space, kind owners, and a purpose, his transformation began. But although he's a much changed animal, Odin will never be one to do a happy dance when an unfamiliar person approaches his gate. And with his cold stare, anvil-like head, and knife-sharp bark punctuating long growls, he might make you rethink your plan to drop by altogether.

But approaching the gate to Odin's yard was a great opportunity to apply some of the lessons I'd been learning about how dogs communicate. Could I quickly but carefully convince this wary animal to tolerate me? Even *like* me? The trick was, of course, to read his signals and speak his language while fighting some of my human urges (it's too soon to snuggle!). Short of sniffing his butt, I needed to *be the dog*.

Here's what I did—and, more important, *didn't* do. I didn't power through the gate, though Odin's owner had said to "just come on in." Odin was right there, stiff in body posture and tail position, growling just a tad, which I read to mean "nope." I obliged. Instead, I *did* turn partway to the side and crouch down to his level, to come on less strongly. I avoided looking back into his eyes as he stared me down—which I took as another nope. I used his name and "good boy" in a pleasantly childlike voice—nothing loud or squeaky or shrill that might increase his general excitement. I didn't stick out a hand, tempting as that is for us primates, instead letting him decide whether to come close enough to sniff me. He did.

And very quickly the growling eased, his posture softened, and he was stretching his neck forward, positioned to investigate. My scent passing muster, he moved his whole body closer and pressed his nose into my leg. Only then did I check his eyes—no longer daggers—and made a slow move to reciprocate contact, choosing to stroke his side instead of reaching to pet his head in a gesture that can feel threatening. Also, who wants their head patted, really? Pat yourself on the head now and see how it feels. Go ahead, do it. Right? Nothing special. But a nice little body rub? Much more pleasant.

Here's what else I *did* do: I continued to keep my head turned slightly away—knowing I must establish trust before holding his gaze (and recalling how, even after all these years, my own wary dog Geddy sometimes avoids a direct look). I even faked a yawn, remembering that dogs may yawn to ease a tense situation with another dog.

Soon, Odin put his full weight against me, despite the bars of the gate between us, and appeared to ask for a deeper massage. I happily complied.

By then I felt confident that our eyes could meet without incident. I slowly opened the gate and again fought the urge to squat down and embrace that big warm head. In the past, I hadn't even considered that it's not at all natural for dogs to hug or be hugged. I stayed strong and held back, letting him decide how much touching was OK. *Be the dog.*

Later, when Odin was sprawled on the couch with me, head in my lap, one leg up so I could scratch his belly, I walked through our introductory interaction in my mind. Odin got an A for communicating how he felt throughout. He did his dog thing, no more or less. All the information was there—in his posture, his eyes, the sounds he made. It was up to me to pay attention and translate. I allowed myself a B+ for my part—because by the end he was nuzzling my ear and then licking my hand, and as I came through the gate still uttering soothing words, he happily trotted beside me, as if welcoming me home.

CHAPTER THIRTEEN

DOG SMARTEST?

We humans measure the "smartest dog in the world" as the one who understands the biggest human vocabulary—never mind the dog-relevant forms of intelligence behind their many abilities. We are so predictable, aren't we?

In 2011, Chaser, a black-and-white border collie, became a viral sensation, proclaimed "smartest" of her kind by media outlets from the BBC and *Paris Match* to the *New York Times* and the *Today* show. With intensive training starting in puppyhood, the dog learned unique proper names for 1,022 different objects, including 800 stuffed animals, 116 balls, 26 Frisbees, and more than a hundred miscellaneous rubber and plastic whatnots—the largest (human) vocabulary ever documented in a nonhuman animal. She also learned that each individual object was part of a *category* of things: toy, ball, Frisbee. When told to "get the X," whether a specific item or a type of object, she could retrieve the right thing with incredible accuracy. Ask me to get my keys and I'll go look for my glasses and find neither. Just sayin'.

Chaser's education was in part inspired by the achievements of Rico, a border collie from Germany whose language learning was documented by scientists at the prestigious Max Planck Institute after his owners taught him the names of more than 200 toys. Chaser's owner, John Pilley, a retired psychology professor from South Carolina's Wofford College, worked with his enthusiastic dog for up to five hours a day. Demonstrating the signature drive of her breed, Chaser quickly came to comprehend the speech of a language not her own—a testament to several types of intelligence at least. Ultimately, she could understand complex combinations of words, including sentences consisting of nouns, prepositions, verbs, and direct objects. She learned not simply to locate a particular named object, but also to manipulate it by rolling it around by "nose" or "paw," or carrying it in her mouth, as Pilley directed, and moving it to sit next to another specified object. Chaser could perform such tasks even when unfamiliar speakers gave her directions.

Both Rico and Chaser were also able to use the logical process of elimination to find items they'd never seen or heard mentioned before. Maybe their thinking went something like, That's Busy Bee, that's Snake, the third one must be the new thing, the "Piggy" they're asking for.

For a 2018 PBS television show on animal intelligence, Chaser demonstrated her prowess to science communicator Neil deGrasse Tyson by using that thought process to retrieve a single novel object with a novel name (Darwin!) from among not just two or three known items, but from seven different toys the *Nova* host randomly selected. Even the Harvard astrophysicist was impressed. Duke University cognitive evolution researcher Brian Hare calls Chaser the "most scientifically important dog in over a century."

Pilley died in 2018, but not before he published two peer-reviewed research papers on Chaser's language skills that brought his superlative pup international acclaim. The reports built on earlier work with Rico to knock deep cracks in the long-standing conceptual wall scientists had built between human and nonhuman language learning abilities. The exploits of Pilley and Chaser also influenced the development of new canine cognition investigations like the Genius Dog Challenge.

And working dogs like border collies aren't the only pups with ears tuned to people talk. Researchers at the University of Memphis tested a "lapdog"—a 12-year-old Yorkshire terrier named Bailey—and confirmed that he could retrieve any of 117 named toys whether the command came from his owner or from people with differing accents and no prior involvement in his training.

A beloved star in her own family and beyond, Chaser died a year after her owner. Her renown illustrates the slow process of changing stubbornly held notions of human exceptionalism, and the overwhelming emphasis we continue to place on human language and the capacity of other animals to understand it. The world's smartest dog wasn't celebrated for any remarkable *dog* things she did: Understanding human speech made her famous.

"Understanding" may be part of Chaser's appeal: She learned to comprehend hundreds of words spoken *to* her, but she never talked back. "I truly believe, deeply, that one reason for our profound love for dogs is that they *don't* talk," Patricia McConnell says. "I really mean that. Look at people trying to increase their spiritual understanding through meditation, through silence. There's incredible power in not using language, and using it can take something away from an interaction. The fact that dogs can't talk back to us is one of the many reasons we love them so much." They don't judge, criticize, or offer unsolicited advice. (Knowing dogs, they probably wouldn't anyway.)

But asking whether dogs are intelligent enough to *speak* human languages is irrelevant: They simply don't have the vocal anatomy required to produce the sounds needed for our speech. With the exception of birds able to mimic human voices, spoken language is essentially a human exclusive; dog anatomy is built for other things. A dog's airway, for example, is adapted to let him smell and breathe while running, which affects the position of the epiglottis, a key apparatus in our speech. A dog's long, toothy muzzle lets it do things we evolved to do with our hands, but its structure limits a dog's flexibility in the lips and face. And so on.

So there it is: We are shaped to be chatty; dogs are not. Still, they get their points across quite well. "It is our all-too-human bias to think that the spoken language is the only thing that is important," Stanley Coren wrote. Because they can't form our sorts of words—instead relying on a perfectly functional language of their own—we've had to get creative in our quest to convince them to *parlez* our way.

Use your words

"Mad," says Bunny. "All done." Bunny looks indignant, as much as a sheepadoodle can. She stands staring hard at Alexis Devine, her owner, as we two humans converse via Zoom. All about Bunny. But Bunny isn't having it. She wants Devine's full attention and doesn't like being an audience to this mindless chatter between *her* person and a strange face on a screen. "Mad," she says again.

"Bunny mad?" Devine asks. "Mom talk other friend now. Mom done soon." Bunny wanders off, and she doesn't have much else to say while Devine and I talk, though periodically the dog comes back into view and we pause, hoping for her input. Despite her shyness that day, Bunny is quite verbal much of the time.

"Verbal," I should say, with quotes around it. Of course, the words don't come from her mouth but from one of the hundred or so button-activated recordings Devine has laid out on large boards on the floor. Using a paw to make her selections, Bunny has the option to talk, human style.

Such keyboards are meant to give dogs access to human language, letting them communicate with us our way. But Devine, I am pleased to hear, has a motive that's a bit less self-centered. "My goal really is to have the best communication and the best relationship possible with her," she tells me as Bunny and the family's younger dog, Otter, romp in front of the camera. "I was really excited to make that happen, doing everything it took," including giving the dog a variety of tools to work with.

Believing in her dog's potential to excel at something new, Devine started by recording an "outside" button, which she'd push every time she let Bunny out, to model the behavior. She worked on paw targeting, too, so the dog could get the feel for the physical action. Within a couple of weeks, Bunny was pressing the button herself when she wanted to go out. So Devine recorded additional common words. Bunny quickly learned them. And the experiment grew from there.

Bunny is one of a long line of pups who are taking (or talking?) after Stella, a chocolate brown Catahoula leopard dog–heeler mix whose owner popularized teaching a pet dog to "speak" with a press of the paw. Stella's owner, Christina Hunger, is a speech pathologist who works with young kids experiencing delayed language development. Taught to presume competence with children, she decided to do the same with her dog. Using a tool of her trade known as augmentative and alternative communication (AAC)—a board of buttons that play recorded words— she set out to give Stella the means to express her wants and needs aloud, in English.

As Hunger writes in her book *How Stella Learned to Talk,* dogs vocalize to get attention and gesture to request action from someone else, combining the two much as a toddler will do. Hunger writes that at two months, Stella was exhibiting more than half of the prelinguistic skills that a nine-month-old baby displays before using recognizable words. She wondered, How else might dogs and babies overlap in the steps toward speech?

Stella was eager, so Hunger adapted the AAC for dogs and recorded a handful of words that seemed most likely to be meaningful to her—"outside," "water," "play"—leaning again on her knowledge that children will use their words more readily if those words are directly relevant to them. As Stella began to catch on and paw the right button at the right time, Hunger encouraged and reinforced the behavior. Over and over and over. And as Stella began "talking" with confidence, Hunger added more complex ideas for the dog to incorporate into her growing lexicon.

Eventually Stella began pairing words with gestures or other words on her own to make her meaning clearer, hitting certain buttons repeatedly for emphasis, and, remarkably, communicating ideas with two-word combinations of her own choosing, a language skill that comes to toddlers at around 18 months of age. Three-word combos followed.

Soon, Stella was expressing herself some 30 times a day, and even got a little insistent: If she asked for "beach" and her owners tried to steer her toward the park instead, she would lie down on the sidewalk and refuse to budge. Deep into the project, "Stella … progressed to a level far beyond what I ever thought possible," Hunger wrote of conversing with her one-year-old pup. She saw it as a revolution happening right there in front of her: Her dog was speaking her language.

Stella won fame, but her owner wasn't the first to teach a pup to talk this way. In 2008, animal behaviorist Alexandre Rossi, of São Paulo, Brazil, reported that he'd trained a rescue mutt named Sofia to ask for food, walks, and petting by choosing lexigrams—nonrepresentational symbols for words often used in communication research with nonhuman primates—on a keyboard and pressing the keys to "speak" words recorded (in Portuguese, naturally). During that experiment, according to Rossi's report, "The dog only utilized the keyboard in the experimenter's presence and gazed to him more frequently after key pressing than before, an indication that lexigram use did have communicative content."

Rossi went on to write that the results suggest dogs may be able to learn a system of signs "that is functionally analogous to spontaneous soliciting behaviors," viewing the keyboard as a potentially fruitful way to study dog communication and cognition. He also trained another rescue dog named Estopinha to answer yes and no questions with buttons, and to communicate on Skype. (Imagine being able to hop on Skype with your dog and ask her to turn on the Crock-Pot!)

But Stella is the dog that people in the English-speaking world know best. Her social media following exploded with Hunger's book publication in 2021, and she's helped spark a community science movement that shows just how smart dogs can be at the human-language game.

And now, back to Bunny. She can be a serious dog, not afraid to leave long pauses between questions and answers. During our video call, she appears thoughtful rather than playful in her use of her keyboard; she certainly doesn't use her words willy-nilly. Devine says her younger dog, Otter, hasn't taken to talking thus far, though he has his own beginner board; after all, he is still a puppy and more interested in tossing the board than speaking his mind with the buttons. But his owner has seen signs that he might be learning that the buttons have value from observing Bunny, and she won't be surprised if he starts using them, too. Devine tries to reinforce every communication—not always by giving Bunny what she's asking for, but at least responding to let her know she's been heard, to encourage her to keep playing the game.

For a time, Devine wondered at her own motivation: Is it about enriching the dog's life or her own? "Early on I started to feel a little *ick* about it—it was so ego-driven to expect a nonhuman animal to communicate in *our* language," Devine says. But Bunny participates willingly—for a "thinking" dog, it's a form of play that lets her intelligence shine through—and Devine isn't asking her to replace dog speak with human words. "In fact, I started trying to understand and respect her intrinsic communication and to learn from her as she's learning from me," she says. "So it felt like this mutually reinforcing growth." She adds, "The steepest learning curve has been mine."

It seems undeniable that Bunny *gets* what she's saying in instances, and the meaning seems clear enough to Devine. If a cat meows outside and she presses "cat, sound," that seems legit, for example. Still, "There are also times when it seems the interaction has solid, communicative intent but I can't find the meaning in it, and I don't want to try too hard," Devine says. The dog may pick a combo of words that are pretty nebulous, looking to Devine "as if [she's] asking, did I say something just then? That exploration, trial and error, seems to be part of her learning process." In those cases, "I walk a fine line, trying to keep boundaries around what truly feels like a communicative event. I fight the bias every day."

It *is* fun to make guesses as to Bunny's inner thoughts. Does she know herself? When she selects "Bunny, human" but "Otter, dog," is she making a point about her status versus Otter's in the household? But Devine stresses that she's "way underqualified" to be assessing what Bunny does or doesn't understand. She's enjoyed simply giving Bunny the opportunity to use her brain in a new way. "Anyway, if you're really paying attention to your dog," Devine says, "you're going to learn what they're saying without the buttons."

If there's anyone who *is* qualified to assess a button-pushing dog's intentions, it might be Federico Rossano, director of the Comparative Cognition Lab at UC San Diego (UCSD). In June 2020, Rossano designed a study to measure scientifically what's going on with Bunny and the other chatty dogs around the world. The general public lined up to enter their dogs into the experiment. Bunny, as the pilot dog and star, was on camera 24/7 for many months, her every button-push available to be analyzed by the UCSD team.

Rossano and his colleagues' approach to understanding the talking dog phenomenon "is less focused on the cognition of the average member of a species than on the potential demonstrated by the existence of the exceptional," according to the team's *TheyCanTalk.org* website. "As such, we are keenly interested in individual differences, idiosyncratic behaviors, and the types of extraordinary skills and communication that a particular human and dog pairing is able to bring about."

In short order, Rossano had more than 10,000 dogs from 47 countries signed up as candidates to participate in the three-phase study. Just a small subset would ultimately "make the cut" to be on camera, but the wave of interest was clearly huge. The enormous global response allowed his team to collect extensive lists of observations, thousands of hours of video, and giant stacks of surveys about the most verbal of the bunch.

It's clear that dogs can learn to use the buttons and to make associations between the recorded sounds and outcomes, Rossano says. But he wants to dive deeper into the question of syntax, and whether the animals truly understand and "talk" about, say, absent entities—a form of expression called displacement. Understanding the latter, Rossano explains, "would answer the question, are dogs stuck in time or can they imagine the future and remember the past?"

It's been difficult to sort out the logistics of getting consistency from human contributors with different board setups and time commitments and ways of training. Plus, there's a real need to scale up operations—and although they've attempted to ground-truth some of the data-collection methods in different households, Rossano has a small team and a limited budget to work with. In other words, it's too soon to know if the talking-dog experiment is going to reveal deep secrets about dog intelligence.

Still, Rossano points to some intriguing tidbits, such as how often the dogs are talking about their people and labeling emotions ("mom, sad"), and even bringing up other animal friends. One dog used the buttons to tell his owner to let the family's *other* dog inside. "It reminds us they have this social mind that does more than tell a cup from a ball," Rossano says. Like most of us, "They are more interested in others than in objects."

There are also reports of dogs describing what they see instead of what they want, "a bit like telling your spouse about your day." It's a phase children go through during speech development, called narrating, Rossano says. He's also impressed with how often the dogs take turns "talking" with their humans, having a real back-and-forth. Rossano is also a fan of clever combinations—as when Bunny used "mad, ouch," followed by "stranger, paw" when she had a thorn in her foot—what Rossano calls a remarkably clear communication of what was, for Bunny, a novel idea.

But in many cases, the combined words don't seem to make sense. That's not surprising, but Rossano doesn't think the odd combos are completely random. Echoing Devine's experience, he says, "Sometimes the dogs play around, but we see them looking at the person—pushing, looking, pushing—not just pawing at the board without purpose. There seems to be real intent."

Rossano also mentions that study participants who have employed the soundboards report quieter households. According to their owners, "Dogs using the word boards do less barking," he says. "Maybe because having an additional way to 'speak,' they are getting their needs met more easily and are less frustrated." Perhaps some iteration of this work will help us to understand what meaning dogs actually ascribe to the sound of a word. Rossano would like to know if, when dogs push "outside," do they think of the place? Of walking out the door? What mental construct goes with that sound?

He'd also like to use the technique to find out just how far language acquisition in dogs might go—hoping that, for instance, it could eventually be a tool for a dog in pain to use to tell her owner where it hurts. And because we seem to care more about animals we think of as "intelligent"—more people worry about how we treat circus elephants than how we treat lizards, for example—"exposing the long reach of dogs' cognitive abilities is a good reason to re-examine their welfare," he says. I'll concur with a *woof*.

To be fair, there's plenty of skepticism about what the animals pawing these buttons really understand. I myself have had many moments watching videos of the popular dogs when I thought, Nope. When I ask Alexandra Horowitz what she thinks about the word-button games, she remarks, "We have a long history of trying to teach nonhumans to speak our language. We know dogs can't do it, but their communications are nonetheless quite rich. While I love that people are interested, why not spend more time looking at what dogs *can* do?"

Still, *this* dog lover finds the concept of giving dogs the keys to human language an entertaining experiment. It certainly illustrates the great lengths we will go to in order to find out what our pets think and how they feel. Patricia McConnell chalks it up to deep-down love, and despite her knowing full well that dogs don't communicate as we do, she is excited by the potential of this tool. Speaking for many of us dog owners, she says, "There's nothing I'd like more than to get inside a dog's head to find out what's really going on there." And I can't deny that it would get my oxytocin flowing if one of my dogs pressed "love you" while giving me puppy dog eyes.

Isn't the possibility of connection what it's all about for us humans? We want our pets to love us back. We look into our dogs' eyes and convince ourselves they feel the same way we do, hoping we're right. We emote all over them and they tolerate us, thank goodness, as we kiss their heads and hug too hard and stick our noses into their yeasty paw pads. And they put up with us missing their dog signals over and over again.

We can certainly do better on that last front, where becoming dog fluent comes into play. What does that mean? It means opening our minds. It means stepping down from our *Homo sapiens* pedestal and appreciating "language" in different forms, just as we're finding many different kinds of intelligence behind a dog's thinking and behavior. Without the dedicated training it takes to create a Chaser or Stella or Bunny, nonhuman animals must continue to rely on their own evolved modes of communication—the ones that have worked for them for millennia. As it should be.

Odin makes himself clear

I am back at Odin's house for a visit and happy to find that our relationship remains intact despite some months apart. His first reaction to my arrival is a protective bark and tense stance. But as I kneel and let him approach, I'm guessing he recognizes my face and voice and fully catches my scent; then everything changes. It takes about eight seconds. A hand through the gate isn't quite enough: He needs more scent and less breeze, I suspect. Breeze takes scent and runs with it, as we've learned.

But once Odin gets a really good whiff of me, his demeanor flips like a switch, his tail beating wildly left and right, and he quickly leans into me for scratches. We have a little playtime, with me throwing the stick, him retrieving the stick, me throwing it again—you know the game—and then I sit in the driveway so our heads are on the same plane and he can do a proper lap sit. We enjoy some calm caresses and a kiss on the head (me, his) before I send him off to lie in the sun and go inside to write about our interaction. "Odin," I say to him before I leave, "I like you very much." And his ear twitches and he gives me that goofy doggy grin before stretching all the way out, belly against the warm concrete, as content dogs will do.

Have I mentioned that Odin is a very intelligent pup, in all the ways I've been writing about? He's got a great nose, and he communicates like a boss. Later, I'll share a story of his emotional intelligence that's truly remarkable. Plus, he quickly learned all the standard pet-dog behaviors, his owners told me—and even a few special ones. To wit: While I was writing the preceding paragraph, the doorbell rang. It was Odin. Yes, after being shown the trick just once or twice, the dog learned to ring the bell with his nose when he wanted to come inside. *Genius.*

CHAPTER FOURTEEN

THE WISDOM
OF THE HEART

I *sense that you feel sad. I know just what that's like, as I, too, have been*
sad. How can I help?

The concept of emotional intelligence comes from human psychology;
it's about being aware of your own feelings, as well as those of others. It's
more than just being agreeable. Highly emotionally intelligent people are
thought to be more empathetic, as their sensitivity to another person's
emotional signals, as well as their ability to identify and manage those
feelings in themselves, gives them a deep understanding of another
human's experience. When emotional intelligence is at work, an act of
kindness is likely on its way.

Dogs, it seems, also respond to our feelings and the needs they signal.
Understanding those needs takes a special kind of interspecies social
intelligence that's been reinforced. Most people who have dogs and love
dogs would never question the animals' emotional capabilities. And as
dogs are masters at noticing the details, the idea that they read us and
"get" what's going on inside, then behave as if they care about it, makes

a lot of sense. "It's one thing that makes dogs so exceptional, one of the secrets to their success," Clive Wynne notes. "They've come to understand the emotions of humans."

The veteran, the darkness, and the dog

Some dogs' emotional sensitivity and dedication save lives. That's the experience of U.S. Marine Corps combat veteran Kenny Bass. He used to have horrible nightmares. A lot of them. The kind that wake you drenched in sweat with a scream scouring your throat. That's not uncommon for military personnel who have served in danger zones, but Bass was especially hard-hit. Injured by an improvised explosive device (IED) in 2003 while on patrol in Iraq, he was left with brain damage that affects his memory and hearing, plus PTSD, among other problems.

The aftermath of Bass's service was poised to destroy his life. And it came frighteningly close. At his lowest point, he was drinking heavily, taking 30 pills a day, and his marriage was falling apart. He couldn't be the dad he wanted to be to his kids. "I never felt more broken, more crazy, more of a burden," he tells me. "I would sit in my garage with a pistol in my hand and think the lowest thoughts. I was suicidal for years."

Not anymore. Bass finally decided to go off the medications, quit drinking, and find a way forward. A counselor he was working with suggested a service dog. That led him to Atlas. Atlas is a German shepherd from an organization called Instinctive Guardians, one of the owners/trainers of which was also a Marine. The dog was initially trained to wake Bass from nightmares, to recognize and interrupt anxiety cues like fidgeting, rapid foot tapping, sweating, and increased breathing rate, and to "block" and "post" in public situations—ways of giving Bass personal space when needed.

Getting the dog in the first place wasn't easy, as service dogs cost many thousands of dollars. Bass, given a Veterans Affairs (VA) prescription for a dog but no funds to buy one, had to raise the money on his own. His struggle to secure Atlas led him to found the Battle Buddy Foundation

(BBF), in collaboration with fellow Marine combat veteran Joshua Rivers. The organization helps veterans get services—especially the tough-to-afford dogs, plus dog training—they need to reenter and to thrive in civilian life. A recent VA study of Vietnam War veterans found that 10 to 30 percent of them suffered from PTSD. Studies have also found that servicemen and -women deployed to combat zones are three times more likely to develop PTSD than other military personnel. BBF aims to help relieve many of the logistical and financial burdens that come with obtaining the help of a service dog, giving former soldiers their lives back after physical, mental, and emotional injuries.

Bass tells me he has fewer nightmares these days, and those he has are much milder than before Atlas began sleeping in a dog bed on the floor next to him. That's because the dog knows Bass's specific signs of sleep distress, which include sweating, rolling around "fighting," and cussing. After just a few days together, Atlas was doing his job—jumping up on the bed at the first signs of trouble and lying across Bass's chest or licking his face. Previously, a bad night would mean fitful sleep, if any, and "a messed-up next couple of days." But by intervening and calming his owner, Atlas helps Bass sleep a full night and feel well in the days that follow. "Just that was huge for me," he says. "That in and of itself has given me my life back."

And Atlas isn't just an interrupter. "He's my sentry. He'll post himself next to me and nudge me with his nose if someone is coming from behind," Bass says. "He's always on alert, reading my mood and providing a barrier between me and others if he senses I need it. He's given me the superpower to go do simple things among other people that I'd lost the ability to do."

The dog knows even better than Bass when panic is imminent. "He'll be sitting under the table and I'm talking to someone, maybe getting more animated, and suddenly I'll feel his chin in my lap. He's not begging for scratches, just asking me to be more self-aware. He reads my breathing, if I'm sweating, if I'm getting agitated, maybe smells something from me, before I notice a thing." Bass adds that sometimes, he sits back and marvels "at how keyed in he is to me. He catches all kinds of things we humans completely miss."

But the hundred-plus-pound service dog is also just "a teddy bear, a big baby," Bass says. "He was there for my daughter's birth and has been her best friend her whole life. We love him to death." What amazes his owner most is Atlas's intelligence when it comes to his "vest on, vest off" behavior: He knows when it's time to work and his demeanor changes for it. When it's not work time, "He's just a dog being a dog."

The power of presence

Time spent just visiting with dogs has been shown to have physical effects, along with psychological ones. In a controlled clinical study in a Canadian hospital, published in March 2022, researchers tested the effects of a short visit with a therapy dog on patients in pain. Such interactions in clinical and other stressful settings are known to reduce anxiety, depression, and loneliness. But in this study, patients in the ER reported significantly lower levels of *physical* pain after just 10 minutes visiting with a dog. The canine interaction also boosted patients' optimism, which in itself may increase a person's pain tolerance and certainly improves the overall hospital experience. Hospital staff, too, had a mood boost from the dog's presence.

"A good therapy dog is sweet and calm and gentle," Chuck Mitchell tells me over a winter breakfast in a Tallahassee café. "A *great* therapy dog is the dog that walks into a room full of people and finds the one who needs her most."

Therapy dogs are different from service dogs. Often the animals who end up doing therapy work are those who didn't quite make it through service training. They aren't defective, though—far from it. In fact, those selected to bring comfort to people are perhaps the most emotionally intelligent creatures in the working dog world. "You can't teach empathy to a dog," Mitchell says. "Some of them just have it."

Mitchell is co-founder of the Tallahassee Memorial Animal Therapy Program and president of Florida Courthouse Therapy Dogs. He did his first therapy work with a golden retriever named Rikki, mostly interacting with kids traumatized by abuse who have to tell their stories in court. Rikki died in 2016, the year Julie Strauss Bettinger's book about Rikki's work with Chuck, called *Encounters with Rikki,* was published. But Chuck—who was instrumental in getting therapy dogs for traumatized children first into deposition rooms and later into courtrooms in Florida—isn't finished sharing Rikki's story.

Rikki landed with Chuck and his wife, Patty, at their home in Tallahassee, after Hurricane Katrina. As she recovered from the devastating experience of the storm and its aftermath, it became clear she had an emotional wisdom that could do the human world good; Mitchell believes Rikki's own trauma made her more empathetic to others. Soon, man and pup were training to be a volunteer therapy dog team. Ultimately, they visited thousands of people who were sick or injured, mentally ill, or in need of a caring friend. No matter the situation, "This dog just knew what to do," Chuck tells me. "All I had to do was create the opportunity and she would take it from there."

Mitchell's main interest has long been tapping an animal's emotional intelligence to support kids who have been abused or traumatized. Considering that at least 1 in 7 children suffered abuse or neglect in the last year in the U.S., according to the Centers for Disease Control and Prevention (CDC), the need is enormous. "Dogs are able to give kids courage to go back to their most horrible memories and know they'll be able to come back out," he says. "With the hardest cases, the dogs can give the hug that we can't give." Also, pups aren't easily thrown off by odd behavior: "One kid might be catatonic, another is bouncing off the walls. But those behaviors aren't who that child is—and the dog seems to understand that and ignores the extra. She gets to the heart of the child, to the real person, and stays there."

These days, carrying with him lessons learned from Rikki, Mitchell does the rounds with a petite golden retriever named Sharon, whom he and Patty got about a year after Rikki died. A high risk for developing hip dysplasia put her out of contention as a guide dog, but with her generosity, big smile, and swishy tail, she had the makings of an excellent comforter. She doesn't have quite the emotional intelligence that Rikki had, but Mitchell says she'll happily latch on to whomever reaches out to her. And more than once, she's found her way to the neediest person in the room all on her own, as Rikki used to do. Plus, she's giving back to Mitchell just as Rikki once did. After particularly difficult days working with traumatized kids, Mitchell will get into the back seat of his car with Sharon and put *his* arms around her, absorbing some of that good stuff she gives so readily.

Mitchell's stories have me recalling Manny, a facility dog for the Center for Hope's Child Advocacy Center whom I met a few months before. His handler, Dr. Kerry Hannan, is the director of forensic services at Center for Hope. We sit there together on a summer afternoon chatting about Manny before taking him for a stroll around the Baltimore neighborhood. Manny comforts children who have been victims of sexual abuse and other traumatic experiences and have to tell their stories during the investigator process, trials, and other stressful events. Manny is an official "facility dog," bred and trained by Canine Companions rather than being plucked from an animal shelter. But the work is mostly the same as Rikki's. Not all states allow courtroom dogs, as there is debate over whether their presence might influence juries and trial outcomes. But about three dozen states do, and nearly 150 dogs are on the job around the country.

Manny greets me sweetly, as black Labs will, and then stretches out alongside my chair. I wonder if he is sensing the electrical buzz of stress that I carry wherever I go. I just want to keep a hand on him, and I notice that he shifts his position so I can reach him better. A child who's allowed to dig her hands into that softness and look into those quiet brown eyes would surely feel some ease. He is also so mouth-gentle—Hannan asks him to pluck a pen off the floor and he does it as if the thing were a fragile bird—and when he brings me his ball, he barely lips my palm handing it over. He is solid and steady, and for a child whose world has been shaken to the core, he would be both a rock and a security blanket. "He's 100 percent, you can count on him entirely," Hannan tells me as I scratch his silky ear. "With people in crisis, he brings the temperature down. His best magic is his presence."

Whether a child is abused directly or witnesses a horrific crime, how they process what has happened to them is shaped by the neurobiology of trauma. Kids may go into fight-or-flight mode when it comes time to talk about the experience; in that emergency state, cognitive abilities like comprehension and memory freeze up, and verbal centers shut down. Work by Boston University psychiatrist Bessel van der Kolk reveals that such traumas can even leave physical lesions on the brain, much as a stroke does. The key is to ease these kids back to higher-level thinking and feeling and to earn their trust, enabling them to recall and verbalize as needed. Sometimes that involves telling their story to the dog in the room instead of to the hovering adults.

"There's no end to the evil," says Brenda Kocher, a guardian ad litem (a lawyer or trained community member, depending on the state, appointed by the court to represent a child's best interests in domestic abuse and related proceedings) for the 13th Judicial Circuit Court in Florida. She describes several cases she's worked—of child neglect, physical and sexual abuse, and worse. "But the dogs offer the kids unconditional acceptance. Whatever they've been through or been a part of, she doesn't care, doesn't judge. She thinks, 'You're fantastic!' She promotes emotional healing."

Her yellow Lab, Tibet, who passed away in 2022, was a courthouse facility dog. Together they worked with more than 1,000 kids over eight years, helping them through unthinkable tragedies, getting their stories on record, and pushing for justice. Tibet was no small part of that process. "We helped with an interview of two little boys, brothers, both of whom were nonverbal," she says. But the "Tibet effect" was strong, and the elder brother, sitting on the floor of the prosecutor's office with Tibet, rocked and raked his fingers through her fur and gave the prosecutor enough information to go forward with the case. "The prosecutor said they wouldn't have gotten that without Tibet," Kocher says.

The dog seemed to know to simply be present and let the child drive the physical interaction. There was no sense of boredom or exasperation during the long sit. At other times, "Kids would be on the couch and she'd climb up and throw her 60 pounds in their lap," Kocher says. "She read them so well," deciding what approach would work best in a given situation. In a meeting with a boy who had witnessed his father murder his family, "Tibet approached him so gingerly. She crawled toward him and gently placed her head in his lap," says Kocher. "It turned out to be exactly the right thing to do."

Studies support that the kind of animal-assisted services facility dogs provide can make a measurable difference. Investigators in 2018 reported on more than 50 kids at a Virginia child advocacy center who were undergoing forensic interviews after sexual abuse, considering whether the presence of a facility dog affected their stress levels. The results for the children interviewed with the dog included significant reduction in heart rate, in systolic and diastolic blood pressure, and in salivary alpha-amylase and intestinal immunoglobulin A—all markers of stress. "It validated what we already knew," Hannan says.

Something I marveled at, talking with Mitchell, Hannan, and Kocher, was how readily the dogs in these situations connect with near strangers—and of another species no less. We forget how remarkable that is, don't we? I think again about wolves, whose social energy is directed entirely toward their own kind, and ask Clive Wynne about dogs' different approach. "Dogs come into the world so ready to look around them. They are primed to form emotional connections with beings of other kinds," he says.

As I know from writing a certain series of books, dogs aren't too proud to befriend a cat, chicken, rat, horse, or whatever creature is willing and available, and often will do so in a way that appears to bring comfort to those animals. "Happily for us, we happen to be on the other side of that sociability," Wynne says. Such openness has helped shape dogs' incredible emotional intelligence, the connective tissue between their hearts and brains and ours. It's a lifeline that can last a lifetime.

Comfort canines

Have you ever had a Great Dane sit in your lap? Arlo, an eight-year-old black-bodied, gray-muzzled giant of 150 pounds, will happily drop his bony butt on your thighs. Having such a titan of a dog choose to share your space makes you feel warm inside, as the residents of the Heritage Assisted Living facility in Hammonton, New Jersey, will tell you. Many of them look forward to the weekly visits from Arlo, his female Great Dane housemate named Moxie, and their squat pit bull–boxer–mastiff mix pal, Ollie, more than any other activity.

The dogs belong to Bruce Compton and Mary Anne Hines, matching animal lovers with white hair and generous smiles. The couple has been bringing their pets to Heritage for more than a decade. When they began visiting in 2010, they had 675 pounds' worth of Great Danes at home, all told, and Compton points out: "We knew we had to share." They come to comfort the elderly and residents with mental challenges, and often the staff as well. I join them at Heritage one November day to watch the dogs do what they do so brilliantly—offer affection, elicit smiles, and in some cases provide a sort of comfort therapy that draws people out of themselves.

Arlo is in tune with people's needs. My favorite scene with him that day involves two tiny ladies who are sharing a floral couch; one speaks only Russian, and the other, who tells me her name is Geneva, has Alzheimer's. And yet, because of the dogs, they are having a conversation. Neither understands the meaning of the other's words, but their common subject is Arlo, who settles his rear fully in the Russian lady's lap. Geneva is a little fearful of the giant dog, but on and off she seems to forget she is scared and leans toward him, reaching out to pet his shoulder, stroke his ear. "That's a whopper!" she says. "What kind of dog is that? It must be the biggest dog there is." (She says it again in a few minutes. And again a few minutes after that.) The other woman offers her thoughts in Russian, and Geneva smiles, nods, and sips her tea. Arlo seems perfectly content to be the ladies' conduit. He leans into each stroke or pat, and otherwise sits tall but relaxed, watching the activity around him.

Nearly a million people in the U.S. live in residential care facilities, according to the CDC, with some experts projecting that number will double by 2030. Inside those facilities, thousands of people suffer from depression, anxiety, and all levels of dementia. These visiting pups do more than just draw smiles as they prance from room to room or resident to resident. Studies from around the world have shown that people choosing to interact with dogs—especially pups trained in animal-assisted therapy—see significant improvements to their mental health. The more interaction, the better the outcome, including reduced agitation, aggressiveness, and depression in people with and without dementia. "We all get therapy out of this," says Hines as we watch the dogs make rounds. She means the caregivers, too, and she's spot on: Both facility professionals and the millions of adults caring at home for an elder or family member with special needs can benefit from interactions with animals.

Do the Danes know what they are doing at Heritage, or do they just behave as they do because it feels good to them? It doesn't really matter. I love the way they move generously among the residents and staff, putting up with hugs and kisses from this bunch of near strangers. They continually make rounds, seeming to want to be inclusive. Arlo, especially, greets everyone who enters the room, tail joyfully thwacking anything in his path. Arlo, Moxie, and Ozzie haven't had any formal training for this job; some dogs just seem to be born to do it. And though some breeds tend to be more socially outgoing than others, how they get along in such a setting is really about an individual dog's temperament and ability to connect. Compton and Hines's beasts sure seem to be made of the right stuff, assessing their audience and bestowing affection accordingly.

"I wouldn't ask them to do my taxes, but they have a very keen emotional intelligence," Compton says of his dogs. Not only are they masters at offering just what a person needs, "They know when to hold back by, say, giving a nervous person space by turning their big heads away. They know how to dial down the intensity of the interaction."

I see that sensitivity in action when Arlo approaches a woman asleep in her wheelchair and gently nuzzles her ear. When he gets no response, he moves on, rather than continuing to poke and demand her attention. Reading the room, considering the individual. These dogs don't force their love. Smart.

The (cognitively) toughest job of all?

My aunt Judy had Alzheimer's during the last few years of her life. I remember the jab to my heart the first time she didn't recognize me. We'd been extremely close: She always told me she thought of me as her daughter, especially after my mom died. For the family of a victim, Alzheimer's may be the cruelest disease of all.

During Judy's struggle, it never occurred to me that a dog could do much for someone with dementia except perhaps assist with general tasks and be a calming influence. How would a dog manage around someone who might not even know themselves?

An Israeli dog trainer named Yariv Ben-Yosef, together with a social worker named Daphna Golan-Shemesh, decided pups have what it takes to do more. Aside from being a daily helper and friend, a dog could be a guide, a protector from harm, and—remarkably—a decision-maker, even for the hardest cases. After learning a bit about Alzheimer's Aid Dogs (also known as AADogs, or more generally, dementia dogs), I would venture that there is no more demanding job for a service dog than walking a person with Alzheimer's safely through their condition.

The demand for service dogs for the elderly is exploding as demographics in many countries are quickly shifting toward older populations. In 2018, globally more people were 64 years or older than children under five for the first time in history. As populations age, the number of people with dementia grows, too. In the United States, at least five million people suffer with Alzheimer's—the most common form of dementia, representing some 70 percent of cases. According to the Alzheimer's Association, by 2050 some 12.7 million people will be living with the disease.

AADogs "aren't just 'smart' in their ability to respond to commands, which of course they do," says Myrna Shiboleth, owner of Netiv HaAyit Collies, based in Israel, who has bred smooth collies for the project. "They have the intelligence and perceptiveness to know when *not* to follow an instruction, or to make their own choice when there's no command to follow."

Like Seeing Eye dogs, military dogs, and police dogs facing dangerous situations, animals helping people with dementia must be masters of intelligent disobedience. When they have better information than their person, they must act on it even if they're being told otherwise. Every time I consider this, I'm floored. These dogs are trained *intensively* to follow human commands, but they must be smart enough to know when it's OK—essential, even—to say no.

And here's where the dementia dog goes a step further: "The Seeing Eye dog is led by the handler; the handler is responsible for managing the dog," says Ben-Yosef. "But the Alzheimer's dog—here, the dog manages the handler. She is responsible. So much is totally up to her." Therefore, she must be skilled—even manipulative—as she's going to have to "convince" a sometimes uncooperative person to do what she knows is right. "Think about that," Ben-Yosef says. "The dog knows when and how to argue, and how to win!"

The training for this work is deeply cognitive, he says, because, for instance, the dog who must get a person back home needs to remember each step along the way, especially in a totally new environment. "You can see it in them—always worrying about and filing away information on how to get back to where they started," Ben-Yosef says. "They have to be cognitively busy all the time, always looking for options." He believes the dogs actually count the roads as they walk as part of their mapping strategy.

Dementia dogs are also fitted with a GPS collar whose "beep," the dog learns, means to begin the journey homeward. It also helps family members locate the pair, if needed, giving the low-tech dog a high-tech assistant. Smart dog plus smartphone can mean a life saved.

Guiding and insisting are just part of the work. The dog also has to "read" and respond to a messy complex of overt and subtle potential problems that Alzheimer's brings, including confusion, agitation, and sudden anger. A person might get lost, forget who they are, or not know the dog belongs to them. The dog has to know when something "isn't right" and respond accordingly. How they figure it out is part of the wonderful mystery of the dog-human relationship. These dogs are also companions and friends, helping to ease anxiety and loneliness in a way only a dog can do. For patients with Alzheimer's, who may feel terribly isolated, this role is as essential as any.

Dementia dogs also need to be responsive to, and even predictive of, fainting spells or seizures. They have to know whom to turn to for help. They must be bonded enough to their people to read needs and confident enough to make decisions on their behalf. As these dogs manage so much unpredictability with so much independence, Shiboleth agrees with my assessment: "Of all the service dogs, the Alzheimer's dog, by necessity, may be the most intelligent," she says.

Dementia dogs are one of the newest entrants to the service dog world and still a relative rarity. Trainers are working out what breeds are most likely to succeed and what traits in an individual dog are most essential. So far, smooth collies—the dogs Shiboleth breeds—seem especially well suited. Generally, these animals bond tightly to their people and are sensitive but not overly sensitive—with the ability, for example, to roll with abrupt changes like a sudden mood swing or outburst and stay focused on the job, taking over as needed under all kinds of circumstances. Dogs who tend to be curious, courageous, and persistent in problem-solving, and have the kind of intelligence that lets them sense a problem and make good choices in response, are essential.

As always, individual dogs may or may not succeed at this job. Promising DNA is an excellent first selection factor, but Shiboleth and others look at each puppy for the right personality and drive. And surely, many individuals of all sorts would shine if given the opportunity. Indeed, organizations elsewhere, including a collaborative, pioneering effort called Dementia Dog in Scotland as well as multiple organizations in the United States, aren't committed to a particular breed.

Developing protocols to train Alzheimer's dogs for the many complex scenarios they may encounter is a work in progress. Like other service dogs, they can easily learn to assist with the basics, from fetching medicine to responding to a door knock to offering physical support. They're also trained to bark if their person falls or has breathing difficulties—some even wear a special collar with a bark-activated transmitter, sensitive to a particular type of bark, that notifies family members of a problem—and, of course, to lead the way home if the person becomes disoriented. One of the first official AADogs, a collie named Polly, went above and beyond on this task: When her owner got confused taking a walk in Paris while on vacation, she led the man back not just to the hotel where they were staying—a place she'd only just been exposed to—but also to the correct *room*. Ben-Yosef says both memory and scent must play a role in such cases.

As for the "smartest" moves, the assessing and independent decision-making that may protect or even save a life? "You can't really train for that," Shiboleth says. "And I don't think we know enough about dog intelligence to fully explain how they know what to do." Fully explainable or not, "the dream is to give people newly diagnosed with this disease a purpose when they wake up in the morning, and way forward as the disease progresses," Ben-Yosef tells me. "The dogs have the heart, mind, and focus to help them through."

The price they pay

Though dogs' extraordinary ability to connect with us even in our most difficult hours offers us humans precious support, it's important that we include the dogs' experiences when thinking about the therapy relationship. Is their experience a positive one? The people I spoke to who handle therapy dogs were adamant that their dogs love what they do—that they get excited when the working harness goes on or as they enter a hospital or nursing home or courthouse to offer comfort to whomever needs it. And I have no doubt that's true. Because, you know, *dogs*.

But the fact is, "Most organizations looking to place dogs as therapy animals use very crude tests" to determine whether they are up for the job, says animal ethicist James Serpell. "They'll expose the dog to situations he might encounter, but mostly, they're looking to ensure the dog won't be reactive, won't run off, and won't do anything dangerous or hazardous. And very few of these dogs fail that test."

That doesn't mean the dog is thrilled by the job, however. "In these tests sometimes they are extremely uncomfortable, filled with anxiety," he says. "They tell us they aren't happy, but even dog experts can be surprisingly insensitive to body language, which can be subtle or fleeting." Though the dog's point of view is more seriously considered now than it has been in the past, Serpell says, there's still room to do better.

He also notes that very few studies have considered positive-welfare measures like an oxytocin boost in dogs working as therapy animals to determine if the experience is actively positive, and not merely "not negative." A postdoctoral student working with Serpell, Sharmaine Miller, reviewed the literature and reported in 2022 that no studies thus far have measured both positive and negative physiological welfare signals alongside an individual dog's temperament—a combination that would go a long way in assessing whether therapy work is right for the animal.

We should also be aware that dogs' emotional intelligence includes a phenomenon called emotional contagion—a primitive form, or building block, of empathy. The strength of that empathy depends in part on the duration of the relationship and the sex of the animals (female dogs do it better). Because dogs are tooled to read our faces, body language, and scent, and "get" how we're feeling, they are necessarily taking in both the good and the bad—a circumstance that has real consequences for them, too. (For example, studies have shown that human stress can cause a boost in dogs' heart rate or cortisol.) Though it's lovely to know that on a biological level dogs "care" about our feelings, we need to acknowledge that emoting all over these animals transfers our stress and affects them physically.

Handlers understand how physically and mentally taxing the dog's work can be. And although many seem to thrive under the rigors of service or therapy, it's only fair to note that being there for us at the worst of times has its downsides. Thank goodness, the best handlers and owners give their working pups time off, replete with opportunities to do dog-relevant things that have little to do with *human* needs, and to exercise their dog-relevant intelligence in ways they may not get to do while on the job. That certainly seems to allow dogs to blow off the steam that accumulates. Maybe that has to be enough.

Odin's gift

Late February is a depressing time in Chicago by any measure, but here I am again. A quick explanation, long overdue: The nursing home where my dad lives is walking distance from Odin's house, and Odin's humans, Margaret and Trevor, have an extra room they rent out. My first time there, we decided we all liked each other, so I became a regular. The location allows me to walk back and forth to spend time with my dad without the extra expense of a rental car. And it has meant making three new friends: two humans, one dog.

I've covered the nursing home experience elsewhere in my writing life, and I don't want to dwell on it here. Briefly, although I'm grateful that skilled nurses are caring for my father, watching him decline has been the hardest thing I've done in my 50-plus years. He'll soon turn 94, and though his body tells that tale, until recently his mind remained fairly robust, able to retrieve the names of his college buddies, the travels he took with Betty Schwartz in grad school, lines of poetry and lyrics of old songs. But now he's losing access to those details. His love for my brother and me (and for chocolate ice cream) is all that remains.

Today his room is stuffy, as usual. His shirt and bedspread are food stained, and the floor around the bed is littered with crumbs and Splenda wrappers. I worry, as I always do, that he doesn't get up and move around enough, despite my reminders. He's legally blind, so the family photos hung on the wall by his bed go mostly unseen. I straighten them anyway. I help him "get things sorted." His glasses are missing (they're on the nightstand), someone took his slippers (they're under the bed), the audiobook player is broken (it's unplugged), the phone is broken (it's off the hook). I hoped to take him outside to the patio for a little fresh air and sunlight, but he's tired and unwilling. We focus instead on the minutiae that now fill his days: the shower schedule, the dinner schedule. He has moments of clarity, and many more moments of profound confusion.

So when I get back to Trevor and Margaret's house, I turn to Odin. He's not a therapy dog by any stretch, but he greets me with a tail thump and a welcoming kind of eye contact, nudging my leg to ask for some love. I squat down in front of him and we look at each other. He lets me put my hands on either side of his face and lean my forehead against his. He licks my nose just once, and I put my arms around him primate style and he lets me hug him. He smells good—like dog, like woodsmoke, like winter. He follows me around the kitchen, his claws on the floor tapping a comforting rhythm. When I finally settle at the table with my head in my hands, he comes over and rests his chin on my knee. It'll be OK, his eyes seem to say. I know I'm reading into them, but so what? It still works wonders.

Later, I bow at Odin in the way that means "Let's play," and he bows back. We are stock-still for a moment, staring each other down: Who will move first? I do. I shoot out a hand at him and he responds with a leap and a spin, then flings himself half in my lap and freezes again, his mouth open but soft against my cheek. How does he know how much pressure is OK to use, how much bite is acceptable? He whaps me with a paw, but not too hard, mouths my arm, and we wrestle without injury. He could easily hurt me playing this game, yet he always holds back, knowing where the line is and not crossing it.

These moments. These are what's so special about a dog. The emotional exchange, the understanding. Social intelligence works magic in both directions—we read one another, giving and taking and giving again. He's more fluent than I am, but I'm getting there.

And honestly, this thing with my dad? It would be immensely harder to do without Odin. He's not even my dog, but he's there for me when I stumble in from the nursing home feeling sad and helpless. He is pure in his intentions and the offer of his gifts. Together, we go to a warm, happy place for a little while, and I'm so grateful for the way his mind works. And his heart.

CHAPTER FIFTEEN

GETTING SMART ABOUT DOG SMARTS

We're never too old, or too smart, to learn new things. And just like dogs, we have an amazing capacity to expand our minds—that is, if we open our minds to the task.

As humans, we tend to consider ourselves the smartest ones in the room, and I think that has limited us in the long run. When we let go of that notion, we discover an open door to an immense storehouse of ideas in our relationships with dogs, from the technological to the existential.

The natural world is filled with fabulous role models, and dogs may be the most approachable, perhaps the wisest, of all our teachers in four-legged form. The anatomy of a sniff, the language of an expression, the value of a moment: Each of these is an opportunity to expand our experience and learn. Why not benefit from opening our minds to the wisdom of our very wise pups?

Sniffing doesn't suck

One morning, Matthew Staymates sent a very special file to the 3D printer in his lab at the National Institute of Standards and Technology. Six hours later, the mechanical engineer had a green acrylonitrile butadiene styrene (ABS) plastic dog nose modeled after the snout of a yellow Lab named Bubbles. His goal was to better understand how air moves when a dog inhales, and to use that knowledge to improve explosives-detection technology.

"We had tried the experiment with a real dog sitting in front of our imaging system and sniffing, but the animal only cooperated for a few minutes before getting grumpy and wandering off," Staymates tells me. Then it occurred to him he had access to a nose that would never stray. His graduate school roommate had originally made the model for his own imaging project, based on the skull of Bubbles, who had died of natural causes. After Staymates printed the nose, he built a tiny mechanism that maneuvered air through the model the way a real sniff does. "We ended up with the world's first anatomically correct actively sniffing e-nose," he says.

The best way to build a superefficient chemical detector is one of many questions that can go to the dogs. If we accept the idea that animals like *Canis familiaris* can be supersmart in areas where our aptitudes may be lackluster, then we'd be wise to let them be our teachers. And if I've discovered anything during my research for this book, it's that dogs have a lot to teach, and we have a lot to learn. That includes both philosophical lessons about how we experience the world, and extremely practical guidance—some of which is leading to next-level opportunities in science and technology with potentially profound effects on human health and welfare.

Many of those opportunities fall under the heading of biomimicry, or using living structures, tissue types, and physiological functions as models for human-made materials and devices. Biomimicry is an increasingly important source of inspiration for developing technologies, but it's not a new strategy: We've been taking cues from the natural world as long as humans have been making things to improve our lives.

Mastering the world of scent has been part of that history. Invisible toxins, some deadly, are common in our world. In certain cases, we've been able to make them detectable to us—for example, by adding a scent to odorless natural gas—so that our own noses can protect us. Such technology has existed in various forms for decades: Home smoke and CO_2 detectors are perfect examples of products that pick up dangerous scents faster or better than we do, setting off alarms that our brains can process.

The first big step on the road to a functional e-nose came with the invention of gas chromatography in the early 1950s, followed in the '60s and '70s by a number of compound-specific sensors built to detect chemicals like ammonia, ethanol, and the extremely flammable and highly toxic compound hydrogen sulfide. A haunting fact regarding ammonia, which is produced in human sweat: The U.S. military employed an electrochemical device during the Vietnam War called a "people sniffer" to locate enemy soldiers hiding (and sweating) in the jungle.

Not until the 1980s did e-nose designs begin to take after mammalian olfaction, employing "intelligent chemical multi-sensor arrays" that could recognize single gases as well as multiple types of odorants and mixed compounds. As new sensing materials and instruments came online in the 1990s, the technology stretched into areas including environmental monitoring (such as air quality), food quality assurance, the detection of explosives and pests, the perfume industry, and medical diagnostics.

As you already know, the physics of a dog sniff are subtle and precise: A tiny exhalation sends air jetting out of both nostrils, moving downward and outward. That moving air entrains, or draws, vapor- and particle-laden air from in front of the nose back toward the nostrils. The following inhalation pulls that air inside. The incoming air splits into two streams—one that goes to the lungs and the other to the olfactory region. In the latter, odor molecules glom on to receptors and accumulate, rather than being exhaled immediately. That pause gives the dog's brain time to analyze a scent in detail and focus on whatever is most interesting.

These complex sniff dynamics make canines extremely sophisticated samplers. Head-to-head comparisons between a dog-style sniffing device and one that simply sucks up air showed that sampling efficiency with the dog-inspired e-nose was four times better at a fairly close distance of 3.9 inches, and 18 times better at 7.9 inches away.

Dogs perform the whole sniff sequence at a rate of about five sniffs a second—that's a frequency of 5 Hz, as scientists measure such things. It turns out that number is breed-independent: A Great Dane and a tiny shih tzu take in different volumes of air, but they both sniff at roughly that same frequency. The behavior is used both for sensing and sampling (the latter being the process of getting data about the scent molecules of interest into the right place in the brain for analysis). You've probably seen a dog shift from sensing mode—catching a first whiff of something intriguing—into sampling mode, with the nose twitching and fluttering and the whole pup obviously intensely focused on figuring out *What is THAT smell?*

"Sampling is very important from an explosives-detection point of view," Staymates says. "And while we engineers are really, really good at developing high-quality sensors, we're not very good at re-creating the analysis part, which is of course crucial." Commercially available detectors may be called "sniffers," he notes, "but they don't really sniff. They suck." (Which is not the word used in the scientific publication about the work, in case you're wondering: "We went with *inspire*," he says.)

That continuous suction—considered passive sampling—just isn't the most effective method for identifying trace chemicals, he says. "The dog sniff is much smarter at getting information where it needs to go." That's why adapting detectors to work more like a "bio-inspired" e-nose could eventually improve not just explosives sampling, but also, for example, instruments aimed at detecting illicit narcotics and pathogens. "I wouldn't be surprised if we start to see more intelligent sampling, modeled after dogs, integrated into the next generation of these technologies," Staymates says.

For robot makers, the dog is a familiar inspiration. At robotics firm Boston Dynamics, agile canid-like machines have paved the way for other animal- and human-inspired designs. Named appropriately, BigDog and Spot were some of the first robots that showed what such machines could do, promising to replace real dogs (or humans) in potentially dangerous scenarios—military operations, on oil and gas rigs, at disaster sites. Like dogs, robots could manage rubble, ice, mud, and other substrates with ease, carry loads into the field, and of course sniff for particular substances and report on their findings. Other animals—from cheetahs to insects—feature in newer robotic designs. But let's thank dogs for being part of this machine-design revolution.

Is that a nose in your pocket?

With what they're learning from the olfactory superpowers of our animal friends, scientists are extending our sensory reach and heading toward some remarkable electronic noses that will likely someday be just another cell phone accessory, able to detect by scent if we're taking care of ourselves.

"The app we're envisioning will be basically like having a dog nose in our pockets that's perpetually sniffing us for signs of ill health," Andreas Mershin, an MIT physicist and inventor, tells me. He's describing an e-nose smaller than a credit card—and shrinking with each iteration—that's built not just to mimic a dog's olfactory prowess but also crafted using actual mammalian olfactory receptors. The proteins are made in the lab: No dog noses are harmed or farmed. The receptors act as sensors, from which a smartphone app can read data. That means your iPhone could message you about a change in your individual scent and what it might mean: a drop in blood sugar, the beginnings of pneumonia, a flare-up of colitis, an early cancer. The app might learn to sniff for environmental threats as well—smoke, CO_2, pollutants, and so on.

It's a huge next step in a line of technologies that aim to exceed even the sensitivity of a dog's nose in a very portable product. Mershin, who co-created the Osmocosm Foundation out of which several start-up companies in olfactory-based tech have emerged, says the latest version of his team's mini-detector is 200 times *more* sensitive than a dog's nose in its ability to detect trace amounts of certain molecules.

However, the app can't interpret what it detects, at least not yet, and it will have to be scaled way up to deal with real-world background odors—problems Staymates faced with his 3D sniffer as well. A dog is still smarter than the devices, as she can make an assessment and, with (and sometimes without) training, communicate her findings consistently. To make the app as intelligent as a dog, Mershin and colleagues are using machine learning, which allows them to input historical data that the software analyzes to predict new output values. "Dogs can infer elusive patterns from a scent that humans aren't able to grasp from a chemical analysis," Mershin says. And because smells are complex things with layers not always clearly defined, dogs have to be able to zoom in. And they can, he says, "because they have this dynamic background reduction algorithm in their head: They're not looking at the whole; they learn to cut through the noise. And that's exactly what we wrote into our machine."

E-nose technologies continue to evolve and enter new spaces. Future e-noses have massive potential to mimic the sophistication of mammalian olfactory intelligence, which will ultimately revolutionize many aspects of how we monitor ourselves and our world. "The dog is the model for new technology," Mershin says. "And from it comes the wisdom to build our own nose that does what a dog's does" with fewer limitations.

The outcome aims to run parallel to the living snout, tweaked to serve our needs. "We should learn from the dog, be inspired by the dog, and then transition to building the nose we need," Mershin says. "In this, the dog is the teacher."

And as it happens, our pups have other, less technological lessons to offer as well. They don't call for smartphones or 3D printers, but for open minds and open hearts. Consider a few bits of furry wisdom with me now.

Do as they do

My pup Geddy is a sun dog. He loves to find that hot spot on the patio slate on a summer afternoon and sprawl out on his side, the rays saturating him with warmth. When his internal thermometer hits red and the panting begins, he gets up and moves, plopping down on a patch of cool grass in the shade. He'll nap there a while, then return to the sunny place when he's ready for another bake. And so it goes.

It's a simple enough behavior pattern, and a familiar one, recalling a beachgoer's move from sun-scorched sand to cool ocean and back again. But sometimes when I spy him cycling this way, I realize I've been going nonstop for hours at something tedious and soul sucking, that I've been tensed up sitting in the air-conditioning's blast, and that I, too, could use some downtime and warming up. Taking to the recliner in the sun until I'm heated through like a fresh biscuit, then stretching out on a blanket in the shade, I let go of thoughts and let in ease. It's a good thing.

I know this is not some great epiphany. When I say we can learn from our dogs, "Pay attention to your body" and "Take a break" aren't exactly shocking lessons—though each is profound in its own way. But the things a nearby dog chooses to do may remind us to do the same, whether sniffing fragrant air or just being in the moment and enjoying the comforts that nature and our bodies allow. That includes finding your own version of dog zoomies: It doesn't even have to be physical, just something that lets you express your pent-up energy in the most buoyant way. It might be throwing paint on a canvas or attempting high notes in the shower rather than running in circles. Just do it.

More broadly, lessons can be learned by climbing inside the dog's *umwelt* and poking around: It's a way we might learn that there's a richer, more textured world to be experienced. Taking a dog's point of view, we can discover how to engage our senses in new ways, how to appreciate facets of our lives and our environments that we may miss or ignore. Be in the moment so deeply that nothing else matters: Think of a dog ignoring your leash tugs as he investigates something new. Spin for joy in rain-soaked grass, mud be damned. Smell something intently that you hadn't thought to smell before, parsing carefully through its layers of aroma. Enjoy.

In fact, we could give our own senses more credit for what they allow us to do! Mostly, I'm thinking of the nose. The human olfactory system has long been thought to play a minor role in our lives: To some degree, over the course of evolution, primates swapped olfactory sensitivity for better vision. And it's true that our sniffing anatomy lost some of its umph over millennia. But what we've got is still a marvel of nature.

And so, inspired by my subjects, I started trying to make better use of my sense of smell—sniffing ingredients more fully when cooking and literally stopping to smell flowers during my walks, for example. This got me thinking about how important scent is to us, even if we don't think about it that way.

The significance of olfactory experience became especially clear when I got COVID-19 in late 2021. I'd read about people losing their sense of smell during infection, so I wasn't entirely surprised when it happened to me. One day it was there, then *poof!* Gone. The condition is called anosmia, and in this case the science suggests the virus directly injures the chemosensory system, knocking back cells that affect neurons in the nose.

But knowing it might happen and experiencing it are very different. Inhaling through my nose became strictly an oxygen-getting exercise. The stream of air felt cold and empty, and my brain struggled to make sense of the void. On a positive note, I couldn't tell if my house smelled like dog. But mostly the experience was disconcerting—and concerning. Our senses work in tandem, with one affecting our experience of another, so flavors were dulled and even my favorite foods were less enticing, including visually. It made me think about a friend who had been a gourmet cook until she permanently lost her sense of smell; with it went her joy of cooking and eating. A terrible loss!

When my olfaction suddenly clicked back on three weeks later over a container of Thai ginger chicken, the steam hitting my nose was a revelation of spicy sweetness that made me hungry and happy and somehow filled the cognitive gap the anosmia had created. It was like my brain had gone black-and-white and suddenly color washed over it, a can of bold paint spilling across concrete. Smells occupy an important place in cognition. Perhaps nothing fills out an experience more than scent. And what drags out a memory, sometimes kicking and screaming, from our brain folds more effectively than a smell from the past? Studies using fMRI have shown that memories prompted by an odor are not only especially emotional and evocative, but they show up in a different spot in the brain than memories from other sensory stimuli.

We might learn from our dogs to pay closer attention—not just to the immediate pleasantness or peculiarity of a smell, but to the effects that sneak up on us. We use scent for more acutely useful things than reliving the past, of course—for example, protecting us from spoiled food, dead things that might carry disease, even from sick people. A Swedish study of the brain's response to "dangerous" smells indicates they are processed unconsciously and extremely fast, prompting the olfactory bulb to instant message the motor cortex, triggering that "back away" response.

Also unconsciously, and also like dogs, we use smells in our social interactions. Mothers and babies know each others' scents. In a study out of the University of California, Berkeley, when women sniffed a chemical found in men's armpit sweat, their cortisol levels—associated with alertness and stress—rose. An earlier study showed that same scent affected women's mood, physiological arousal, and brain activity. Smell may even help us choose a healthy mate whose family tree grows far enough from our own to ensure good genetic diversity. (Online dating has its limits.)

So we shouldn't give the human nose short shrift: It serves our survival needs and makes life richer. And though dogs' smell sensitivity can be a thousand times greater than ours, in some cases we have a lower scent threshold than they do. For example, we are superdetectors of the aromas of flowers and fruits, which are relevant to us as omnivores but not terribly important to carnivorous canids.

And here's another way we can indulge in the power of smell: Instead of balking at what your dog's nose is into, why not dip your own into the grass or leaf pile alongside your pup to get the true animal experience? (Don't linger too long; the neighbors are watching.) The onslaught of information pinballing between your dog's nose and brain when he sniffs is hard to fathom, but we can make an effort. You'll notice I was careful in my suggestions of where to put our noses. But go ahead, sniff that yellow snow if you're curious.

Though I've had the nose on the brain of late, I would suggest we give more of a workout to *all* our senses. How refreshing it is to mindfully appreciate, perhaps one at a time, what our eyes, ears, tongues, and skin experience as we move through the world. That's not to mention the many other sensations our bodies allow. I, for one, often copy my dogs' *big stretch* in the morning, and it feels glorious. Another lesson from dogs: Shake things off! Fart! Create ease in your body in whatever ways you can! We may not have a dog's nose power, but we can enjoy the sensory potluck that the world provides.

Express yourself as they do

Thanks to dogs, I'm also taking a closer look at body language in my interactions. For instance, when I'm considering a walk with Monk, just for fun I'll see if I can keep my intentions secret for a while. I'll deliberately endeavor not to "Clever Hans" the situation (remember the "counting" horse taking subtle cues from his owner?) with an inadvertent glance or gesture toward him, his leash, my shoes. I won't say words or even spell words aloud that might cue him, though I might speak to my husband in what I feel confident is code, continuing whatever I was doing to further obscure the plan. It'll be at a random hour of the day, so the time isn't giving me away. From my perspective, the idea is still under wraps.

And yet, *somehow he knows.* Suddenly he becomes extra alert, watching my face, tail up. Something in what I thought was irrelevant chatter holds a message, or maybe my plan has a scent. He comes closer and keeps his eyes on me. I ignore him but he's too smart to buy it. And if our eyes meet, it's all over: He starts his pre-walk rituals, dancing in circles, rushing to his water bowl for a quick drink, giving a couch pillow a death shake, grabbing a shoe to parade around. The rapid-fire *click-click* of his nails on the wood floor tells me how sure he is of what's coming.

I won't go so far as to say dogs can read our minds. But sometimes it seems they come close. At least, it appears, they may be able to understand whether a human's intentions are good or ill. In a 2022 study out of Vienna by comparative psychologist Christoph Völter and colleagues, the tester offered dogs treats following different protocols: In one scenario she'd snatch the bite away repeatedly before the pup could grab it; in another she'd fumble, appearing to drop the treat over and over by mistake. The dogs' behavior and body language, including clues from tail wags, indicated the animals got more frustrated when they were being teased than when the tester was simply "clumsy." On some level, the dogs seemed to realize that in the latter scenario, the human was trying her best.

And of course, they read each other just as well, or likely better, than they read humans. We read one another, too, though perhaps not as effectively. With us, distractions, preconceived notions, self-doubt, or conceit often get in the way of clear communication. Might we do better?

Let me say up front: Regardless of what analysts like to observe about the position of the hands or eyebrows of a politician on the podium, no single gesture or expression can reliably reveal someone's intentions, thoughts, or emotions. (Pinocchio's nose is not a thing!) How we feel or what we intend manifests outwardly in various ways simultaneously, including such subtleties as when a change in emotional state increases blood flow to the surface of the skin, changing the appearance of the face. As with dog postures, that can mean one thing or its opposite depending on context. Therefore, emotions behind even the most "obvious" human facial expressions, experts caution, aren't in fact obvious at all. Still, without making a sound, we can say a lot—just like our dogs.

We speak with our bodies, whether with a scrunched-nose *Ewww, that's sour!* facial expression (which dogs also have, and it's adorable!), or we may assume a protective posture when threatened, expressing the strength of a warrior with a purposeful yoga pose. And we can express vulnerability, sadness, or joy through a simple dance routine. That we derive meaning from expressive body language is clear—fMRI has even offered clues about what parts of the brain are involved. Exactly how the brain makes heads or tails of a body or face in motion, though, is unknown.

We don't have to fully understand the science of brains and behavior to make better use of both. Perhaps being more dog smart in our approach to other humans—more mindful of those with whom we interact most—would help us navigate our own social world with more understanding. With more intelligence.

So when your friend says she's *fine* to go to the party despite her recent breakup, you'll examine what she *isn't* saying—through the stiffness of her smile, the tension of her jaw muscles, the way she curls into herself sitting on the couch. She's the timid pup being drawn into a mosh pit of wrestling dogs when she really wants to sit this one out. Take notice. Suggest a night at home instead. Watch her shoulders relax and her face soften.

And if, for example, we paid better attention to each other's accumulating signals before an argument—like a dog takes another's stiff posture or raised lip seriously—we might be able to de-escalate rather than lunge ahead sometimes. Dogs don't miss a thing. We could stand to emulate that.

Many of us could take some instruction in frankness, too. Dogs communicate their wishes, needs, likes, and fears quite consistently; we don't always read them correctly, but they are pretty straight-up in how they express themselves to each other and to us. I can't think of too many passive-aggressive dog behaviors. Try the Woof Way: Say what you mean.

Mean what you say. Don't dance around what you want or don't want. Be clear.

My socially smart dogs have made me consider something else about body language, and that is just how much physical expressiveness is being lost as we evolve into screen-addicted creatures with our butts perpetually in chairs. Especially now that working from home and communicating mostly by video is commonplace, how much body language is being lost, and how much more common is misinterpretation of another's meaning? Sitting at a computer, are we even emoting, gesturing, showing how we feel as much as before? If we are, can others even tell?

I can't help but think immobile and less expressive communications make our social interactions less effective. Less meaningful or satisfying. Less human. What to do about it? Be more demonstrative online? More jazz hands during Zoom calls? I don't know.

But I'll add that the reduced physicality is a loss in and of itself, and another area where dogs have a lesson for people. Canines tend to exhibit a lot of "kinesthetic intelligence"—the natural capacity for movement and body control in space that makes them a joy to watch run and play—and many of us have at least some of that, too. But are we making use of it? Are we dancing enough? (Re)connecting with our sensory and physical selves can guide us toward a fuller appreciation of our own experiences. It can give us entry into worlds we may not have realized are within our reach.

Accept others as they do

I can't help myself: With my passion for interspecies relationships, some of my favorite stories about animals' social and emotional intelligence are about the trust and affection dogs show toward unusual people and other animals needing care or comfort: the dog who nuzzles up, undeterred, to the child with severe autism as she shrieks and flaps her arms. The dog who chooses to guide and protect a blind deer, or becomes the "greeter" at an animal rescue, moving among the orphans, whatever their species, to offer a welcoming gesture.

This stuff is irresistible to me. Dogs, more than any other animal, seem to have all the right moves when it comes to making and keeping friends both among their own kind and outside their species (though of course not all dogs share this temperament). Often, such friendships seem to form in an instant: Think of the dog park, where unfamiliar animals come together and accept one another into the game within seconds. Unless they feel threatened, many dogs have an openness about them that only calls attention to people's often less generous treatment of strangers. There's a strong lesson in there about acceptance and kindness toward our fellow humans.

That's the story I've always told kids when presenting about my *Unlikely Friendships* books: Look at these animals ignoring or embracing their differences, finding common ground. Why can't we be more like them?

That's not to say dogs aren't wary when they need to be and that they always keep the peace. But preconceptions tied to prejudices just aren't there. If, say, high schools or neighborhoods were a bit more like dog parks (minus the poop piles and humping, please), a new student or a new resident of a different color, culture, size, or belief system could come in and—if her intentions are good and honest—be welcomed by all instead of judged, ignored, or rejected.

How wonderful it would be if we were more dog smart in the way we *human*.

CHAPTER SIXTEEN

BEING BETTER HUMANS FOR OUR SMART DOGS

This book is packed with smart dogs—some of a particular breed, others a mix and match, each with a unique story. But in at least one way they're the same: All have had *opportunity*. With the exception of an itchy Costa Rican beach dog who certainly missed out on K-9 classes, the animals featured here have been given opportunities to show off their natural aptitudes and build on them through training and experience. And across the board, they have succeeded brilliantly as a result. As dog owners and companions, we are the ones to offer those opportunities; we can choose to set up our dogs for success or leave them to flail about in an environment of our making. Seems like a clear choice to me.

I'm excited to think that I can empower my dogs to be their smartest selves, and I'm hopeful others feel the same. So, how do we do it? After spending so much time with so many impressive pups and learning from the people who care for them, I have some ideas. See what you think.

Learn to speak dog

Learning how dogs communicate, in all their watchful, raised-lip, twitchy-tail glory, can help us ensure our pets are happy and healthy. Understanding canine "language" will also equip us to discover our pup's natural aptitudes and recognize her preferences. Improving our fluency in Doggish will enable deeper engagement with our furry companions—and give us a greater appreciation for how hard they're working to understand *us*. "Dogs are profoundly sophisticated in their ability to communicate with each other, while we are shockingly bad at reading their signals," Patricia McConnell says. A large part of "speaking dog," then, is simply being more observant. "As we are such a visual species, you wouldn't think we'd have to be taught to watch our dogs," she adds. "And yet that's one of the first things trainers tell their clients. Watch your dog, really see what the animal is doing. There are messages in each little behavior."

An observant owner can learn to read her dog extremely well in any context—at home, on the street, at the dog park, with other people, with other animals. Dogs tell us their preferences and their limits all the time. And it's important to consider that touch, for instance, can be soothing in some contexts and agitating in others, McConnell notes. "That's the kind of awareness we owe to our dogs," she says. Like us, animals have thresholds beyond which touch may be unwelcome; we can learn where those boundaries are and stay within them.

In a photo-driven examination of dogs' responses to being hugged, Stanley Coren found that 80 percent of the pups showed "at least one sign of discomfort, stress, or anxiety," when embraced, he wrote in a blog post about the work. Among those signals: "half-moon eyes," a lowered tail, lip licking, and an effort to turn away from the hugger. Slicked-back ears, yawning, and raising one paw are other signs of agitation. A dog might also tuck his tail, go rigid, or start panting. Most obvious: "If you hear growling or see your dog bare teeth, chances are that they're very upset and might even bite you," Coren wrote.

We've already delved into canine body language in these pages, so I won't repeat those details here. But it's easy to find resources that lay it out in pictures—great for a visual species like us. The takeaways: Once we know what to look for, we can do a better job of removing stimuli that cause anxiety or unwanted behavior. And we can aim to give our dogs more of the kinds of interactions and levels of touch they enjoy while easing up on the encounters they've asked us time and again to avoid.

Though I've become a big proponent of learning dogs' language to help us communicate with them better, that doesn't mean I've quit talking to my own pups, hoping they understand what I'm saying. Even if it's all *blah blah blah* to their ears, it feels good to me—they're great nonjudgmental listeners. And based on what scientists know about how canine brains respond to our words, they are primed to at least *try* to understand. Veterinarian and animal behavior expert Ian Dunbar agrees that we should keep talking. "Silly conversations with our dogs mesmerize them," he says. To enhance both training and bonding, "Commune with your dog, get him to focus, talk to him, tell him a hundred reasons you love him."

Set your dog up for success

We owe it to our dogs to tell them what we expect of them before expecting it—and certainly before demanding it. As Dunbar says, "A trained dog is a happy dog: He understands the rules, which lets him have a much closer relationship with his owner and a better quality of life." Researchers at the University of Milan found that dogs trained for agility competition and for search and rescue work were more engaged with their humans than untrained dogs who lived simply as household pets.

It's a little counterintuitive, isn't it? Wouldn't you imagine that a pet, asked only to be a pampered companion, would be the most purely attached to her people? But flip the script for a minute. Think about dating someone who is physically affectionate and repeats "I love you" a lot, but not much else goes on between you. It sounds romantic at first, but over time, how engaged would you really feel with that person, compared with someone with whom you share goals, activities, and accomplishments? A picnic, a hand of cards, a trip to a new city, a joint charitable project: These are the ties that bind. Dogs are like great dates: We connect best when we *do things* together.

Training our pet dogs nurtures both our bonds and their intelligences. Dunbar would say it's immoral *not* to train them: "If a dog is not educated, he doesn't know how to live with people, doesn't know what the rules are," he says. "And then if he's not compliant people get frustrated, and take it out on the dog." Failing to train sets our pets up for failure. "We shouldn't deny them the education that lets them get it right," he says.

If dogs are allowed to go where you're going, take your pup with you. Introduce her to lots of people and other dogs early in life. Play both mental and physical games and offer challenges. Let her try new things— and let her fail, get frustrated, and figure out another way. Why? Because life experience helps shape what a dog knows, how she thinks, whether she looks to us for help or solves her own problems. Studies have shown that social species raised in enriched conditions do better at problem-solving tasks than animals growing up solo, without chances to socialize and explore.

It's important not to designate instantaneous obedience as the sole measure of intelligence. Consider your dog's choices when she's *not* just following directions—why is she doing X instead of Y? What preferences and judgments did that choice express? And, wherever you can, make use of what you observe to ensure that what you're teaching feels like a natural part of the dog's life. Coren wrote about using "auto training" with young dogs, naming and praising behavior a dog is already doing to reinforce it. So, as your pup is coming toward you, pat your leg and say with excitement, "Fido, come! Good boy!" It's a simple and effective way to give the dog agency while also teaching him what you want him to know.

Letting a dog "figure it out" rather than always showing her the way is also worthwhile. K-9 nose work instructor Lisa Holt talks about watching her Parkinson's-sniffing dogs "sort through the background scents," giving them three runs at a set of samples before accepting their answer about whether signs of the disease were present in any of them. In an essay on selecting and training dogs for scent work, Ohio trainer-handler Sherri Minhinnick writes that when a dog can work "in a natural, unforced way, without coercion and intrusion by a human, [it] permits the dog to cognitively discover successes on their own, which in turn adds further motivation and decision-making toward future training goals."

That's a formal way of describing what I experienced learning back handsprings as a young gymnast: My confidence bloomed when the spotter quietly stepped away and it was all me. Suddenly, I was flying down the mat, one flip after another, and, realizing I hadn't needed the spotter's help, I was immediately ready to try the next, more difficult, move.

Nurture their brains

Brains grow and change with experience; intelligence is not fixed. Even what Coren calls "instinctive intelligence," with its genetic underpinnings, has wiggle room.

A famous study in the 1960s compared rats caged alone in environmentally impoverished conditions against littermates given toys, friends, and spaces to investigate. The lucky rats grew heavier and thicker cerebral cortexes and had higher concentrations of certain brain enzymes associated with the ping-pong of information from one part of the brain to another. That study and others since have shown that exploration and decision-making stimulate the growth of dendrites and axons, the brain branches that carry information to and from nerve cells. And these, in turn, spark new connections—a phenomenon called use-induced plasticity. Enriched early experiences change the brain in the same way as formal training.

There are lots of resources out there for games to play with your dogs to give their brains a workout. But the tasks don't have to be high-tech or complex for your average mutt to benefit from them. Coren came up with a series of exercises for those who want to determine just how smart their dog is. Though I'm not as interested in the "IQ test" component of his method, the tasks can be both fun and brain-enhancing. For example, putting food under a can or up on a platform, or tossing a towel over a dog's head, gives the pup a quick problem to solve. Hiding food in a room while the dog watches, then leading him out and back in, lets him use his short-term memory. Doing the same but with a longer wait tests longer-term memory; both are good for the brain.

Smart dogs really do crave structure and direction, and it's important to give them both, says Super Collies owner-trainer Sara Carson. But that doesn't require outdated and scientifically debunked "alpha" posturing. "Dogs want a leader, whether it's you or another dog in the pack," Carson says. "But the 'be the alpha' mantra has confused the issue. You don't have to dominate to be in charge; you can still give your dog choices and opportunities without foregoing structure."

A wildly irregular feeding schedule, for example, is confusing and frustrating for animals. Playtime also benefits from some regularity: Dogs who know and trust that fun activities are coming soon, as they do every day, are likely happier, better-behaved members of the household.

Start the learning early

You've already heard how trainer Julie Case starts exposing pups to all kinds of stimuli practically at birth. Before their eyes are open, her dogs are experiencing the world. "We start puppy stimulation exercises on day three of their lives, and they're then handled every day after," she says.

It's advice worth repeating: Offering a dog diverse stimuli at a very young age can help shape the animal into a smart, well-rounded, even-tempered pup. Dunbar tells me, "Even as neonates, you can make a difference by exposing them to everything (except diseases, of course).

Put them in a room with metal balls and crinkly plastic bottles, seesaws and boxes, toys and uneven floors. Bring in children to handle them and scream and sing. Have a party and invite friends of all sizes, sexes, and races. Play music, slam doors!" The idea is that by the time a dog is eight weeks old, "he'll be bombproof," says Dunbar. "If you've done it right, there's almost nothing he'll meet in the real world that will be truly novel and therefore frightening."

When I visited Auburn University, where scientists study the effects of very early exposure to odor on their sniffer-dogs-to be, I was impressed with their puppy stimulation room, a tiny space off the kennel filled with hanging cups, paintbrushes and cans, ramps, toys, blocks—even a television. It was quiet at the time, but when the room is packed with pups, I'm told, it's educational pandemonium.

I asked around and found that very few breeders, who have the most access to young puppies, offer early enrichment to this degree—which frustrates Dunbar to no end. "That's what all should be doing," he tells me. "Because when we deny them enrichment early on, we pay for it later when the dog is filled with fear."

Let them learn all life long

Our pups age as we do in many ways—especially cognitively. With time, dogs' thinking tends to slow down, their brains tend to shrink, their ability to learn and remember and problem-solve declines. Sound familiar? Some even end up with canine cognitive dysfunction, the dog version of Alzheimer's disease. Sadly for both of our species, some aspects of intelligence are simply on a bell curve over our lifetimes.

But we know from studies in people that physical activity can help protect human brain function, and reports based on the lives of nearly 40,000 pet dogs around the world coming out of the Dog Aging Project—a community science initiative launched at the University of Washington in 2014, with many collaborating institutions—suggest the same is true for dogs. Researchers from the Clever Dog Lab at the

Messerli Research Institute in Vienna have found that in some cases, old dogs learn new tricks just as well as younger ones. The scientists say it's worthwhile not only to keep giving your elder pup cognitive challenges, with activities like nose work and trick training, but also to simply keep playing with him. He may not have the energy or strength to roughhouse anymore—maybe you don't, either?—but he'll continue to benefit from the kind of thinking that any form of play requires.

These findings got me thinking about older working dogs: What happens when they stop working? Is there a feeling of loss? As we still don't really know exactly how a dog's sense of self is constructed, it's impossible to gauge if "self-worth" is diminished with the end of a career.

A police officer in Atlanta told me a story about his retired patrol dog: The gray-muzzled shepherd would lie by the front door and when his owner left for work with his new, younger K-9 partner, the elder dog was utterly miserable. It seemed more than just the dog not wanting to be left behind. "I really felt he wanted to be a part of *this thing*. He missed all parts of the job and still wanted to work," the officer said.

But the ex-working dog was no longer spry enough to handle the rigors of the job, and the department's policy was to retire K-9s when they turned 10, giving them some ease after a life of service. It occurs to me now that this is a case where letting the dog choose to keep "working"—by offering him occasional rides in the patrol car with the siren on, for instance, or by letting him have the chance to do a little nose work on a parked car each week, if he was willing—would have been both a true kindness and a cognitive gift, a way to keep his mind working while giving him some of his self-esteem back instead of closing the door on everything he'd been before.

Make learning happy

We owe it to our dogs to treat them humanely in all areas of their lives, and that includes training them in the kindest way possible. What does that look like? "I use lures and a little bit of science and a whole lot of fun and games," Ian Dunbar tells me.

The long history of aversive, or punishment-based training methods, and the ongoing, evidence-based transition to positive, reward-based strategies among the most highly respected and successful trainers—including the men and women who train military and law enforcement canines—has been well documented. But there's no doubt in my mind that compassionate, respectful teaching methods are better than the alternative, including in their impacts on our dog's physical welfare. A 2020 report by an international team of experts concurs, finding that aversive-based training—especially when used "in high proportions"—is stress inducing (measured chemically and behaviorally) both during and after training. It's also associated with "pessimism" and stress behaviors in dogs asked to perform a cognitive task outside of the training scenario.

As Pat Miller writes in *The Power of Positive Dog Training,* "Dogs just want to get good things and avoid bad things." Punishment isn't necessary to make a behavior "not rewarding." You just have to make the wanted behavior *more* rewarding than the unwanted one. And the formula is quite simple: "You accomplish this by rewarding the behaviors you want and ignoring or preventing those you don't want."

Considerate teaching also requires us to be consistent in what we ask and how we ask it. As McConnell notes in *The Other End of the Leash,* "Almost every dog training book ever written advises dog owners to pick simple commands and use them consistently, and almost every dog owner in the world violates that rule repeatedly." Not only do we repeat; we lob mixed-up commands padded with extra words and expect pups to pick out the single keyword and make sense of it. For example: You've taught your dog "sit," but then you say, "OK, you, time to sit. Come here and sit! Hey goofball, I said sit! Will you just sit down! I said SIT DOWN! GET OVER HERE AND SIT! Damn it, SIT YOUR BUTT DOWN!" How is even a very good boy supposed to know what to do?

Here are a few quick tips for smart training from the experts:

Use the dog's name first, then give the single word command, in that order. The name lets the dog know to pay attention. The command tells him what you want him to do. Period. No repeating. (It's hard!) Eryka Kahunanui, a former Army K-9 handler, suggests that we can suppress our primate compulsion to chatter by singing the alphabet song silently to ourselves after speaking the command word in a training session. "Depending on your tempo," she says, "it takes 10 to 15 seconds to get through the song. That's not an unreasonable amount of time to give a member of another species to hear and understand an instruction, and to decide how to carry it out."

Next, be aware of yet another way we constantly sabotage our own efforts to manage our dogs' behavior: ignoring the fact that dogs, with their social animal instincts, naturally join in when they hear a member of their group vocalizing. So even if the word we're barking out is "Quiet!" our louder and louder yapping only encourages more noise in response. Anyone with a husky or other howler knows what I mean.

Finally, experts suggest not choosing training words that sound similar but mean different things. (My example: "Sit" is better paired with "go poop" than with another option.) We also love rearranging the order of words we use with our pups, despite the fact that "asking a dog to understand the rules of human grammar is asking for the moon," McConnell writes. Be clear. Be concise. Be consistent. It's not boring. It's kind, and it works.

These are just a few of the ways we confuse our dogs, then wonder why they seem to ignore or disobey or willfully misunderstand what we want. They look for predictable patterns from us, and we can do a better job of providing them. Instant compliance with lousy instruction shouldn't be the defining characteristic of a "good dog." Disobedient dogs aren't dumb, nor are they *trying* to be difficult. Often, they're telling us *we're* not being *clear.*

Who's the smart one now?

Follow the science

"We owe it to dogs to be intellectually curious about their inner lives," Cat Warren said to me recently. I agree wholeheartedly. Though not everyone has the time or inclination to keep up with all the scientific papers coming from the growing amount of dog-cognition research around the world, we know more now than ever before about dogs' thoughts, feelings, and behavior, and that knowledge is useful. It's worth being aware of what scientists are learning about our canine friends, and then weaving relevant insights into our own relationships.

There are more and more opportunities to contribute. When scientists at the University of Massachusetts were collecting data for their Darwin's Ark project some years ago, I eagerly went online and added Monk's and Geddy's information to the mix. Now that papers are coming out assessing the piles of data they collected—in part to consider the role of genetics in behaviors we think of as breed-specific—it's fun to know that my pups were a tiny part of it. I pointed to results from a few such community science projects earlier in these pages; more are still going on, and others are just getting started. Many require in-person (and in-dog) appearances, but others only call for online surveys. Think about getting involved.

Research results can feel abstract and highly technical, of course, but they can also offer very quick-and-easy practical applications. For example, several studies document a reduction in stress markers in dogs when they are exposed to familiar humans. So a pup seeing or smelling his or her person "in a sense gets a blip of Xanax, a moment of calm," notes aggressive-dog researcher Jim Crosby. "So if I'm working with a dog who trusts me but who is anxious or distracted, I know if I get her to look at me, I'm giving her a burst of neurochemicals that might help her through a tough situation." The right kind of intervention, he says, "gives a neurochemical advantage that you can use to address stress or even change bad behaviors."

Consider, too, that knowing something about the science of dog cognition and behavior can help us problem-solve at home when pup-related mysteries arise.

Understanding Odin

Let's return to that very special canine friend of mine, Odin the mountain cur. Yet again, he provided unique insight into how we can be smarter partners to our differently smart pups.

Just after Halloween 2022, Odin started chewing holes in blankets. First, he shredded part of a treasured quilt that always sat on top of Margaret and Trevor's bed. Margaret made him get off the bed, told him no, and gave him a bone to distract him. The next morning, as she cooked breakfast, he was back at it—bone abandoned outside, quilt balled up between his paws. Margaret made him get down again, and this time she took the quilt away. Next morning, he went to work on the next layer of bedding, a white cotton blanket. More holes.

This was new behavior for Odin. He's not a destructive dog and had never chewed on household items before. But there he was, gnawing away.

Knowing I was writing about dogs, and that I have a special love for Odin, Margaret texted to ask what I thought about this behavior. It seemed to me to be a stress response. He was likely self-soothing with the kneading and chewing. So, what was going on in their lives that might have upset him?

It turns out he'd hurt his paw on Halloween night. The slice across his pad had required a trip to the vet, with antibiotics and pain meds prescribed. The blanket chewing started soon after. So, that seemed like a reasonable explanation—pain, vet trip, drugs, reduced activity during recovery. Stressful! Except oddly, even after the paw was healed and he was fully active again, Odin kept chewing. So, was there anything else? Anything at all?

It turns out, yes. Margaret had neglected to mention one major change in their household: *She was pregnant.* She'd just found out, and the timing of Odin's compulsive behavior coincided with the probable start of this new development.

I loved this new plot twist. Maybe Odin could smell a change in Margaret and had taken to a Margaret-smelling item to work out his feelings about it. Because Margaret didn't know she was pregnant until after the behavior started, we couldn't blame some outward excitement or stress behavior on her part for tipping him off. It had to be something else. Olfactory intelligence seemed likely.

We wanted a more expert perspective, though, so I turned to Mark Spivak, the Atlanta trainer and dog behaviorist you met earlier. Spivak has a broad knowledge of current cognitive, behavioral, and veterinary research. We laid out the case. He asked for many specific details about the timing of events, the medications Odin had taken, who had lain on the blanket, whether under or atop, whether Odin is closer to Margaret than to Trevor, and so on. The man is very thorough.

His analysis was that the new behavior likely stemmed from several factors working together. The injury and subsequent low-activity period, the medications, and the pregnancy—each can cause stress on its own, but combined they would be especially powerful, disrupting Odin's sense of security enough to prompt an obsessive-compulsive behavior. And yes, as the blankets carried Margaret's scent, and Margaret is definitely Odin's favorite (sorry, Trevor), the dog may have chosen that bedding in particular as especially comforting.

As for the pregnancy's contribution, though Spivak knows of no peer-reviewed studies to prove it, he agrees scent was the likely factor. "There are multiple anecdotal reports of dogs undergoing behavioral changes, which include chewing behavior, coinciding with the first trimester pregnancy of a female owner," he wrote in an email. "The likelihood of a dog possessing the ability to detect hormonal, human volatilome changes associated with pregnancy is very high." That would also help explain why, once the paw healed, Odin didn't stop chewing: Margaret's body was still sending out pregnancy signals. Plus, "compulsive chewing may release dopamine, which provides a sensation of pleasure and reward that increases the probability of the act habitually and addictively recurring," wrote Spivak. In other words, Odin had a new drug.

The trainer offered various strategies to get Odin to kick the habit. In keeping with the idea that nurturing dogs' natural intelligences is essential to their health and happiness, Spivak recommended, first, increased exercise and sessions of cognitive training to keep the pup's body and mind active. Also on the list was interrupting the behavior, giving Odin acceptable items to chew and praising his use of them, and, if needed, enlisting various holistic calming strategies and products. Sedating medication would be very much a last resort.

A few weeks on, with Margaret giving him lots of extra attention, walks, and other distractions, and blocking his access to the bedroom, Odin was less interested in blankets but had turned to compulsively licking his own body, creating hot spots. The original injury had long since healed; the pregnancy continued. It certainly seemed that Margaret's new hormonal state was the trigger for Odin, who was communicating his angst in a very doggy way. Of course, the more he licked, the more Margaret fretted about him, which he could no doubt sense. So he licked some more. Vicious cycle. Efforts to ease the anxiety continued. As a different species trying to speak dog language and read dog emotions, sometimes it takes time, and many tries, for us to find the right answer.

Dogs aren't automatons where one cause equals one effect, any more than human beings are. Sometimes we may wish they were—it would sure make the job of caring for them easier. But a dog's experience is complex, and it takes being dog smart, and patient, to see how each piece fits the puzzle (and even what those pieces are). If we take too simplistic an approach to a problem, we are likely to miss the mark in our response. And though it may take diverse minds to truly understand our canine friends—including cognitive, behavioral, and veterinary experts, to name just a few contributors—it all comes down to the one-on-one relationship between human and dog.

How closely each of us pays attention to the details in our own pets' lives truly matters if we are to act in an informed and dog-forward way. The more dog smart the human, the more dog smart our answers to our pups' needs and desires, and the better the outcome down the line. For all of us.

CHAPTER SEVENTEEN

LETTING OUR DOGS BE DOGS

C at Warren is serious about her cadaver dogs. Over the years she
has meticulously trained her pups to find the dead, working with
them daily, asking them to bring their extraordinary olfactory intelligence
to bear when they're needed to help humans solve some of our most
heartbreaking problems.

But when their services aren't required by our species, Warren offers
them opportunities to indulge in more dog-driven activities. "I really try
to give them time when I'm not asking them to *do* anything," she says.
What she calls decompression walks, for example, are long off-leash
outings during which the pups can wander and sniff and play on their
own terms, monitored for their safety but otherwise minimally managed.
"Any parent with an adventurous child knows that feeling of being a little
bit fearful," she says, "but these are the experiences that let them develop.
Dogs deserve that same chance," employing the tools unique to their
species that let them develop fully as the animals they are.

Not all of us have a place where our dogs can run completely free, but

243

there are many ways to let dogs be dogs. "Even silly things like letting my dogs open the Chewy box when it comes, and letting them tear it apart when it's empty—there's something deep in their canine soul that finds this enormously satisfying," she says.

So, never mind the mess. Because no matter how well we treat them, their *dog* lives are constrained because of their roles as our companions and pets. "By making them adapt to our world and ignoring their point of view, we've stunted their cognitive growth," Warren says. "We owe them these moments of cognitive joy."

What we owe our dogs—and how to ensure that they have a good life not just as our pets but also as autonomous creatures—has been on my mind of late. Because we ask them to give up a lot of themselves, don't we? To be our very good boys and girls, we ask dogs to stop sniffing, drooling, chewing, barking, marking, and humping. We expect them to learn human manners. We expect them to fight their natural urges and ignore other dogs or prey animals or squealing children, and not be protective or guard resources, despite their every natural impulse.

We ask hunting dogs to chase and retrieve, but not to kill or eat, herding dogs just to chase. The war dog must ignore sounds, sights, and smells that could drive any living thing to terror and flight. Assistance dogs must work on command and focus fully on the needs of a single person they did not choose. Therapy dogs are asked to absorb stress and sadness and stay still for long stretches, to accept overzealous hugs, erratic behavior, and pulled tails. We demand a level of self-control in all of our working dogs that goes beyond what we'd ask of any child—and many adults— often requiring them to shove instincts that have helped them survive for millennia *waaaaay* down inside.

Can we be more mindful of all that we ask and all that we take away? Doing better by our dogs doesn't require upending the dynamics of the human-dog relationship—we will undoubtedly remain in charge, and we will always expect them to adapt to whatever we throw at them. But it's not hard to give the animals back something of themselves, to put more woof into their everyday. I think we owe them that much. We can give them a meaningful life that suits the beings they are, not just the beings they become as our companions. We can give them access to experiences relevant to their dogness.

Prime among those characteristics, as we've learned, is the brilliance of the canine nose. So first, make sure your pup has plenty of opportunities to deploy her olfactory superpower.

Let them sniff

Did you know that sniffing boosts a dog's optimism? When allowed to play smell-finding games versus heeling exercises, the animals in a 2019 study by Alexandra Horowitz became more optimistic over time, as quantified by cognitive testing before and after a week of activities.

Why? Sniffing lets them explore freely. It lets them do what they do best, tapping into their own best language. Horowitz told me that her findings were "consistent with the notion that olfaction is important to their welfare. That it gives them the chance to think about and do something more ecologically relevant to dogs."

That's one reason to give our dogs time to sniff. Also, it helps to remember just how much information about other dogs—and other local species—they pick up through the nose. Letting them sniff is letting them socialize. Do you chat with your neighbors when you're out walking? Notice who bought a new car or who hasn't taken down their holiday lights? Dogs like to do the same, through the nose. When we pull our dogs away, we're refusing them access to the neighborhood news. I could certainly give my pups more time at their favorite task. I aim to fight the urge to yank them away.

That said, when my dogs want to *roll* in smelly things, it's harder to say OK. Why they do it is a bit of a mystery. It may be a holdover from wilder evolutionary times, an attempt at camouflage or intra- or interspecies communication. Whether or not such an ancient trait is useful to a homed dog, it remains a natural inclination. So maybe once in a while, it's not so awful to let 'em roll and stew in it for a bit. Hold off on the hose for as long as you can. "Love of the putrid is inherent in canines," Warren writes in *What the Dog Knows*. For the most part it's against *our* nature to root around in stink, but why should we deprive dogs of something that's such an important part of their nature?

This goes for eating "gross" stuff, too. Although I get why we intervene (and wonder if their smarts are offline) when they go for it, even eating poop (technically called coprophagia) can be healthy for dogs. The feces may act as a probiotic, contributing bacteria to the pup's gut microbiome, according to veterinarian Ian Billinghurst. As scavengers, dogs "receive valuable nutrients from materials that we humans find totally repugnant … like vomit, feces, and decaying flesh," he writes.

Now, I would never call you out for grabbing a cat turd or a squirrel carcass out of your dog's mouth or stopping him from licking up his own vomit—especially if he shares your bed. (I mean, there's morning breath and then there's MORNING BREATH.) The point is, the seemingly icky things dogs do aren't signs of stupidity nor are they even weird for a nonhuman animal. The behaviors are often purposeful. Even intelligent? Perhaps.

But it's asking a lot of humans to change our attitude about coprophagia. Maybe letting dogs be dogs has its limits, and this is one of them. I can live with that.

Let them play with others

It's been a while since I took Monk to a dog park, but I'm thinking it's time to get back there. Although not *all* dogs are a good fit for these pup parties (Geddy is never invited, because he's an asshole), Monk seems to really enjoy sizing up and then romping and wrestling with strangers; I love seeing him get some of his wild energy out among his own kind.

Because dogs are social beings, finding ways to ensure that they have social interactions is part of our commitment to them. And that means exercising their social intelligence not just with us but also with other dogs, if possible. Not everyone can have multiple dogs, or even multiple pets that get along safely and happily. But it's a good thing for those who have the option to let dogs be dogs among dogs—or, in a pinch, among goats, cats, or whatever other animal is at hand.

Let them choose

"If I could identify the single most significant problem facing homed dogs right now, it would be lack of adequate agency," writes bioethicist Jessica Pierce in a *Psychology Today* article. Lacking that sense of control, she argues, "has significant fallout for their physical and especially their psychological well-being."

More and more trainers and owners seem to be addressing the agency issue, bringing choice into the mix—and I love it. For me, giving my dogs choice is as simple as letting them set the pace, the direction, and the duration of a walk (within reason); making real use of a long leash and extreme patience when it's safe to do so; letting them take some time interacting with the environment around them; pulling less, scolding less. Small stuff, but important nonetheless.

Giving dogs the option to train at a particular time is another promising trend. "If he's not showing interest in the game, I stop and try again later," trainer Vidhyalakshmi Karthikeyan tells me about working with her dog, Beanie, on math and reading games. Others say the same, whether training basic behaviors or those done just for fun.

Consider their experience

Looking at the world we share through our dogs' eyes is something we should do more often. For example, Australian trainer Shannon Carroll has observed detailed ways dogs may be hypersensitive to sensory input, with some having a canine form of ADHD; others have symptoms of autism. All of these can affect their ability to process cues and to stay on task, to enjoy learning and to effectively problem-solve. Though we can't always know exactly what our dog is experiencing, it pays to be aware that something beneath the surface—a personality trait, an anxiety disorder, even just a gassy gut—might be interfering with the animal being all he can be.

Keeping your dog's sensory experiences in mind can help you create a more comfortable environment for him. Remember, dogs live by the nose. And some smells are known to repel dogs, even causing physical irritation and discomfort. They include citrus, vinegar, chili pepper, rubbing alcohol, nail polish, and chlorine; I'm sure there are many more. And we all know dogs who are distressed by loud noises, like fireworks, thunder, lightning—even the vacuum cleaner or the heat pump cycling on. Though we can't control public celebrations or the weather, it pays to know your dog's particular triggers and do what you can to dampen their effects.

Know your breed's tendencies

If you have a purebred dog or a mix whose genetic makeup is clear, being aware of how he might express his genetic leanings can be useful. Yes, your border collie has the urge to herd and maybe nip ankles. Yes, your rat terrier mix will likely hunt the rodent living under your deck. Yes, your Jindo is going to go after that rabbit.

Although DNA doesn't make promises, and breed stereotypes are much more loosey-goosey than previously thought, genes are important shapers of behavior. "DNA is powerful, and it's important to know your breed and what tendencies it might bring," says Lucia Lazarowski, a cognitive and behavioral scientist who works with detection dogs at Auburn University. "And it's important not to fault dogs for doing what's tied to breed. It may be unwanted behavior, but they're not bad dogs; they just need a different outlet. Speak their language, find them the world they belong in, and join them there."

Sara Carson, whose high-flying Super Collies' DNA no doubt shapes their need for full-on physical activity and play every day, points out that knowing a breed's inclinations *before* you choose a pet is essential. "If you don't like to do the things that kind of dog is likely to enjoy, don't get that dog," she says. And if you already have him? Just throw the ball. THROW THE BALL.

Know your dog as an individual

DNA is just one component of your dog's makeup. It's never nature versus nurture—it's always both. Plus, there is no "the dog," as I pointed out earlier in this book. Each of the billion-ish canines on the planet has needs, desires, joys, and fears. Like us, every dog is a mixed bag of genes and environment and experience, plus a pinch of this and a dash of that. What's most important is to know your particular dog and his individual temperament and preferences. And then try to take them to heart.

Something as simple as finding the "right" kind of play for an individual dog is important, says Horowitz. "Some like rough and tumble, some prefer a toy, some enjoy other dogs. You have to learn your own dog's personality and preferences so you can set up a world more suited to that individual."

I've paid attention to Monk, for example, in all aspects of his behavior. I know he's terrified of storms, fireworks, gunshots, flashing lights, and the sudden quiet of a power outage, and he needs me to have a hand on him while he suffers through these disasters. Hugs are OK during these episodes; at other times he might stiffen up or shrug me off if I try to cuddle. He needs to run, full throttle, at least every other day, or he's likely to get a little destructive. Chasing him during his zoomies makes him very happy. He will reliably grab a shoe and prance around with it when he has to poop. He doesn't mind kids, but after a quick lick to assess the flavor of their sticky faces, he's pretty much done with them. He is relentlessly cheerful, other than when he's afraid, so when he's not upbeat, something is amiss. And so on.

These are not breed characteristics, nor traits he seems to share with his Kai Ken parents or littermates. This is just Monk. When I keep all this in mind, I do better by him as a result.

It's very give-and-take, our relationship with our dogs. But when it comes to giving them a good and dog-relevant life that nurtures their multiple intelligences, we humans could stand to take less and give more. In all the roles they play, dogs deserve our appreciation, our intellectual curiosity, and our commitment to their physical and cognitive well-being. That means acknowledging their experience of the world as different from ours, and doing all we can to ensure that experience is not just humane but dog-friendly; when possible dog-centric; and always dog-enhancing.

Odin, uninterrupted

Moraine Beach is a narrow band of sand and rocks at the base of a ravine on Lake Michigan in Highland Park, Illinois. On a cold and cloudy January afternoon, wave action made it feel like the ocean, though the smell gave it away as fresh water instead of sea. Odin is used to being off leash on trails when he goes hiking with his people, and he is allowed to run free at Moraine.

Nothing is quite as heady as watching a very good boy realize that he is free and seize the moment. Unhooked from his leash when we arrived at the water's edge, Odin paused, looked at Margaret and me, and then took off. Briefly his head was down, his tail wagging as he trotted around nosing the washed-up flotsam. But soon he hit the packed sand with a new stride—ears back, big grin into the wind, grit and lake foam flying out from under his feet.

He leaped a tumbledown pier, then a concrete barrier, landed on the next beach over, then zoomed up a steep hill. At the top, silhouetted against the gray sky, he ran along the edge of the bluff, then headed back down, side-sliding in the slippery leaf litter and righting himself near the bottom. Back on the beach, he tiptoed over a pile of boulders—knowing an ankle breaker when he saw it—before kicking back into high gear, vaulting another barrier and continuing his adventure. We watched him get smaller and smaller until he veered into the woods again and disappeared.

We called his name, half-heartedly. Now and then we'd spy movement between trees as he looped around not exactly making his way back. We didn't panic: Odin was in dog mode, but he knew where he was, and where we were, and that we expected his return. He is smart that way.

Finally, he reappeared *way* down the beach and began his full-on sprint back. Again with the goofy grin, flattened ears, racing-dog grace, muscles rippling as he flew, showing off the full expression of his body in space. The scent of his muck-caked paws and lake foam dripping from his belly reached us before he arrived. Oh yes, he stank. But who cared? Odin didn't. Even we didn't.

The exhilaration of the entire scene grabbed me and shook away my weariness. This was what it meant to be dog smart as a human—to let your dog be a dog to the utmost. In those moments, there's no question Odin knew what he was and how to be happy in his skin. He skidded to a stop before Margaret, accepted her praise for (sort of) obeying, and then sprawled out at her feet, tongue hanging low, saliva dripping in the sand. He was filthy and wet, he reeked of dead fish and algal slop, and he was as content as I'd ever seen him.

Every dog deserves time to be a total canine, whatever that looks like for the individual and whatever extra scrubbing it might mean for that animal's caregiver. For Odin, putting his all into his physical being, his kinesthetic intelligence on full display, was clearly *his* happy thing—a way to work his doggiest abilities to the max. And the bath when we got home? Despite plenty of side eye from him as we lathered him up and rinsed him down, I'm confident he would agree even that was worth it.

I'll end with this: When we let our dogs express their dogness however they choose, using whatever aspect of intelligence they tap in to, it feels so, so good to give back that freedom and power—and to witness their brilliance, the perfect manifestation of joy.

CATCHING UP WITH JESSE

Some months after my special experience with guide dog Jesse in New York, I decide to follow up and see how she's faring. When I reach out to The Seeing Eye to ask, I am thrilled to learn that not only did she excel at the rest of her training, but she is also now with a new owner in Florida, and things are going brilliantly.

When she was seven years old, Janette Noe, who manages collections and digital resources for Florida's Martin County Library system, was diagnosed with retinitis pigmentosa. The degenerative eye condition has taken much of her vision in the last two decades, leaving her with a line of sight "like looking through a paper towel tube," she tells me. "I see just enough to get me into serious trouble on my own!"

For years she denied her struggles, but finally, tired of bumped elbows and bruised shins, she opened herself up in 2014 to various assistive devices, computer technologies, and the iconic white cane. "They all have their place," she says. "For a time the cane was my godsend." But as an animal lover, she realized that a guide dog would offer her so much more than just a tool for managing day-to-day. "I wanted something to pour my trust and love into, something that gives back in a way no artificial intelligence ever could."

She and Jesse got together in January 2022, their pairing based on a long list of factors The Seeing Eye staff considered. Noe gets a little emotional talking about their initial meeting, with Jesse "sitting like a tiny statue in the hall" waiting to be introduced, followed by her "soft, gentle, wiggly greeting. She has a very welcoming way about her that I love." Unlike her previous pup, Annie, also from The Seeing Eye, who was "all serious business when the harness came out, Jesse wiggles the whole time. She's such a happy girl."

Jesse's smarts on the job were evident right off, and she impresses Noe daily with her thoughtful assessments of the path ahead (no matter how much of an obstacle course), as well as with her gentle maneuvering to keep Noe safe. "I feel her take a moment to analyze her options," Noe says.

With practice, their partnership is becoming more and more seamless. The pair chews up the miles on foot, and having the dog not only encourages more social interaction than the cane did, but the relationship also gives Noe confidence the cane just couldn't provide, especially in a crowded city. "With Jesse I am really free to pay attention to what I'm able to see, and to the sounds, the smells, good and bad," she says. "When we go to New York City, we move easily through malls and into stores, but there's nothing more fun than to walk staring up at the buildings, listening to all the people speaking different languages, to feel the culture of the city. And I can do that with Jesse, trusting her to navigate the crowded sidewalks. I can focus on the skyline ahead and know I'm safe."

Recognizing the inevitable deterioration of the vision she has left, Noe has a "bucket list of things I want to see while I still can," she says. Together they've been exploring U.S. cities. And wherever they go, "my husband documents the journey from behind us, taking pictures of Jesse and me heading across the bridge or the street toward the next thing. It shows us on our way, moving forward." I love that image so much—the two of them as partners, thinking as one, unstoppable.

And of course, there's the emotional connection. Jesse sleeps with her head under Noe's chin or tucked up against her legs. She reads Noe's moods and gives her love at all the right times. Plus, there are morning kisses, "a lovely way to start the day."

So. Jesse turns out to be one very special, very smart pup.

Not that there was ever a question.

ACKNOWLEDGMENTS

W riting a book about dogs, I met a lot of dogs. I knew it would take plenty of woof to pull this thing off—and the book was the perfect excuse for me to get my dog fix wherever I went. So many dogs! And I loved every encounter. They showed off the most extraordinary canine superpowers and exposed me to a different perspective—a dog's perspective—on what intelligence means and just how smart *Canis familiaris* can be.

I'm forever grateful to all the good boys and girls I met, was told about, and read about along the way, including the demonstrators, history makers, and bed warmers, and especially those who indulged my inner primate as I neglected the dog smart rules and embraced them with open arms. With apologies for any omissions, I offer remote belly scratches in thanks to Jesse, Luna, Roger, Monty, Griffin, Fletch, Shiraz, Wick, Lorna, Warrior, Bunny, Chaser, Stella, Hawkeye, Marvel, Coral, Beanie, Bonnie, Arlo, Moxie, Ozzie, Cash, Rikki, Sharon, Manny, Tibet, Atlas, Jasper, Casey, Socha, Eba, Tucker, Zeus, Selma, Jumbo, Kozak, Darwin, Angie, Tangle, Daisy, McKenzie, Callie, Armstrong, Danielle, Mack, Charity, Alepo, Zern, Shugga, Mia, Bendy, Bubba, Hudson, Bailey, FLA Highway Stray, the Hero Dogs trainees, Prudence, Caspian, Forrest, Green Bean, Bruce, Midas, Tetley, Sam, and Bo.

And of course, special love goes out to my main canid muses: Mr. Ball Dangles, Gretel, Waits, Geddy, Monk, and Odin.

But I don't want to neglect the people behind the pups—the researchers, trainers, handlers, owners, and other friends of dogs—who have turned enthusiastic interest in *Canis familiaris* into a long-term commitment to working with and understanding them. More than a hundred people made time to answer my interview questions, and dozens more allowed me to visit them and observe their work firsthand. You've heard many of their voices in these pages. Regardless of who was or wasn't quoted, all those connections proved not only exceedingly helpful to the book content, but also wonderfully meaningful on a personal note. I met my heroes. I made new friends.

My sources' dog-forward attitudes and trailblazing work were only part of it: Their generosity as human beings impressed me the most. Whether hosting my field research trips both on land and at sea, sharing incredibly personal stories about the dogs they love who love them back, or battling technical glitches to answer endless questions on Zoom, people exceeded my expectations at every turn.

Quick demonstrations turned into full-afternoon hands-on adventures, followed by dinner (and, once, bubble tea). I'd sit down with one source and walk away with a list of three more people to talk to; a lab visit meant access to a full team of enthusiastic interviewees. People made detailed arrangements for me to see and do things not easily seen and done. People said yes to me sitting in on conferences; observing competitions, classes, and workshops; and following them (and their dogs) for hours—peppering the humans with questions and the pups with squeaky-voiced praise. Those yeses made my job easy.

No less generous were those who fed and housed me and loaned me a car or shuttled me here and there during my field reporting around the country. Friends new and old, friends or family of friends, I'm so, so grateful to all of you for making my time away from home so comfortable, fruitful, and fun.

Then there are those whose excellent research and writing laid the foundation for my thinking about animal sentience and intelligence and about how to be the best friends to our dogs we can be. You continue to push our species toward a new appreciation of and better ways of interacting with our nonhuman kin, and I'm right behind you. I've read many of your books and papers and I quoted your words in this text to help support my own. Thank you.

Back at the office: A big thanks to my agent, Alice Martell, who I can always count on for straight talk, bold plans, and a confidence boost, and to my National Geographic editor, Hilary Black, who gave me the push I needed to take on this project, supported my ever shape-shifting approach, and never doubted that I'd pull it off. Thank you both for your confidence and enthusiasm at all the right moments. I'm grateful also to Elisa Gibson and Katie Dance for building a terrific cover that we're all proud of, and associate editor Gabriela Capasso for keeping everything on schedule. Others on the editorial and production teams have my deep appreciation: editorial project manager Ashley Leath, associate production editor Becca Saltzman, proofreader Mary Stephanos, and copy editor Heather McElwain. To the excellent PR team, Ann Day and Alex Serrano, and marketing honcho Daneen Goodwin, thank you for your promotional wisdom, and I look forward to continued work together! Looking ahead, a quick thanks to whomever ends up helping me make a TikTok video, which I'm determined to do despite my advanced age and having exactly three followers.

Lucky writers, like me, have great friends and families to support them along the way. I'm grateful to my posse of gal pals (you know who you are) and my closest kin, including my dear old dad, wise stepdad, enthused brother, wonderful in-laws, and supersmart and creative niece and nephews. To my pup-loving husband, John, thank you for your unwavering confidence, even when I was flailing, and your willingness to hold down the fort while I did my thing. Again.

One final, essential acknowledgment goes to my dear friend and sister wordsmith Lynne Warren, who was my deep-dive research assistant, judicious editor, idea bouncer, thread follower, and late-night cheerleader. Her wisdom is woven through the text. Her repeated advice, *ADD MORE DOG,* is still scrawled on a sticky note taped to my laptop. Without her, *Dog Smart* would be a lesser book, if it existed at all. LW, it's hard to put my thanks into words. And so, if I may: *Aaarroooooo!*

SELECTED
SOURCES

I t's easy to fall down all kinds of rabbit holes doing book research. One conversation leads to another, one link connects to many, a video brings you to two more, and each of those to many more still. The ideas you've encountered in *Dog Smart* have evolved from interviews with dozens of experts, and from collecting and consulting hundreds of other sources, including books, original papers, government reports, doctoral dissertations, newspaper and magazine articles, web pages, video presentations, press releases, course materials—anything that promised genuine insight into the canine experience.

Though much of that material helped shape my thinking, I hope to serve readers best by presenting the most crucial sources for the facts and ideas that appear in these pages, rather than including endless pages of citations. So here you'll find a (still plentiful) list of the books I found particularly enlightening, along with a chapter-by-chapter list of research publications where key observations and analyses were first or most clearly expressed.

For any of the subjects that appear in *Dog Smart*, know that there's a great deal of other valuable material out there, and that the depth and breadth of research on canine cognition is growing all the time. So consider what's offered here—quite a lengthy list despite my attempt to pick and choose—as a good place to start.

SUGGESTED READING AND BIBLIOGRAPHY

Balcombe, Jonathan. *Second Nature: The Inner Lives of Animals.* New York: Palgrave Macmillan, 2011.

Bekoff, Marc. *Canine Confidential: Why Dogs Do What They Do.* University of Chicago Press, 2018.

Bekoff, Marc. *Dogs Demystified: An A-to-Z Guide to All Things Canine.* Novato, CA: New World Library, 2023.

Bekoff, Marc. *The Emotional Lives of Animals: A Leading Scientist Explores Animal Joy, Sorrow, and Empathy—and Why They Matter.* Novato, CA: New World Library, 2008.

Bekoff, Marc, and Jessica Pierce. *Unleashing Your Dog: A Field Guide to Giving Your Canine Companion the Best Life Possible.* Novato, CA: New World Library, 2019.

Berns, Gregory. *How Dogs Love Us: A Neuroscientist and His Adopted Dog Decode the Canine Brain.* Seattle, WA: Lake Union, 2013.

Berns, Gregory. *What It's Like to Be a Dog: And Other Adventures in Animal Neuroscience.* New York: Basic Books, 2017.

Bettinger, Julie Strauss. *Encounters with Rikki: From Hurricane Katrina Rescue to Exceptional Therapy Dog.* Oakland, CA: Inkshares Publishing, 2016.

Billinghurst, Ian. *Give Your Dog a Bone: The Practical Commonsense Way to Feed Dogs for a Long Healthy Life.* Bathurst: Warrigal Publishing, 1993.

Bradshaw, John. *Dog Sense: How the New Science of Dog Behavior Can Make You a Better Friend to Your Pet.* New York: Basic Books, 2011.

Charleson, Susannah. *The Possibility Dogs: What A Handful of "Unadoptables" Taught Me About Service, Hope, and Healing.* Detroit: Wheeler, 2013.

Clothier, Suzanne. *Bones Would Rain from the Sky: Deepening Our Relationships with Dogs.* New York: Grand Central, 2005.

Coppinger, Raymond, and Lorna Coppinger. *What Is a Dog?* University of Chicago Press, 2016.

Coppinger, Raymond, and Mark Feinstein. *How Dogs Work.* University of Chicago Press, 2015.

Coren, Stanley. *How Dogs Think: What the World Looks Like to Them and Why They Act the Way They Do.* New York: Simon & Schuster, 2005.

Coren, Stanley. *How to Speak Dog: Mastering the Art of Dog-Human Communication.* New York: Fireside, 2001.

Coren, Stanley. *The Intelligence of Dogs: A Guide to the Thoughts, Emotions, and Inner Lives of Our Canine Companions.* Rev. ed. New York: Atria, 2006.

Derr, Mark. *How the Dog Became the Dog: From Wolves to Our Best Friends.* New York: Overlook Duckworth, 2013.

de Waal, Frans. *The Age of Empathy: Nature's Lessons for a Kinder Society.* New York: Crown, 2010.

de Waal, Frans. *Are We Smart Enough to Know How Smart Animals Are?* New York: W. W. Norton & Co., 2016.

Dunbar, Ian. *Barking Up the Right Tree: The Science and Practice of Positive Dog Training.* Novato, CA: New World Library, 2023.

Dunbar, Ian. *Before and After Getting Your Puppy: The Positive Approach to Raising a Happy, Healthy and Well-Behaved Dog.* Novato, CA: New World Library, 2004.

Francis, Richard C. *Domesticated: Evolution in a Man-Made World.* New York: W. W. Norton & Co., 2015.

Frankel, Rebecca. *War Dogs: Tales of Canine Heroism, History, and Love.* New York: Palgrave Macmillan, 2014.

Frydenborg, Kay. *A Dog in the Cave: The Wolves Who Made Us Human.* Boston: Houghton Mifflin Harcourt, 2017.

Gardner, Howard. *Frames of Mind: The Theory of Multiple Intelligences.* 3rd ed. New York: Basic Books, 2011.

Goodavage, Maria. *Doctor Dogs: How Our Best Friends Are Becoming Our Best Medicine.* New York: Dutton, 2019.

Goodavage, Maria. *Soldier Dogs: The Untold Story of America's Canine Heroes.* New York: Dutton, 2012.

Grandin, Temple, and Catherine Johnson. *Animals Make Us Human: Creating the Best Life for Animals.* Boston: Houghton Mifflin Harcourt, 2009.

Guest, Claire. *Daisy's Gift: The Remarkable Cancer-Detecting Dog Who Saved My Life.* London: Virgin Books, 2016.

Ha, James C., and Tracy L. Campion. *Dog Behavior: Modern Science and Our Canine Companions.* London: Academic Press, 2019.

Handelman, Barbara. *Canine Behavior: A Photo Illustrated Handbook.* Wenatchee, WA: Dogwise, 2008.

Hare, Brian, and Vanessa Woods. *The Genius of Dogs: How Dogs Are Smarter Than You Think.* New York: Dutton, 2013.

Hare, Brian, and Vanessa Woods. *Survival of the Friendliest: Understanding Our Origins and Rediscovering Our Common Humanity.* New York: Penguin Random House, 2020.

Higgins, Jackie. *Sentient: How Animals Illuminate the Wonder of Our Human Senses.* New York: Atria, 2022.

Hobgood-Oster, Laura. *A Dog's History of the World: Canines and the Domestication of Humans.* Waco, TX: Baylor University Press, 2014.

Holland, Jennifer S. *Unlikely Friendships: Dogs: 37 Stories of Canine Compassion and Courage.* New York: Workman, 2016.

Holland, Jennifer S. *Unlikely Heroes: 37 Inspiring Stories of Courage and Heart from the Animal Kingdom.* New York: Workman, 2014.

Horowitz, Alexandra. *Inside of a Dog: What Dogs See, Smell, and Know.* New York: Scribner, 2010.

Horowitz, Alexandra. *Our Dogs, Ourselves: The Story of a Singular Bond.* New York: Scribner, 2019.

Hunger, Christina. *How Stella Learned to Talk: The Groundbreaking Story of the World's First Talking Dog.* New York: HarperCollins, 2021.

Jennings, Herbert Spencer. *Behavior of the Lower Organisms.* New York: Columbia University Press, 1906.

Jezierski, Tadeusz, John Ensminger, and L. E. Papet, eds. *Canine Olfaction Science and Law: Advances in Forensic Medicine, Conservation, and*

Environmental Remediation. Boca Raton, FL: CRC Press, 2016.

Leaver, Kate. *Good Dog: Celebrating the Dogs Who Change, and Sometimes Even Save, Our Lives.* New York: Harper Collins, 2021.

Lewis, Tim. *Biology of Dogs: From Gonads through Guts to Ganglia.* Wenatchee, WA: Dogwise Publishing, 2020.

Long, Lorie. *A Dog Who's Always Welcome: Assistance and Therapy Dog Trainers Teach You How to Socialize and Train Your Companion Dog.* Hoboken, NJ: Howell Book House, 2008.

McConnell, Patricia. *For the Love of a Dog: Understanding Emotion in You and Your Best Friend.* New York: Ballantine, 2007.

McConnell, Patricia. *The Other End of the Leash: Why We Do What We Do Around Dogs.* New York: Ballantine, 2003.

Miklósi, Ádám. *Dog Behaviour, Evolution, and Cognition.* Oxford University Press, 2007.

Miller, Pat. *Do Over Dogs: Give Your Dog a Second Chance for a First Class Life.* Wenatchee, WA: Dogwise Publishing, 2010.

Miller, Pat. *The Power of Positive Dog Training.* 2nd ed. Hoboken, NJ: Howell Book House, 2008.

Pierce, Jessica. *Run, Spot, Run: The Ethics of Keeping Pets.* University of Chicago Press, 2016.

Pilley, John W., with Hilary Hinzman. *Chaser: Unlocking the Genius of the Dog Who Knows a Thousand Words.* Boston: Mariner Books, 2013.

Powell, Neil. *Search Dogs and Me: One Man and His Life-saving Dogs.* Belfast: Blackstaff Press, 2011.

Pryor, Karen. *Reaching the Animal Mind: Clicker Training and What It Teaches Us About All Animals.* New York: Scribner, 2010.

Ramirez, Ken. *The Eye of the Trainer: Animal Training, Transformation, and Trust.* Boston: Karen Pryor Clicker Training, 2020.

Safina, Carl, *Beyond Words: What Animals Think and Feel.* London: Picador, 2016.

Serpell, James, ed. *The Domestic Dog: Its Evolution, Behavior and Interactions with People.* 2nd ed. Cambridge University Press, 2017.

Shapiro, Beth. *Life as We Made It: How 50,000 Years of Human Innovation Refined—and Redefined—Nature.* New York: Basic Books, 2021.

Shipman, Pat. *Our Oldest Companions: The Story of the First Dogs.* Cambridge, MA: Belknap Press, 2021.

Slobodchikoff, Con. *Chasing Doctor Dolittle: Learning the Language of Animals.* New York: St. Martin's Press, 2012.

Spotte, Stephen. *Societies of Wolves and Free-Ranging Dogs.* Cambridge University Press, 2012.

Todd, Zazie. *Wag: The Science of Making Your Dog Happy.* Vancouver, BC: Greystone Books, 2020.

Van der Kolk, Bessel. *The Body Keeps the Score: Brain, Mind, and Body in the Healing of Trauma.* New York: Penguin Publishing Group, 2015.

von Uexküll, Jakob. *A Foray into the Worlds of Animals and Humans: With a Theory of Meaning.* Translated by Joseph D. O'Neil. Minneapolis: University of Minnesota Press, 2010.

Warren, Cat. *What the Dog Knows: Scent, Science, and the Amazing Ways Dogs Perceive the World.* New York: Touchstone, 2013.

Wohlleben, Peter. *The Inner Life of Animals: Love, Grief, and Compassion—Surprising Observations of a Hidden World.* Translated by Jane Billinghurst. Vancouver, BC: Greystone Books/David Suzuki Institute, 2021.

Wynne, Clive. *Dog Is Love: Why and How Your Dog Loves You.* Boston: Mariner Books, 2019.

Yong, Ed. *An Immense World: How Animal Senses Reveal the Hidden Realms Around Us.* New York: Penguin Random House, 2022.

RESEARCH PUBLICATIONS

CHAPTER 1: WHAT MAKES A DOG A DOG?

Bergström, Anders, David W. G. Stanton, Ulrike H. Taron, Laurent Frantz, Mikkel-Holger S. Sinding, Erik Ersmark et al. "Grey Wolf Genomic

History Reveals a Dual Ancestry of Dogs." *Nature* 607 (2022).

Bray, Emily E., Gitanjali E. Gnanadesikan, Daniel J. Horschler, Kerinne M. Levy, Brenda S. Kennedy, Thomas R. Famula, and Evan L. MacLean. "Early-Emerging and Highly Heritable Sensitivity to Human Communication in Dogs." *Current Biology* 31, no. 14 (2021).

Call, Joseph, Juliane Bräuer, Juliane Kaminski, and Michael Tomasello. "Domestic Dogs *(Canis familiaris)* Are Sensitive to the Attentional State of Humans." *Journal of Comparative Psychology* 117, no. 3 (2003).

Correia-Caeiro, Catia, Kun Guo, and Daniel S. Mills. "Visual Perception of Emotion Cues in Dogs: A Critical Review of Methodologies." *Animal Cognition* 26, no. 3 (June 2023).

Cuaya, Laura V., Raul Hernández-Pérez, and Luis Concha. "Our Faces in the Dog's Brain: Functional Imaging Reveals Temporal Cortex Activation During Perception of Human Faces." *PLoS One* 11, no. 3 (2016).

D'Aniello, Biagio, Gün R. Semin, Alessandra Alterisio, Massimo Aria, and Anna Scandurra. "Interspecies Transmission of Emotional Information via Chemosignals: From Humans to Dogs *(Canis lupus familiaris)*." *Animal Cognition* 21, no. 1 (2018).

Debutte, Bertrand L., and A. Doll. "Do Dogs Understand Human Facial Expressions?" *Journal of Veterinary Behavior* 6, no. 1 (2011).

Frank, Jens, Olof Liberg, and M. Eriksson. "At What Distance Do Wolves Move Away From an Approaching Human?" *Canadian Journal of Zoology* 85, no. 11 (2007).

Grimm, David. "Earliest Evidence for Dog Breeding Found on Remote Siberian Island." *Science,* May 26, 2017. www.science.org/content/article/earliest-evidence-dog-breeding-found-remote-siberian-island.

Guérineau, Cécile, Miina Lõoke, Anna Broseghini, Giulio Dehesh, Paolo Mongillo, and Lieta Marinelli. "Sound Localization Ability in Dogs." *Veterinary Science* 9, no. 11 (2022).

Howell, Tiffani J., Tammie King, and Pauleen C. Bennett. "Puppy Parties and Beyond: The Role of Early Age Socialization Practices on Adult Dog Behavior." *Veterinary Medicine* (Auckland) 6 (April 2015).

Kaminski, Juliane, Andrea Pitsch, and Michael Tomasello. "Dogs Steal in the Dark." *Animal Cognition* 16, no. 3 (2013).

Kaminski, Juliane, Bridget M. Waller, Rui Diogo, Adam Hartstone-Rose, and Anne M. Burrows. "Evolution of Facial Muscle Anatomy in Dogs." *Proceedings of the National Academy of Sciences* 116, no. 29 (June 2019).

Lampe, Michelle, Juliane Bräuer, Juliane Kaminski, and Zsófia Virányi. "The Effects of Domestication and Ontogeny on Cognition in Dogs and Wolves." *Scientific Reports* 7, no. 11690 (2017).

Lazarowski, Lucia, Andie Thompkins, Sarah Krichbaum, L. Paul Waggoner, Gopikrishna Deshpande, and Jeffrey S. Katz. "Comparing Pet and Detection Dogs *(Canis familiaris)* on Two Aspects of Social Cognition." *Learning & Behavior* 48, no. 3 (2020).

Lindblad-Toh, Kerstin, Claire M. Wade, Tarjei S. Mikkelsen, Elinor K. Karlsson, David B. Jaffe, Michael Kamal, Michele Clamp et al. "Genome Sequence, Comparative Analysis and Haplotype Structure of the Domestic Dog." *Nature* 438, no. 7069 (2005).

Lord, Kathryn. "A Comparison of the Sensory Development of Wolves *(Canis lupus lupus)* and Dogs *(Canis lupus familiaris)."* *Ethology* 119, no. 2 (February 2013).

MacLean, Evan L., and Brian Hare. "Dogs Hijack the Human Bonding Pathway: Oxytocin Facilitates Social Connections Between Humans and Dogs." *Science* 348, no. 6232 (April 2015).

Nagasawa, Miho, Shouhei Mitsui, Shiori En, Nobuyo Ohtani, Mitsuaki Ohta, Yasuo Sakuma, Tatsushi Onaka et al. "Oxytocin-Gaze Positive Loop and the Coevolution of Human-Dog Bonds." *Science* 348, no. 6232 (2015).

Nagasawa, Miho, Misato Ogawa, Kazutaka Mogi, and Takefumi Kikusui. "Intranasal Oxytocin Treatment Increases Eye-Gaze Behavior Toward the Owner in Ancient Japanese Dog Breeds." *Frontiers in Psychology* 8, no. 1624 (2017).

Range, Friederike, Sarah Marshall-Pescini, Corinna Kratz, and Zsófia Virányi. "Wolves Lead and Dogs Follow, but They Both Cooperate with Humans." *Scientific Reports* 9, no. 3796 (2019).

Stoeckel, Luke E., Lori S. Palley, Randy L. Gollub, Steven M. Niemi, and Anne E. Evins. "Patterns of Brain Activation When Mothers View Their Own Child and Dog: An fMRI Study." *PLoS One* 9, no. 10 (2014).

Thompkins, Andie M., Lucia Lazarowski, Bhavitha Ramaiahgari, Sai S. R. Gotoor, Paul Waggoner, Thomas S. Denney, Gopikrishna Deshpande, and Jeffrey S. Katz. "Dog-Human Social Relationship: Representation of Human Face Familiarity and Emotions in the Dog Brain." *Animal Cognition* 24, no. 2 (March 2021).

VonHoldt, Bridgett M., Emily Shuldiner, Ilana Janowitz Koch, Rebecca Y. Kartzinel, Andrew Hogan, Lauren Brubaker, Shelby Wanser et al. "Structural Variants in Genes Associated With Human Williams-Beuren Syndrome Underlie Stereotypical Hypersociability in Domestic Dogs." *Science Advances* 3, no. 7 (2017).

Wynne, Clive D. L. "The Indispensable Dog." *Frontiers in Psychology* 12, no. 656529 (2021).

CHAPTER 2: DOG SMART SCIENCE

Berns, Gregory S., Andrew M. Brooks, and Mark Spivak. "Scent of the Familiar: An fMRI Study of Canine Brain Responses to Familiar and Unfamiliar Human and Dog Odors." *Behavioral Processes* 110 (2015).

Hare, Brian, and Michael Tomasello. "Human-Like Social Skills in Dogs?" *Trends in Cognitive Science* 9, no. 9 (2005).

Karl, Sabrina, Magdalena Boch, Anna Zamansky, Dirk van der Linden, Isabella C. Wagner, Christoph J. Völter, Claus Lamm, and Ludwig Huber. "Exploring the Dog-Human Relationship by Combining fMRI, Eye-Tracking and Behavioural Measures." *Scientific Reports* 10, no. 22273 (2020).

Salomons, Hannah, Kyle C. M. Smith, Megan Callahan-Beckel, Margaret Callahan, Kerinne Levy, Brenda S. Kennedy, Emily E. Bray et al.

"Cooperative Communication with Humans Evolved to Emerge Early in Domestic Dogs." *Current Biology* 31, no. 14 (2021).

Soproni, Krisztina, Ádám Miklósi, József Topál, and Vilmos Csányi. "Dogs' *(Canis familiaris)* Responsiveness to Human Pointing Gestures." *Journal of Comparative Psychology* 116, no. 1 (March 2002).

Willgohs, Kaitlyn Rose, Jenna Williams, Elaina Franklin, and Lauren E. Highfill. "The Creative Canine: Investigating the Concept of Creativity in Dogs *(Canis lupus familiaris)* Using Citizen Science." *International Journal of Comparative Psychology* 35 (2022).

CHAPTER 3: HOW SMART DOGS GET SMARTER

Aulet, Lauren S., Veronica C. Chiu, Ashley Prichard, Mark Spivak, Stella F. Lourenco, and Gregory S. Berns. "Canine Sense of Quantity: Evidence for Numerical Ratio-Dependent Activation in Parietotemporal Cortex." *Biology Letters* 15, no. 12 (2019).

Berghänel, Andreas, Martina Lazzaroni, Giulia Cimarelli, Sarah Marshall-Pescini, and Friederike Range. "Cooperation and Cognition in Wild Canids." *Current Opinion in Behavioral Sciences* 46 (August 2022).

Berns, Gregory S., Andrew M. Brooks, Mark Spivak, and Kerinne Levy. "Functional MRI in Awake Dogs Predicts Suitability for Assistance Work." *Scientific Reports* 7, no. 43704 (March 2017).

Cassella, Carly. "This Single-Celled Animal Makes Complex 'Decisions' Even Without a Nervous System." *Science Alert* (December 4, 2019).

Catania, A. Charles, and Terje Sagvolden. "Preference for Free Choice Over Forced Choice in Pigeons." *Journal of the Experimental Analysis of Behavior* 34, no. 1 (July 1980).

Cook, Peter F., Ashley Prichard, Mark Spivak, and Gregory S. Berns. "Awake Canine fMRI Predicts Dogs' Preference for Praise *vs* Food." *Social Cognitive and Affective Neuroscience* 11, no. 12 (December 2016).

Dexter, Joseph P., Sudhakaran Prabakaran, and Jeremy Gunawardena. "A Complex Hierarchy of Avoidance Behaviors in a Single-Cell

Eukaryote." *Current Biology* 29, no. 24 (December 2019).

Frazer, Jennifer. "Can a Cell Make Decisions?" *Scientific American,* May 22, 2021.

Fugazza, Claudia, and Ádám Miklósi. "The 'Do as I Do' as a New Method for Studying Imitation in Dogs: Is the Dog a Copycat?" *Dog Behavior* 3, no. 3 (December 2017).

Fugazza, Claudia, and Ádám Miklósi. "Social Learning in Dog Training: The Effectiveness of the Do as I Do Method Compared to Shaping/Clicker Training." *Applied Animal Behaviour Science* 171 (2015).

Fugazza, Claudia, Alexandra Moesta, Ákos Pogány, and Ádám Miklósi. "Social Learning From Conspecifics and Humans in Dog Puppies." *Scientific Reports* 8, no. 9257 (2018).

Fugazza, Claudia, Ákos Pogány, and Ádám Miklósi. "Spatial Generalization of Imitation in Dogs *(Canis familiaris)."* *Journal of Comparative Psychology* 130, no. 3 (August 2016).

Hare, Brian, Michelle Brown, Christina Williamson, and Michael Tomasello. "The Domestication of Social Cognition in Dogs." *Science* 298, no. 5598 (2002).

Jia, Hao, Oleg M. Pustovyy, Paul Waggoner, Ronald J. Beyers, John Schumacher, Chester Wildey, Jay Barrett et al. "Functional MRI of the Olfactory System in Conscious Dogs." *PLoS One* 9, no. 1 (January 2014).

Karthikeyan, Vidhyalakshmi. "The Layer Cake Approach: What Are Complex Behaviors Made Of?" The Lemonade Conference, May 7–9, 2021. thelemonadeconference.com/wp-content/uploads/2021/05/TLC-2021-Schedule.pdf.

MacNulty, Daniel R., Aimee Tallian, Daniel R. Stahler, and Douglas W. Smith. "Influence of Group Size on the Success of Wolves Hunting Bison." *PLoS One* 9, no. 11 (November 2014).

MacPherson, Krista, and William A. Roberts. "Can Dogs Count?" *Learning and Motivation* 44, no. 4 (2013).

Nieder, Andreas. "The Adaptive Value of Numerical Competence." *Trends in Ecology & Evolution* 35, no. 7 (2020).

Prichard, Ashley, Peter F. Cook, Mark Spivak, Raveena Chhibber, and Gregory S. Berns. "Awake fMRI Reveals Brain Regions for Novel Word Detection in Dogs." *Frontiers in Neuroscience* 12 (October 2018).

Range, Friederike, Zsófia Viranyi, and Ludwig Huber. "Selective Imitation in Domestic Dogs." *Current Biology* 17, no. 10 (May 2007).

CHAPTER 4: WHEN LEARNING MATTERS MOST

Bray, Emily. "Making the Grade: Development of Cognition and Temperament in Assistance Dogs." Assistance Dogs International (ADI) Virtual Conference, September 12–15, 2021. assistancedogsinternational.org/about/2021-adi-conference.

DeChant, Mallory T., Cameron Ford, and Nathaniel Hall. "Effect of Handler Knowledge of the Detection Task on Canine Search Behavior and Performance." *Frontiers in Veterinary Science* 7, no. 250 (May 2020).

Hall, Nathaniel J., Angie M. Johnston, Emily E. Bray, Cynthia M. Otto, Evan L. MacLean, and Monique A. R. Udell. "Working Dog Training for the Twenty-First Century." *Frontiers in Veterinary Science* 8, no. 646022 (July 2021).

Kaste, Martin. "Eliminating Police Bias When Handling Drug-Sniffing Dogs." National Public Radio, November 20, 2017. www.npr.org/2017/11/20/563889510/preventing-police-bias-when-handling-dogs-that-bite.

Lit, Lisa. "Handler Beliefs Affect Scent Detection Dog Outcomes." *Animal Cognition* 14, no. 3 (May 2011).

CHAPTER 5: WALKING TOGETHER IN DIFFERENT WORLDS

Andrews, Erica F., Raluca Pascalau, Alexandra Horowitz, Gillian M. Lawrence, and Philippa J. Johnson. "Extensive Connections of the Canine Olfactory Pathway Revealed by Tractography and Dissection." *Journal of Neuroscience* 42, no. 33 (August 2022).

Bálint, Anna, Attila Andics, Márta Gácsi, Anna Gábor, Kálmán Czeibert, Chelsey M. Luce, Ádám Miklósi et al. "Dogs Can Sense Weak Thermal Radiation." *Science Reports* 10, no. 3736 (February 2020).

Benediktová, Kateřina, Jana Adámková, Jan Svoboda, Michael Scott Painter, Luděk Bartoš, Petra Nováková, Lucie Vynikalová et al. "Magnetic Alignment Enhances Homing Efficiency of Hunting Dogs," *eLife* 9 (June 2020).

Byosiere, Sarah-Elizabeth, Philippe A. Chouinard, Tiffani J. Howell, and Pauline C. Bennett. "What Do Dogs *(Canis familiaris)* See? A Review of Vision in Dogs and Implications for Cognition Research." *Psychonomic Bulletin and Review* 25, no. 5 (October 2018).

Coren, Stanley. "How Good Is Your Dog's Sense of Taste?" *Canine Corner* (blog), *Psychology Today,* April 19, 2011. www.psychologytoday.com/us/blog/canine-corner/201104/how-good-is-your-dogs-sense-taste.

Gibbs, Matthew, Marcel Winnig, Irene Riva, Nicola Dunlop, Daniel Waller, Boris Klebansky, Darren W. Logan et al. "Bitter Taste Sensitivity in Domestic Dogs *(Canis familiaris)* and Its Relevance to Bitter Deterrents of Ingestion." *PLoS One* 17, no. 11 (November 2022).

Hall, Nathaniel J., Franck Péron, Stéphanie Cambou, Laurence Callejon, and Clive D. L. Wynne. "Food and Food-Odor Preferences in Dogs: A Pilot Study," *Chemical Senses* 42, no. 4 (May 2017).

Nahm, Michael. "Mysterious Ways: The Riddle of the Homing Ability in Dogs and Other Vertebrates." *Journal of the Society for Psychical Research* 79, no. 920 (May 2019).

Sexton, Courtney. "How Do Dogs Find Their Way Home? They Might Sense Earth's Magnetic Field." *Smithsonian,* July 27, 2020. www.smithsonianmag.com/smart-news/how-did-lassie-find-timmy-all-those-times-it-may-have-been-magnetic-180975414.

CHAPTER 6: NOSE SMART

Aviles-Rosa, Edgar O., Gordon McGuinness, and Nathaniel J. Hall. "Case Study: An Evaluation of Detection Dog Generalization to a Large Quantity of an Unknown Explosive in the Field." *Animals* (Basel) 11, no. 5 (May 2021).

Bainbridge, David. "The Anatomy of the Canine Nose." In *Canine Olfaction Science and Law,* edited by Tadeusz Jezierski, John Ensminger, L. E. Papet. Boca Raton, FL: CRC Press, 2016.

Concha, Astrid R., Claire Guest, Rob Harris, Thomas W. Pike, Alexandre Feugier, Helen Zulch, and Daniel S. Mills. "Canine Olfactory Thresholds to Amyl Acetate in a Biomedical Detection Scenario." *Frontiers in Veterinary Science* 22 (January 2019).

DeChant, Mallory T., Paul C. Bunker, and Nathaniel J. Hall. "Stimulus Control of Odorant Concentration: Pilot Study of Generalization and Discrimination of Odor Concentration in Canines." *Animals* (Basel) 11, no. 2 (January 2021).

Hall, Nathaniel J., Kelsey Glenn, David W. Smith, and Clive D. L. Wynne. "Performance of Pugs, German Shepherds, and Greyhounds *(Canis lupus familiaris)* on an Odor-Discrimination Task." *Journal of Comparative Psychology* 129, no. 3 (August 2015).

Hall, Nathaniel J., Franck Péron, Stéphanie Cambou, Laurence Callejon, and Clive D. L. Wynne. "Food and Food-Odor Preferences in Dogs: A Pilot Study." *Chemical Senses* 42, no. 4 (May 2017).

Horowitz, Alexandra. "Smelling Themselves: Dogs Investigate Their Own Odours Longer When Modified in an 'Olfactory Mirror' Test." *Behavioral Processes* 143 (October 2017).

Hurt, Aimee, Deborah A. (Smith) Woollett, and Megan Parker. "Training Considerations in Wildlife Detection." In *Canine Olfaction Science and Law,* edited by Tadeusz Jezierski, John Ensminger, L. E. Papet. Boca Raton, FL: CRC Press, 2016.

Kauer, John, Joel White, Timothy Turner, and Barbara Talamo. "Principles of Odor Recognition by the Olfactory System Applied to Detection of Low-Concentration Explosives." Final report by the Tufts University School of Medicine for the U.S. Army Soldier and Biological Chemical Command, Soldier Systems Center, Natick, Massachusetts. Defense Technical Information Center (January 2003).

Kokocińska-Kusiak, Agata, Martyna Woszczyło, Mikołaj Zybala, Julia Maciocha, Katarzyna Barłowska, and Michał Dzięcioł. "Canine Olfaction: Physiology, Behavior, and Possibilities for Practical Applications." *Animals* (Basel) 11, no. 8 (January 2021).

Lazarowski, Lucia, and David C. Droman. "Explosives Detection by Military Working Dogs: Olfactory Generalization From Components to Mixtures." *Applied Animal Behaviour Science* 151 (February 2014).

Lazarowski, Lucia, Bart Rogers, L. Paul Waggoner, and Jeffrey S. Katz. "When the Nose Knows: Ontogenetic Changes in Detection Dogs' *(Canis familiaris)* Responsiveness to Social and Olfactory Cues." *Animal Behaviour* 153 (July 2019).

Lazarowski, Lucia, Paul Waggoner, Bethany Hutchings, Craig Angle, and Fay Porritt. "Maintaining Long-Term Odor Memory and Detection Performance in Dogs." *Applied Animal Behaviour Science* 238 (May 2021).

Lenkei, Rita, Tamás Faragó, Borbála Zsilák, and Péter Pongrácz. "Dogs *(Canis familiaris)* Recognize Their Own Body as a Physical Obstacle." *Science Reports* 11, no. 2761 (February 2021).

Siniscalchi, Marcello. "Olfaction and the Canine Brain." In *Canine Olfaction Science and Law,* edited by Tadeusz Jezierski, John Ensminger, L. E. Papet. Boca Raton, FL: CRC Press, 2016.

Yang, Lu M., Sung-Ho Huh, and David M. Ornitz. "FGF20-Expressing, Wnt-Responsive Olfactory Epithelial Progenitors Regulate Underlying Turbinate Growth to Optimize Surface Area." *Developmental Cell* 46, no. 5 (September 2018). See also: Washington University School of Medicine. "New Details in How Sense of Smell Develops: Findings Could Help Determine How Dogs Evolved Such Good Noses." *ScienceDaily* (August 2018). www.sciencedaily.com/releases/2018/08/180810091607.htm.

CHAPTER 7: POOPER SNOOPERS

Biddinger, David, Greg Krawczyk, Michela Centinari, Flor Edith Acevedo, Cain Hickey, and Heather Leach. "Spotted Lanternfly Management in Vineyards." Penn State Extension, April 20, 2021. extension.psu.edu/spotted-lanternfly-management-in-vineyards.

Hardbarger, Mary. "Calling All Canines: Help Sniff Out the Dangerous Spotted Lanternfly." *Virginia Tech News,* April 11, 2023. news.vt.edu/articles/2023/04/cals-spottedlanternfly-dogdetection.html.

Kardos, Marty, Yaolei Zhang, Kim M. Parsons, A. Yunga, Hui Kang, Xun Xu, Xin Liu et al. "Inbreeding Depression Explains Killer Whale Population Dynamics." *Nature Ecology & Evolution* 7, no. 5 (March 2023).

Murray, Cathryn C., Lucie C. Hannah, Thomas Doniol-Valcroze, Brianna M. Wright, Eva H. Stredulinsky, Jocelyn C. Nelson, Andrea Locke, and Robert C. Lacy. "A Cumulative Effects Model for Population Trajectories of Resident Killer Whales in the Northeast Pacific." *Biological Conservation* 257 (2021).

Ward, Eric J., Elizabeth E. Holmes, and Ken C. Balcomb. "Quantifying the Effects of Prey Abundance on Killer Whale Reproduction." *Journal of Applied Ecology* 46, no. 3 (2009).

Wasser, Sam, Jessica I. Lundin, Katherine Ayres, Elizabeth Seely, Deborah Giles, Kenneth Balcomb, Jennifer Hempelmann et al. "Population Growth Is Limited by Nutritional Impacts on Pregnancy Success in Endangered Southern Resident Killer Whales *(Orcinus orca)*." *PLoS One* 12, no. 6 (June 2017).

Watson, George. "Researcher Receives Grant to Sniff Out Invasive Pests, Species in Agriculture." *Texas Tech Today,* Stories, February 8, 2021. today.ttu.edu/posts/2021/02/Stories/Hall-Ag-Detection-Dogs.

Wild Fish Conservancy Northwest v. *Barry Thom, Regional Administrator, National Marine Fisheries Service et al.,* Case No. 2:20-cv-00417-MLP. (W.D. Wash. 2020). Declaration of Dr. Deborah Giles, Ph.D., filed April 16, 2020. wildfishconservancy.org/wp-content/uploads/2021/12/014.2.giles_.decl-2.pdf.

CHAPTER 8: THE SCENTS OF A HUMAN

Berns, Gregory S., Andrew M. Brooks, and Mark Spivak. "Scent of the Familiar: An fMRI Study of Canine Brain Responses to Familiar and Unfamiliar Human and Dog Odors." *Behavioral Processes* 110 (January 2015).

Dror, Shany, Andrea Sommese, Ádám Miklósi, Andrea Temesi, and Claudia Fugazza. "Multisensory Mental Representation of Objects in Typical and Gifted Word Learner Dogs." *Animal Cognition* 25 (2022).

Gallagher, Michelle, Charles J. Wysocki, J. J. Leyden, Andrew I. Spielman, X. Sun, and George Preti. "Analyses of Volatile Organic Compounds from Human Skin." *British Journal of Dermatology* 159, no. 4 (September 2008).

Glavaš, Vedrana, and Andrea Pintar. "Human Remains Detection Dogs as a New Prospecting Method in Archaeology." *Journal of Archaeological Method and Theory* 26, no. 1–3 (September 2019).

Jacobi, Keith P. "Cadaver Detection in Forensic Anthropology and Criminology." In *Canine Olfaction Science and Law,* edited by Tadeusz Jezierski, John Ensminger, L. E. Papet. Boca Raton, FL: CRC Press, 2016.

Katz, Brigit. "Who's a Good Archaeologist? Dog Digs Up Trove of Bronze Age Relics." *Smithsonian,* September 19, 2018.

Starr, Michelle. "A Very Good Doggo Just Found Incredible Bronze Age Treasure in Czechia." *Science Alert* (September 17, 2018).

Wang, Nijing, Lisa Ernle, Gabriel Bekö, Pawel Wargocki, and Jonathan Williams. "Emission Rates of Volatile Organic Compounds from Humans." *Environmental Science and Technology* 56, no. 8 (2022).

CHAPTER 9: SICKNESS STINKS

Ensminger, John. "Medical Alerting to Seizures, Glycemic Changes, and Migraines: Significance of Untrained Behaviors in Service Dogs." In *Canine Olfaction Science and Law,* edited by Tadeusz Jezierski, John Ensminger, L. E. Papet. Boca Raton, FL: CRC Press, 2016.

Feil, Charlotte, Frank Staib, Martin R. Berger, Thorsten Stein, Irene Schmidtmann, Andreas Forster, and Carl C. Schimanski. "Sniffer Dogs Can Identify Lung Cancer Patients From Breath and Urine Samples." *BMC Cancer* 21 (August 2021).

Jezierski, Tadeusz. "Detection of Human Cancer by Dogs." In *Canine Olfaction Science and Law,* edited by Tadeusz Jezierski, John Ensminger, L. E. Papet. Boca Raton, FL: CRC Press, 2016.

Juge, Aiden E., Margaret F. Foster, and Courtney L. Daigle. "Canine Olfaction as a Disease Detection Technology: A Systematic Review." *Applied Animal Behaviour Science* 253 (August 2022).

Kantele, Anu, Juuso Paajanen, Soile Turunen, Sari H. Pakkanen, Anu Patjas, Laura Itkonen, Elina Heiskanen et al. "Scent Dogs in Detection of COVID-19: Triple-Blinded Randomised Trial and Operational Real-Life Screening in Airport Setting." *BMJ Global Health* 7, no. 5 (2022).

Liu, Shih-Feng, Hung-I Lu, Wei-Lien Chi, Guan-Heng Liu, and Ho-Chang Kuo. "Sniffer Dogs Diagnose Lung Cancer by Recognition of Exhaled Gases: Using Breathing Target Samples to Train Dogs Has a Higher Diagnostic Rate Than Using Lung Cancer Tissue Samples or Urine Samples." *Cancers* (Basel) 15, no. 4 (February 2023).

Maurer, Maureen, Todd Seto, Claire Guest, Amendeep Somal, and Catherine Julian. "Detection of SARS-CoV-2 by Canine Olfaction: A Pilot Study." *Open Forum Infectious Diseases* 9, no. 7 (July 2022).

Mount Sinai Medical Center. "Lung Cancer Screening Dramatically Increases Long-Term Survival Rate." Press release, November 22, 2022. www.mountsinai.org/about/newsroom/2022/lung-cancer-screening -dramatically-increases-long-term-survival-rate.

Shirasu, Mika, and Kazushige Touhara. "The Scent of Disease: Volatile Organic Compounds of the Human Body Related to Disease and Disorder." *Journal of Biochemistry* 150, no. 3 (September 2011).

Sonoda, Hideto, Shunji Kohnoe, Tetsuro Yamazato, Yuji Satoh, Gouki Morizono, Kentaro Shikata, Makoto Morita et al. "Colorectal Cancer

Screening With Odour Material by Canine Scent Detection." *Gut* 60, no. 6 (January 2011).

Trivedi, Drupad K., Eleanor Sinclair, Yun Xu, Depanjan Sarkar, Caitlin Walton-Doyle, Camilla Liscio, Phine Banks et al. "Discovery of Volatile Biomarkers of Parkinson's Disease From Sebum." *ACS Central Science* 5, no. 4 (March 2019).

Wang, Peiyu, Qi Huang, Shushi Meng, Teng Mu, Zheng Liu, Mengqi He, Qingyun Li et al. "Identification of Lung Cancer Breath Biomarkers Based on Perioperative Breathomics Testing: A Prospective Observational Study." *Lancet* 47 (May 2022).

Willis, Carolyn M., Susannah M. Church, Claire M. Guest, W. Andrew Cook, Noel McCarthy, Anthea J. Bransbury, Martin R. Church et al. "Olfactory Detection of Human Bladder Cancer by Dogs: Proof of Principle Study." *British Medical Journal* 329, no. 7468 (September 2004).

CHAPTER 10: THE WHIFF THAT WARNS

Blanka, Pophof, Bernd Henschenmacher, Daniel R. Kattnig, Jens Kuhne, Alain Vian, and Gunde Ziegelberger. "Biological Effects of Electric, Magnetic, and Electromagnetic Fields From 0 to 100 MHz on Fauna and Flora: Workshop Report," *Health Physics* 124, no. 1 (January 2023).

Hart, Vlastimil, Petra Nováková, Erich Pascal Malkemper, Sabine Begall, Vladimír Hanzal, Miloš Ježek, Tomáš Kušta et al. "Dogs Are Sensitive to Small Variations of the Earth's Magnetic Field." *Frontiers in Zoology* 10, no. 1 (December 2013).

Powell, Neil A., Alastair Ruffell, and Gareth Arnott. "The Untrained Response of Pet Dogs to Human Epileptic Seizures." *Animals* (Basel) 11, no. 8 (July 2021).

CHAPTER 11: BORN TO BOND

Bekoff, Marc. "Playful Fun in Dogs." *Current Biology* 25, no. 1 (January 2015).

Faragó, Tamás, Péter Pongrácz, Friederike Range, Zsófia Virányi, and

Ádám Miklósi. "'The Bone Is Mine': Affective and Referential Aspects of Dog Growls." *Animal Behaviour* 79, no. 4 (April 2010).

Fenzi, Denise. "Zooming: Impulse Control or Stress?" Denise Fenzi (blog), March 28, 2016. denisefenzi.com/2016/03/zooming -impulse-control-or-stress.

Fugazza, Claudia, Attila Andics, Lilla Magyari, Shany Dror, András Zempléni, and Ádám Miklósi. "Rapid Learning of Object Names in Dogs." *Scientific Reports* 11, no. 1 (January 2021).

Fugazza, Claudia, B. Turcsan, Andrea Sommese, Shany Dror, Andrea Temesi and Ádám Miklósi. "A Comparison of Personality Traits of Gifted Word Learner and Typical Border Collies." *Animal Cognition* 25, no. 6 (August 2022).

Horowitz, Alexandra. "Attention to Attention in Domestic Dog *(Canis familiaris)* Dyadic Play." *Animal Cognition* 12, no. 1 (January 2009).

Mellor, David J. "Tail Docking of Canine Puppies: Reassessment of the Tail's Role in Communication, the Acute Pain Caused by Docking and Interpretation of Behavioural Responses." *Animals* (Basel) 8, no. 6 (2018).

Murata, Kaori, Miho Nagasawa, Tatsushi Onaka, Nobuyuki Kanemaki, Shigeru Nakamura, Kazuo Tsubota, Kazutaka Mogi et al. "Increase of Tear Volume in Dogs After Reunion With Owners Is Mediated by Oxytocin." *Current Biology* 32, no. 16 (2022).

Panksepp, Jaak. "Can PLAY Diminish ADHD and Facilitate the Construction of the Social Brain?" *Journal of the Canadian Academy of Child and Adolescent Psychiatry* 16, no. 2 (May 2007).

Simonet, Patricia R., Molly Murphy, and Amy Lance. "Laughing Dog: Vocalizations of Domestic Dogs During Play Encounters." Paper presented at the meeting of the Animal Behavior Society, Corvallis, OR, July 2001.

Siniscalchi, Marcello, Rita Lusito, Giorgio Vallortigara, and Angelo Quaranta. "Seeing Left- or Right-Asymmetric Tail Wagging Produces Different Emotional Responses in Dogs." *Current Biology* 23, no. 22 (November 2013).

Siviy, Stephen M., and Jaak Panksepp. "In Search of the Neurobiological Substrates for Social Playfulness in Mammalian Brains." *Neuroscience & Biobehavioral Reviews* 35, no. 9 (October 2011).

Volsche, Shelly, Hannah Gunnip, Cameron Brown, Makayla Kiperash, Holly Root-Gutteridge, and Alexandra Horowitz. "Dogs Produce Distinctive Play Pants: Confirming Simonet (2001)," *International Journal of Comparative Psychology* 35 (2022).

Walker, Reena H., Andrew J. King, J. Weldon McNutt, and Neil R. Jordan. "Sneeze to Leave: African Wild Dogs *(Lycaon pictus)* Use Variable Quorum Thresholds Facilitated by Sneezes in Collective Decisions." *Proceedings of the Royal Society B: Biological Sciences* 284, no. 1862 (September 2017).

CHAPTER 12: CANINE NETWORKING

Bálint, Anna, Huba Eleőd, Lilla Magyari, Anna Kis, and Márta Gácsi. "Differences in Dogs' Event-Related Potentials in Response to Human and Dog Vocal Stimuli: A Non-Invasive Study." *Royal Society Open Science* 9, no. 4 (April 2022).

Couchoux, Charline, Jeanne Clermont, Dany Garant, and Denis Réale. "Signaler and Receiver Boldness Influence Response to Alarm Calls in Eastern Chipmunks." *Behavioral Ecology* 29, no. 1 (January/February 2018).

Crosby, James. "Dog Bite Injuries and Behavioral Projections: What We Have Learned About Fatal Attacks by Following the Evidence." The Lemonade Conference, February 11–13, 2022. thelemonade conference.com.

Crosby, James, and Chelsea Rider. *Decoding Canine Body Language Quick Reference Guide.* In *Law Enforcement Dog Encounters Training (LEDET): A Toolkit for Law Enforcement.* U.S. Department of Justice Community-Oriented Policing Service (COPS), November 2019. portal.cops .usdoj.gov/resourcecenter/Home.aspx?page=detail&id=COPS-W0882.

McConnell, Patricia. "Play Bows as Meta-Communication." *The Other*

End of the Leash (blog), December 14, 2012. www.patriciamcconnell.com/theotherendoftheleash/tag/puppy-pauses.

Sommese, Andrea, Ádám Miklósi, Ákos Pogány, Andrea Temesi, Shany Dror, and Claudia Fugazza. "An Exploratory Analysis of Head-Tilting in Dogs." *Animal Cognition* 25, no. 3 (2022).

CHAPTER 13: DOG SMARTEST?

Bastos, Amalia P. M., and Federico Rossano. "Soundboard-Using Pets? Introducing a New Global Citizen Science Approach to Interspecies Communication." *Interaction Studies* (forthcoming).

Griebel, Ulrike, and D. Kimbrough Oller. "Vocabulary Learning in a Yorkshire Terrier: Slow Mapping of Spoken Words." *PLoS One* 7, no. 2 (February 2012).

Kaminski, Juliane, Josep Call, and Julia Fischer. "Word Learning in a Domestic Dog: Evidence for 'Fast Mapping.'" *Science* 304, no. 5677 (June 2004).

Pilley, John W. "Border Collie Comprehends Sentences Containing a Prepositional Object, Verb, and Direct Object." *Learning and Motivation* 44, no. 4 (November 2013).

Pilley, John W., and Alliston K. Reid. "Border Collie Comprehends Object Names as Verbal Referents." *Behavioural Processes* 86, no. 2 (February 2011).

Rossi, Alexandre P., and César Ades. "A Dog at the Keyboard: Using Arbitrary Signs to Communicate Requests." *Animal Cognition* 11, no. 2 (2008).

Smith, Gabriela E., Amalia P. M. Bastos, Ashley Evenson, Leo Trottier, and Federico Rossano. "Use of Augmentative Interspecies Communication Devices in Animal Language Studies: A Review." *WIREs Cognitive Science* (2023).

Wood, Heather. "Rico the Wonder Dog." *Nature Reviews Neuroscience* 5, no. 599 (2004).

CHAPTER 14: THE WISDOM
OF THE HEART

Carey, Ben, Colleen Anne Dell, James Stempien, Susan Tupper, Betty Rohr, Eloise Carr, Maria Cruz et al. "Outcomes of a Controlled Trial With Visiting Therapy Dog Teams on Pain in Adults in an Emergency Department." *PLoS One* 17, no. 3 (March 2022).

Huber, Annika, Anjuli L. A. Barber, Tamás Faragó, Corsin A. Müller, and Ludwig Huber. "Investigating Emotional Contagion in Dogs *(Canis familiaris)* to Emotional Sounds of Humans and Conspecifics." *Animal Cognition* 20, no. 4 (April 2017).

Katayama, Maki, Takatomi Kubo, Toshitaka Yamakawa, Koichi Fujiwara, Kensaku Nomoto, Kazushi Ikeda, Kazutaka Mogi et al., "Emotional Contagion From Humans to Dogs Is Facilitated by Duration of Ownership." *Frontiers in Psychology* 10 (July 2019).

Krause-Parello, Cheryl A., Michele Thames, Colleen M. Ray, and John Kolassa. "Examining the Effects of a Service-Trained Facility Dog on Stress in Children Undergoing Forensic Interview for Allegations of Child Sexual Abuse." *Journal of Child Sexual Abuse* 27, no. 3 (April 2018).

Miller, Sharmaine L., James A. Serpell, Kathryn R. Dalton, Kaitlin B. Waite, Daniel O. Morris, Laurel E. Redding, Nancy A. Dreschel, and Meghan F. Davis. "The Importance of Evaluating Positive Welfare Characteristics and Temperament in Working Therapy Dogs." *Frontiers in Veterinary Science* 9 (April 2022).

Müller, Corsin A., Kira Schmitt, Anjuli L. A. Barber, and Ludwig Huber. "Dogs Can Discriminate Emotional Expressions of Human Faces." *Current Biology* 25, no. 5 (March 2015).

Schnurr, Paula P. "Epidemiology and Impact of PTSD." U.S. Department of Veterans Affairs, National Center for PTSD. www.ptsd.va.gov/professional/treat/essentials/epidemiology.asp.

CHAPTER 15: GETTING SMART ABOUT DOG SMARTS

Arasaradnam, Ramesh P., Chuka U. Nwokolo, Karna D. Bardhan, and J. A. Covington. "Electronic Nose Versus Canine Nose: Clash of the Titans." *Gut* 60, no. 12 (2011).

Chandler, David L. "Toward a Disease-Sniffing Device That Rivals a Dog's Nose." *MIT News,* February 17, 2021. news.mit.edu/2021/disease-detection-device-dogs-0217.

Forbes, Thomas P., and Matthew Staymates. "Enhanced Aerodynamic Reach of Vapor and Aerosol Sampling for Real-Time Mass Spectrometric Detection Using Venturi-Assisted Entrainment and Ionization." *Analytica Chimica Acta* 957 (March 2017).

Grimm, David. "Are You Clumsy—Or Just Mean? Your Dog May Know the Difference." News from *Science,* July 21, 2022. www.science.org/content/article/are-you-clumsy-or-just-mean-your-dog-may-know-difference.

Iravani, Behzad, Martin Schaefer, Donald A. Wilson, Artin Arshamian, and Johan N. Lundström. "The Human Olfactory Bulb Processes Odor Valence Representation and Cues Motor Avoidance Behavior." *Proceedings of the National Academy of Sciences* 118, no. 42 (October 2021).

Staymates, Matthew, William A. MacCrehan, Jessica L. Staymates, Roderick R. Kunz, Thomas Mendum, Ta-Hsuan Ong, Geoffrey Geurtsen et al. "Biomimetic Sniffing Improves the Detection Performance of a 3D Printed Nose of a Dog and a Commercial Trace Vapor Detector." *Scientific Reports* 6 (December 2016).

Völter, Christoph J., Lucrezia Lonardo, Maud G. G. M. Steinmann, Carolina Frizzo Ramos, Karoline Gerwisch, Monique-Theres Schranz, Iris Dobernig et al. "Unwilling or Unable? Using Three-Dimensional Tracking to Evaluate Dogs' Reactions to Differing Human Intentions." *Proceedings of the Royal Society B: Biological Sciences* 290, no. 1991 (January 2023).

Wyart, Claire, Wallace W. Webster, Jonathan H. Chen, Sarah R. Wilson,

Andrew McClary, Rehan M. Khan, and Noam Sobel. "Smelling a Single Component of Male Sweat Alters Levels of Cortisol in Women." *Journal of Neuroscience* 27, no. 6 (February 2007).

CHAPTER 16: BEING BETTER HUMANS FOR OUR SMART DOGS

Berns, Gregory S., Andrew M. Brooks, and Mark Spivak. "Scent of the Familiar: An fMRI Study of Canine Brain Responses to Familiar and Unfamiliar Human and Dog Odors." *Behavioral Processes* 110 (January 2015).

Coren, Stanley. "The Data Says 'Don't Hug the Dog!'" *Canine Corner* (blog). *Psychology Today,* April 13, 2016. www.psychologytoday.com/us/blog/canine-corner/201604/the-data-says-dont-hug-the-dog.

Hall, Nathaniel, Kelsey Glenn, David W. Smith, and Clive D. L. Wynne. "Performance of Pugs, German Shepherds, and Greyhounds *(Canis lupus familiaris)* on an Odor-Discrimination Task." *Journal of Comparative Psychology* 129, no. 3 (May 2015).

Horowitz, Alexandra. "Smelling Themselves: Dogs Investigate Their Own Odours Longer When Modified in an 'Olfactory Mirror' Test." *Behavioral Processes* 143 (2017).

Karl, Sabrina, Magdalena Boch, Anna Zamansky, Dirk van der Linden, Isabella C. Wagner, Christoph J. Völter, Claus Lamm, and Ludwig Huber. "Exploring the Dog-Human Relationship by Combining fMRI, Eye-Tracking and Behavioural Measures." *Scientific Reports* 10 (2020).

Marshall-Pescini, Sarah, Chiara Passalacqua, Shanis Barnard, Paola Valsecchi, and Emanuela Prato-Previde. "Agility and Search and Rescue Training Differently Affects Pet Dogs' Behaviour in Socio-Cognitive Tasks." *Behavioral Processes* 81, no. 3 (July 2009).

Minhinnick, Sherrie, L. E. Papet, Carol Merry Stephenson, and Mark R. Stephenson. "Training Fundamentals and the Selection of Dogs and Personnel for Detection Work." In *Canine Olfaction Science and Law,* edited by Tadeusz Jezierski, John Ensminger, L. E. Papet. Boca Raton, FL: CRC Press, 2016.

Pilla, Rachel, and Jan S. Suchodolski. "The Role of the Canine Gut Microbiome and Metabolome in Health and Gastrointestinal Disease." *Frontiers in Veterinary Science* 6 (January 2020).

Schöberl, Iris, Manuela Wedl, Andrea Beetz, and Kurt Kotrschal. "Psychobiological Factors Affecting Cortisol Variability in Human-Dog Dyads." *PLoS One* 12, no. 2 (February 2017).

Vieira de Castro, Ana Catarina, Danielle Fuchs, Gabriela Munhoz Morello, Stefania Pastur, Liliana de Sousa, and I. Anna S. Olsson. "Does Training Method Matter? Evidence for the Negative Impact of Aversive-Based Methods on Companion Dog Welfare." *PLoS One* 15, no. 12 (December 2020).

Wallis, Lisa J., Zsófia Virányi, Corsin A. Müller, Samuel Serisier, Ludwig Huber, and Friederike Range. "Aging Effects on Discrimination Learning, Logical Reasoning and Memory in Pet Dogs." *Age* 38, no. 1 (2016).

CHAPTER 17: LETTING OUR DOGS BE DOGS

Carroll, Sharon. "Working with Sensitive Sport Dogs." The Lemonade Conference, February 11–13, 2022. thelemonadeconference.com.

Duranton, Charlotte, and Alexandra Horowitz. "Let Me Sniff! Nosework Induces Positive Judgment Bias in Pet Dogs." *Applied Animal Behaviour Science* 2011 (February 2019).

Pierce, Jessica. "Why Dogs Should Have More Control Over Their Lives." *All Dogs Go to Heaven* (blog). *Psychology Today,* May 18, 2022. www .psychologytoday.com/us/blog/all-dogs-go-heaven/202205/why-dogs -should-have-more-control-over-their-lives.

Promislow, Daniel. "The Effects of Age on Activity and Cognition: Results from the Dog Aging Project." The Lemonade Conference, February 11–13, 2022. thelemonadeconference.com.

VIRTUAL CONFERENCES

The Lemonade Conference 2021 and 2022:
Including talks by Sharon Carroll, Dr. Jim Crosby, Denise Fenzi, Dr. Susan Friedman, Vidhyalakshmi Karthikeyan, Dr. Kathryn Lord, Dr. Daniel S. Mills, Dr. Daniel Promislow, Michael Shikashio, Zazie Todd, Shade Whitesel, and Dr. Sue Yanoff.
thelemonadeconference.com/schedule

Assistance Dogs International 2021:
Theme: "The Power of Positivity" in training and human-dog interactions. Including talks by Dr. Emily Bray, Dr. Ian Dunbar, and other leaders in the assistance-dog world.
assistancedogsinternational.org/about/2021-adi-conference

Osmocosm 2021:
Theme: Emerging technologies in olfaction science, including machine olfaction for detecting human ailments.
osmocosm.org/program-1

CANINE RESEARCH CENTERS*

Arizona State University: Canine Science Collaboratory
psychology.asu.edu/research/labs/canine-science-collaboratory

Auburn University: Comparative Cognition Lab
webhome.auburn.edu/~katzjef/index.html

---

* A robust, but not necessarily inclusive, list

Barnard College, Columbia University: Horowitz Dog Cognition Lab
dogcognition.weebly.com

Boston College: Canine Cognition Center and Social Learning Laboratory
sites.bc.edu/doglab

Brown University: Brown Dog Lab
sites.brown.edu/browndoglab

CONICET: National Scientific and Technical Research Council
(Argentina): Grupo de Investigación del Comportamiento en Cánidos
canids.com.ar

Dalhousie University (Canada): Wildlife Ethology and Conservation Canine Lab
www.gadbois.org/simon

Duke University: Duke Canine Cognition Center
evolutionaryanthropology.duke.edu/research/dogs

Eckerd College: Comparative Psychology Lab
cplab.eckerd.edu/home

Emory University: Center for Neuropolicy
neuropolicy.emory.edu

Eötvös Loránd University (Hungary): The Family Dog Project
ethology.elte.hu/Family_Dog_Project

Illinois Wesleyan University: IWU Dog Scientists
efurlong2.wixsite.com/dogscience

La Trobe University (Australia): Anthrozoology Research Group Dog Lab
latrobe.edu.au/school-psychology-and-public-health/anthrozoology
  -research-group-dog-lab

Oregon State University: Human-Animal Interaction Lab
thehumananimalbond.com

Texas Tech University: Canine Olfaction Lab
depts.ttu.edu/afs/people/nathan-hall/CanineOlfactionLab/index.php

Universities of Milan and Parma (Italy): Canis Sapiens Lab—-Compara-
  tive Cognition and Human-Animal Interaction
comportamentoanimale.it/en

University of Arizona: Arizona Canine Cognition Center
dogs.arizona.edu

University of Auckland (New Zealand): Clever Canine Lab
clevercaninelab.auckland.ac.nz

University of Bristol Veterinary School (UK): Animal Welfare and
  Behaviour
bristol.ac.uk/vet-school/research/welfare-behaviour

University of Kentucky: Comparative Cognition Laboratory,
  Science Dogs Program
www.uky.edu/~zentall/sciencedogs.html

University of Lincoln (UK): Animal Behaviour, Cognition and
  Welfare Research Group
lincoln.ac.uk/lifesciences/research/animalbehaviourcognitionandwelfare

University of Maryland: Canine Language Perception Lab
dogs.umd.edu/index.html

University of Nebraska–Lincoln: Canine Cognition and Human
Interaction Lab
dogcog.unl.edu

University of Washington: Center for Environmental Forensic Science
cefs.uw.edu

Veterinary Medicine University (Austria): Clever Dog Lab
vetmeduni.ac.at/cleverdoglab

Yale University: Canine Cognition Center
doglab.yale.edu

INDEX

ABOUT THE
AUTHOR

J ennifer S. Holland is a science writer, conservation biologist, and the
author of the *New York Times* best-selling *Unlikely Friendships* book
series, the first volume of which spent more than 46 weeks on the bestseller
list and was translated into more than 30 languages. A longtime contrib-
utor to *National Geographic* magazine, Holland has traveled the world
writing about natural history, animal behavior, wildlife conservation, and
the glory of wild places. Her adventures include diving with tiger sharks
in the Bahamas, climbing rainforest trees in Borneo, exploring panda
breeding in China, camping on a live volcano in Hawaii, floating in zero
gravity over the Gulf of Mexico, and camping out with the Indigenous
people of Papua New Guinea.

Holland's work has also appeared in *National Wildlife, Nature Conservancy* magazine, the *New York Times,* the *Washington Post,* and numerous
web-based publications, including *Atlas Obscura* and *Hakai;* she also
regularly contributes essays to the highly regarded science blog *The Last
Word on Nothing.* With her husband, (very smart) dogs, and pet geckos,
Holland splits her time between the D.C. area and a cabin in the woods
in central Virginia. *Dog Smart* is her fifth book.